T0317292

CULTURE, PLACE, AND NATURE

STUDIES IN ANTHROPOLOGY AND ENVIRONMENT

K. Sivaramakrishnan, Series Editor

CULTURE, PLACE, AND NATURE

Centered in anthropology, the Culture, Place, and Nature series encompasses new interdisciplinary social science research on environmental issues, focusing on the intersection of culture, ecology, and politics in global, national, and local contexts.
Contributors to the series view environmental knowledge and issues from the multiple and often conflicting perspectives of various cultural systems.

BEING AND PLACE

among the TLINGIT

Thomas F. Thornton

UNIVERSITY OF WASHINGTON PRESS

SEATTLE AND LONDON

in association with

SEALASKA HERITAGE INSTITUTE

JUNEAU

University of Washington Press
P.O. Box 50096, Seattle, WA 98145 U.S.A.
www.washington.edu/uwpress

Library of Congress Cataloging-in-Publication Data
Thornton, Thomas F.
Being and place among the Tlingit / Thomas F. Thornton.
p. cm.—(Culture, place, and nature)
Includes bibliographical references and index.
ISBN-13: 978-0-295-98749-1 (pbk. : alk. paper)
ISBN-10: 0-295-98749-9 (pbk. : alk. paper)
1. Tlingit Indians—Social life and customs. 2. Names,
Geographical—Social aspects—Alaska. 3. Cultural property—
Alaska 4. Geographical perception—Alaska. 5. Alaska—Social
life and customs. I. Sealaska Heritage Institute. II. Title.
E99.T6T55 2007 305.897'270798—dc22 2007023887

CONTENTS

ILLUSTRATIONS

TLINGIT SPELLING AND PRONUNCIATION GUIDE

The spelling of Tlingit words conforms to the accepted popular orthography first developed by Constance M. Naish and Gillian L. Story and revised by Jeff Leer and Nora Marks Florendo Dauenhauer in 1972 (see Dauenhauer and Dauenhauer 1987:38–46). Important Tlingit concepts and names for places are italicized within the text. Personal and social group names, however, are not.

Coastal Tlingit has four long vowels and four short vowels, represented and pronounced as follows:

Tlingit vowel	As in the English	Tlingit example
A	Was	tás (thread)
Aa	Saab (a Swedish automobile)	taan (sea lion)
E	Ten	té (stone)
Ei	Vein	yeis (horse clams)
I	Hit	hít (house)
Ee	Seek	s'eek (black bear)
U	Push	núkt (male grouse)
Oo	Moon	xóots (brown bear)

Vowels may be pronounced with either a high (á) or a low (à) tone. In northern Tlingit the low tone is unmarked. In southern Tlingit both tones are marked.

Consonants in Tlingit include more than two dozen sounds not found in English. The technical sound chart below (see Dauenhauer and Dauenhauer 1987; Leer 1991) provides a basic guide to the spelling and pronunciation of consonants in Tlingit words.

Tlingit Consonantal Sound Chart

	Alveolar	Lateral	Palatal	Velar Plain	Velar Round	Uvular Plain	Uvular Round	Glottal Plain	Glottal Round
Stop									
plain	d			g	gw	g̲	g̲w	.	.w
aspirated	t			k	kw	k̲	k̲w		
	t'			k'	k'w	k̲'	k̲'w		
glottalized									
Affricative									
plain	dz	dl	j						
aspirated	ts	tl	ch						
	ts'	tl'	ch'						
glottalized									
Fricative									
plain	s	l	sh	x	xw	x̲	x̲w	h	hw
	s'	l'		x'	x'w	x̲'	x̲'w		
glottalized									
Nasal	n								
Glide			y	w					

PREFACE

I first became interested in researching Tlingit concepts of place during the summer of 1989, when, as a young graduate student, I was employed by the Alaska Department of Fish and Game, Division of Subsistence, to study the historical and contemporary use of a famous but dwindling red salmon fishery in northern Southeast Alaska, known as Sitkoh Bay. Sitkoh Bay lay on the border between Sitka and Angoon, two Tlingit communities with historical ties to the place and stakes in its management. Upon my first visit to Angoon, I was directed to see Matthew Fred Sr. and Mary Willis, elders of the Deisheetaan clan, which was said to have "owned" and "taken care of" that bay. Approaching the leaders of the right social group was extremely important; indeed, as I was to learn, the social and physical geography are inseparable in Tlingit concepts of place. This was my first lesson. I shall not soon forget the first thing Matthew Fred Sr. said to me, for it was perhaps the singular lesson not only about Sitkoh Bay but about Tlingit geography as a whole: "You have to understand. There's a history about that place. We've got stories on it." My first encounter with Mary Willis was similarly poignant. I knocked on her door and, after introducing myself, nervously stated my desire to learn something about the sockeye salmon fishery at Sitkoh Bay. She simply nodded and, leaving the door open, turned and walked back toward the kitchen table and began to narrate: "I've been worried about it. I don't like what's happening to that place. . . . My uncle used to take care of it." Mary Willis had Sitkoh Bay on her mind. And the rest was history—literally. For this reason, history and social groupings have remained central to my inquiry into Tlingits' senses of place.

After returning to Alaska the following summer for a short stint of fieldwork, I joined the Division of Subsistence as a resource specialist.

I was fortunate in that this work took me to communities throughout Southeast Alaska and enabled me to become familiar with the people and geography of the Southeast region from Yakutat to Saxman. Although most of the projects I was involved in concerned fish and wildlife harvest patterns, this research led quite naturally into discussions of place. Tlingits tend to hunt and fish in areas that they know and to which they have social ties. In addition to housing desirable natural resources, these places have other cultural values, which people invoke in myriad ways. Through this work, I learned another valuable lesson: hunting and fishing in particular and production in general are fertile contexts for learning, thinking, and speaking about places. Conversely, just as subsistence is central to place-making, so too is place central to Alaska Native subsistence lifeways, although federal and state subsistence laws protect only "customary and traditional uses" of resources, not places.

My knowledge of the multifaceted relationships among Tlingit subsistence, history, social organization, and landscape was further developed when I became involved, along with the Division of Subsistence, the Hoonah Indian Association, and the National Park Service, in a formal attempt to map Tlingit place-names in the vicinity of Glacier Bay National Park and Preserve. This map spawned tremendous interest in the Tlingit names placed on the land and what they mean and helped the Huna Tlingits and the Park Service move their relationship from one of contention over resource rights to one of increasing collaboration (see HIA 2006).

In the course of this work, and in my own studies, I continued to record and analyze Tlingit place-names with support from numerous institutions, organizations, and individuals to whom I am exceptionally grateful. My fieldwork in Angoon, Sitka, and Yakutat was supported from grants from the Jacobs Fund of the Whatcom Museum and the Phillips Fund of the American Philosophical Society. Additional research on place-names was funded through three generous grants by the Language and Heritage grant program of the National Park Service through the Southeast Native Subsistence Commission under the leadership of Harold Martin and Gordon Jackson; the results of this region-wide survey are being published separately through the Sealaska Heritage Institute and the University of Washington Press. I also benefited from a

National Endowment for the Humanities Fellowship in 1997 and received support on a range of place-related projects from the following: University of Alaska Southeast, National Oceanic and Atmospheric Administration, National Park Service, Sealaska Corporation, Sealaska Heritage Foundation (now Institute), Central Council of Tlingit and Haida Indian Tribes of Alaska, Sitka Tribe of Alaska, Hoonah Indian Association, Auk Kwáan Tribe, Angoon Community Association, Chilkat Indian Village, Chilkoot Indian Association, Skagway Traditional Council, Yakutat Tlingit Tribe, Carcross-Tagish First Nation, Ketchikan Indian Association, Douglas Island Indian Association, Juneau Tlingit and Haida Community Council, Pelican Tlingit and Haida Community Council, Tenakee Springs Indian Community Association, Native Village of Saxman, Organized Village of Kake, Organized Village of Kasaan, Hydaburg Cooperative Association, Klawock Cooperative Association, Craig Community Association, Petersburg Indian Association, Wrangell Cooperative Association, Alaska Rural Systemic Initiative, Alaska Native Language Center, Portland State University, Saint Lawrence University, and Trinity College.

An earlier version of chapter 2 was published in *Ethnology* (Fall 1997) by the University of Pittsburgh and appears herein with permission in revised form. Parts of the central arguments in chapters 3, 4, and 5, also reprinted with permission, appeared in summary form in an essay titled "The Geography of Tlingit Character," in *Coming to Shore* (2004), edited by Marie Mauzé, Michael Harkin, and Sergei Kan and published by the University of Nebraska Press in Lincoln.

In analyzing names I was fortunate to have some formal linguistic training from the late Richard Newton and Dr. Walter Soboleff and plenty of assistance with "unpacking" names from linguists Jeff Leer and Nora and Richard Dauenhauer, and a host of Tlingit speakers, most especially, Herman Kitka Sr. and John Marks.

In 1993 this project took an exceptionally enriching and embracing turn when Herman Kitka Sr. agreed to work with me on compiling a personal geography—a survey of his knowledge of named places and their associations. He proved to be my greatest teacher, friend, and brother. Through his extraordinary intellect, memory, patience, humor, and wisdom he taught and continues to teach me what Tlingit places mean and how they fit into the order of things. When I asked for a lesson in Tlingit geography, he taught me a course, which continues. His geographic life history proved so rich that I became interested in it as a text itself. I compiled and analyzed a preliminary version of that text as part of my 1995 dissertation, but since then this project has continued to grow considerably and will culminate in a separate publication. In recognition of his status as teacher, Herman Kitka Sr. was invited to participate in my thesis defense at the University of Washington in Seattle. In the spring of 1996 we taught a course together at the University of Alaska Southeast, providing further opportunity for collaboration and understanding of the ways Tlingits construct and relate to landscapes in Southeast Alaska. In a ceremony during that semester Herman bestowed upon me the ultimate gift: adoption into his family as his brother, giving me the name *Yaan Jiyeet Gaax*, carried by his late brother David and many distinguished Kaagwaantaan before him. For this exceptional embrace I am eternally grateful, humbled, and indebted.

My thinking on place-names and senses of place has been greatly enhanced by Eugene Hunn, my mentor at the University of Washington, and by the exceptional work of a wide range of scholars and artists inside and outside of anthropology, especially David Abram, Keith Basso, William Bright, Robert Bringhurst, Julie Cruikshank, Nora and Richard Dauenhauer, Robert Davis, Susan Fair, Walter Goldschmidt, A. I. Hallowell, Michael Harkin, Dell Hymes, Stephen Jett, Leslie Main Johnson, Miriam Kahn, Sergei Kan, James Kari, Steve Langdon, Michael Krauss, Jeff Leer, Frederica de Laguna, Marie Mauzé, Dan Montieth, Fred Myers, Richard Nelson, Priscilla Schulte, Brian Thom, Anthony F. C. Wallace, Thomas Waterman, Gary Witherspoon, and others.

I would also like to thank colleagues, associates, and former students at the University of Alaska, Saint Lawrence University, and Trinity College, especially Rosita Worl, Wallace Olson, Ginny Mulle, Clive Thomas, Judy Andree, Pat Fitzgerald, Robin Walz, John Pugh, Hans Chester, Yarrow Vaara, Deborah McBride, Mary Kapsner, Norio Matsumoto, Nikki Morris, Ali Pomponio, Richard Perry, John Collins, Eve Stoddard, Celia Nyamweru, Margaret Bass, David Katz, Saurabh Gupta, Fred Errington, Jane Nadel-Klein, Beth Notar, Hugh Ogden, and Jim Trostle. Finally, I thank the expert staff at the University of Washington Press, especially Lorri Hagman, Pam Canell, Marilyn Trueblood, and Jane Lichty.

Like all contemporary ethnographers of the Tlingit, I labor in the shadow of Frederica de Laguna, whose classic works have laid the foundation for nearly all subsequent work. It was her Boasian attention to ethnogeographic detail that first drew my attention to Tlingit places and place-names and to the role of the past and of the clan in shaping Tlingit conceptualizations of space and place. She also graciously furnished me with copies of her unpublished notes on Tlingit place-names.

In Alaska I would like to extend *a tlein gunalchéesh* (a big thank-you) to all those people who taught me something of Tlingit places, especially Mary Willis, Amy Marvin, Richard Dalton, Jessie Dalton, Vesta Dominicks, Charlie Joseph, Oscar Frank, John Bremner, Cecelia Kunz, Paul James, Charles Johnson, Richard Sheakley, Kelly St. Clair, Wilbur "Jumbo" James, Mary Johnson, Gilbert Mills, Edith Bean, Kelly James, Richard Newton, Frank Gordon, George Jim, Matthew Fred, Martha Kitka, Esther Shea, and Mark Jacobs, who have all walked into the forest. In addition, I would like to thank Harold Martin, George Davis, Ruth Demmert, Clarence Jackson, Mike Jackson, Lydia George, Gabriel George, Jimmy George, Matthew Kookesh, Joe Hotch, Marsha Hotch, Tom Jimmie, Paul and Marilyn Wilson, Lance Twitchell, Wanda Culp, Mary and Paul Rudolph, Charles Jack, Ken Grant, Sam Hanlon, Pat Mills, Frank White, Lilly White, George Ramos, Elaine Abraham, Judy Ramos, Ray Sensemeir, Walter Johnson, John and Roby Littlefield, Ethel Makinen, Vida Davis, Nels Lawson, Dan Marino, Andy Hope, Fred and Margaret Hope, Richard Stokes, Walter Soboleff, and others too numerous to mention. For intellectual and logistical support, I am especially grateful to Nora and Richard Dauenhauer, Nancy Yaw Davis, Andy Hope, Bob Schroeder, Robi Craig, Martha Betts, Rob Bosworth, Herman Kitka Jr., Harvey Kitka, Mike Turek, Karl Gurcke, Wayne Howell, Theresa Thibault, Dick and Rosemarie Isett, Margo Waring, and Doug Mertz.

Finally, in addition to my Tlingit brother Herman Kitka Sr., I thank the rest of my family for their invaluable assistance, herculean tolerance, and unwavering support, especially my wife, Tia, whose understanding and intelligence informs this project in so many ways, and our children, Mariah, Liam, and Roan. In me you hold a special place.

BEING AND PLACE AMONG THE TLINGIT

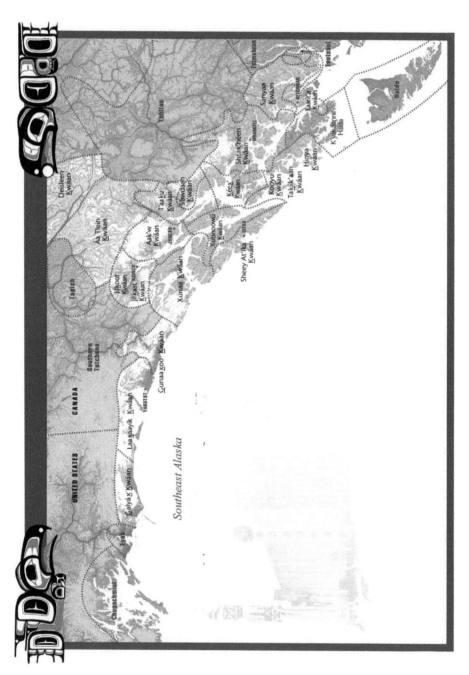

MAP 1.1. *Lingít Aaní*, Tlingit Country. Historical and Contemporary Ḵwáan Territories; courtesy of Tlingit Readers, Inc.

1 INTRODUCTION

Place and Tlingit Senses of Being

These lands are vital not only to our subsistence, but also to our sense
of being as Tlingit people. —GABRIEL GEORGE

In the summer of 1990, I attended a public hearing staged by the U.S.
Forest Service in Angoon (*Aangóon*, Isthmus Town, in Tlingit), a pre-
dominately Tlingit village of some six hundred residents located on
Admiralty Island in the center of the Tongass National Forest in Southeast Alaska. The "810 subsistence hearing," referring to section 810
of the Alaska National Interest Lands Conservation Act of 1980 (P.L.
96-487), was designed to solicit public response to a proposed commercial timber harvest in nearby Kelp Bay and its potential impacts
on subsistence fish and wildlife users. A number of Tlingits testified at
the hearing, as did some non-Natives. Most Angoon residents opposed
the proposed logging and in general were critical of Forest Service logging practices and resource management. Others spoke more broadly
on the concept of subsistence, which extends to many dimensions
beyond its legal definition, and on the meaning of Kelp Bay to Angoon
residents.

A simple statement by Gabriel George, a middle-aged fisherman, particularly struck me. He said, "These lands are vital not only to our subsistence, but also to our *sense of being* as Tlingit people." He did not
elaborate on what he meant by that statement or by the phrase "sense
of being," for it seemed self-evident to the mostly Tlingit audience (and
painfully irrelevant to the professional planners assembled on behalf of
the U.S. Forest Service). But the phrase has echoed in my mind ever since.
In many ways this project is an ethnographic attempt to understand
that statement.

3

In a fundamental sense, the landscape is part of every individual's sense of being, not just that of Tlingits, or Native Americans, or indigenous peoples. Historically—and even in the contemporary age of globalization and generic "non-places" (Auge 1995)—landscape and place have been central to culture in all societies, from the production and maintenance of cultural materials, knowledge, and values, to the formation of individual and group identity. Place can be said to constitute a cultural system (cf. Geertz 1973; Kruger 1996). As geographer Edward Relph (1976:43) puts it, "There is for virtually everyone a deep association with and consciousness of the places where we were born and grew up, where we live now, or where we have had particularly moving experiences. This association seems to constitute a vital source of both individual and cultural identity and security." Archeologist Christopher Tilley (1994:15) echoes this sentiment: "Personal and cultural identity is bound up with place; a topoanalysis is one exploring the creation of self-identity through place. Geographical experience begins in places, reaches out to others through spaces, and creates landscapes or regions for human existence."

At the same time, one cannot deny the special relationships that indigenous peoples maintain with the landscapes they have inhabited for hundreds, if not thousands, of years. Especially among indigenous hunting and gathering peoples, the importance of these relationships is exemplified in their basic metaphysics, which posits a cosmos that is alive, sentient, empowered, and moral. This animated, enchanted view of the universe as inhabited by a community of beings constantly in communication and exchange with human beings underlies processes of *interanimation* (Basso 1996) that define and enliven people in places and places in people. Thus, for Tlingits, and perhaps all indigenous peoples, place is not only a cultural system but *the* cultural system on which all key cultural structures are built.

How, then, does one analyze and understand a people's sense of being in a particular geographic environment? Clearly this enterprise involves a topoanalysis not only of the particular physical environment and people's interactions with specific places but also of how individuals and social groups define these places and express their being in relationship to them. As Arturo Escobar (2001:143) suggests, "From an anthropological perspective, it is important to highlight the emplacement of all cultural practices."

Studies of place represent old and venerable domains of inquiry in both the humanities and the social sciences, and recently they have undergone a renaissance. The philosopher Aristotle emphasized the remarkable, fundamental power of place and characterized it as "prior to all things," an indispensable aspect of every substance, and a "vessel" or container that frames and holds things—perceptions, memories, feelings, and so on (cf. Casey 1993:13–16; 1997:ix–xi). Aristotle's theory of the primordiality of place has been expanded by phenomenologists, such as Martin Heidegger (1962, 1977), Edward Casey (1993, 1997), and David Abram (1996), who have explored perceptual aspects of sensing place. Similarly, humanistic geographers (e.g., Tuan 1974, 1975, 1977; Relph 1976, 1987; Meining 1979; Buttimer and Seamon 1980; Pickles 1985; Agnew and Duncan 1989; Entrikin 1991; Sack 1997), noting the shortcomings of purely quantitative and positivist analyses of specific environments, have charted a more experientialist approach to the study of place.

In sociology, this new interest in place prompted E. V. Walter (1988:215) to launch an ambitious new subfield called "topistics," which he defines as "a holistic mode of inquiry designed to make the identity, character, and experience of place intelligible." Similarly, psychologists have begun to formulate a "social psychology of place" based on factors contributing to place identity and place attachment (cf. Altman and Low 1992; Stedman 2002). And within anthropology are found attempts to formulate an anthropology of landscape (Hirsch and O'Hanlon 1995; Bender and Winer 2001), space and place (Low and Lawrence-Zúñiga 2003), and senses of place (Feld and Basso 1996). At the same time, postmodern studies across the disciplines have underscored the importance of recognizing multiplicities of location and place in cultural analyses, the inextricable connections between space, power, and knowledge in human societies, and the enduring significance of localization and place-based struggles amid the flows and seemingly homogenizing processes of globalization (cf. Appadurai 1996; Rodman 1992; Gregory 1994; Gupta and Ferguson 1997; Low 2000; Escobar 2001).

A basic assumption underlying all this work is that to understand places one must understand the people who inhabit them. The dialectic between physical and cultural landscapes was well laid out by the geographer Carl O. Sauer (1927), who rejected the environmental determinism of his day in favor of a cultural historical approach that recognized human transformations of the land over time. Thus, landscapes and places are human constructions and relational fields, not just geographic determinants. A corollary to this idea is the notion that relationships between individuals and places are unique, complex, and dialectical. People affect places, and places affect people in countless ways. While it is still constructive to generalize about "a culture's" views of space and place, it is also true that individuals within cultures do not view or relate to the landscape in exactly the same ways. For example, if one were to map the land-use biographies of individuals within the same culture, even within the same village or household, as Hugh Brody (1981) did with Beaver Indians of northeast British Columbia, one would find that no two map biographies are alike. This is because the configuration of every individual's place experiences is unique. Similarly, as Margaret Rodman (1992:643) suggests, "places, like voices, are local and multiple" such that "for each inhabitant, a place has a unique reality, one in which meaning is shared with other people and places." Thus, to speak about a Tlingit's sense of being in relation to place is not to suggest a monolithic image tied to a single geographic landscape. On the contrary, as shall be shown, Tlingits relate to places through a variety of cultural processes that mediate activity and shape meaning. The means by which relationships with place are forged, maintained, and broken are the focus of this study.

If places are largely human constructions, then it should follow that, in order to understand people, one must know something of their places. Unfortunately, however, anthropologists have not always been as attentive to this side of the equation. As Rodman (1992:640) points out, "anthropologists, who take pains to lead students through the minefields of conceptualizing culture often assume that place is unproblematic," not a determinant but a given, simply the setting or location "where people do things."[1] But to decouple culture from place is to ignore the rich roles that place and landscape play in cultural systems. As I suspect is true in all indigenous cultures, when certain elements of social life among the Tlingit—their names, stories, songs, and art—become abstracted or otherwise wrenched from their geographic moorings, they lose a vital part of their meaning and wholeness. Much of what I have witnessed among Tlingits in Southeast Alaska and elsewhere involves just the opposite process, namely, one of binding and rebinding themselves and their culture to specific places and landscapes. This book, then, is also an attempt to understand the anchoring role of place in Tlingit identity and being.

Relationships with place are a matter not just of living and evolving in specific environments but also of imagining them. Humans not only study the land in order to make a living but also theorize about their ontological relationships to it. These musings and bits of empirical knowledge about the landscape accumulate over generations and become part of oral traditions, traditions that make people and place inseparable. As writer Barry Lopez points out (1986:244–45), "Even what is unusual does not become lost and therefore irrelevant. . . . The perceptions of any people wash over the land like a flood, leaving ideas hung up in the brush, like pieces of damp paper to be collected and deciphered." If, as a newcomer, one views the landscape as a "wilderness" to be learned and experienced only directly and anew, then one misses these bits and pieces of place knowledge and thought that have evolved and become sedimented in indigenous cultures. However, if one only studies maps or photos, or reads narratives about the geography, culture, and folklore of a place, without experiencing it directly, then one is similarly lost. In this sense anthropology, with its emphasis on cultures and on "being there," seems especially well suited to the study of place.

Most of the popular literature on indigenous peoples' conceptions of places has tended to contrast implicitly or explicitly "their" intimate, enchanted union with the landscape with "our" (Euro-American) mechanistic or estranged view. Obviously, such an approach is limited, if not flawed, and often yields a superficial or one-dimensional view of the complex and unique relations of peoples to the places they inhabit throughout the world. Here again, I believe an anthropological approach can help by providing conceptual tools and a framework for ethnographic studies of place.

As a general framework for an anthropological analysis of place making, I have identified four key cultural structures that are fundamental in mediating human relationships to place. These are (1) social organization, which groups and distributes people on the landscape and helps to coordinate their spatial world and interactions with place; (2) language and cognitive structures, which shape how places are perceived and conceptualized; (3) material production, particularly subsistence production, which informs how places are used, not used, or misused to sustain human life; and (4) ritual processes, which serve to symbolize, sanctify, condense, connect, transform, and transcend various dimensions of time, space, and place in ways that profoundly shape human place consciousness, identity, and experience. Each of these cultural structures is at once a response to the physical environment and a constitutive element of the human environment. As such, they are fundamental to understanding the relationship between people and places across cultures.

As analytical frames for the study of place-making processes, the four cultural structures are especially useful for two reasons. First, they constitute discrete variables that can be examined independently over time. Second, and more significantly, they are the four most important means by which Tlingits themselves "reciprocally appropriate" the landscape, to borrow Scott Momaday's (1974:80) felicitous phrase. It is through these media that Tlingits "invest themselves in the landscape" and, at the same time, "incorporate" the landscape into their "most fundamental experience" (80). How Tlingits use each of these structures to culturalize space and spatialize culture and to construct and maintain social, intellectual, material, and spiritual ties to places will be taken up in detail in subsequent chapters.

Changes in language, material production, social organization, and ceremonial life have affected both the quantity and quality of Tlingit interactions with place, particularly in the postcontact era since 1800. Understanding these changes requires a diachronic and ethnohistoric perspective on place. In the case of language and cognition, these changes, particularly the displacement of the Tlingit language by English in public and private discourse, have led to a loss of the rich and sensuous information content embedded in traditional linguistic domains, such as place-names. However, many of the cognitive and symbolic principles that inform the Tlingit views of place and the environment have been maintained and even enhanced despite competing worldviews and pressures to assimilate and develop. Continuity and changes in cognitive orientations toward place, while difficult to evaluate, are evident in expressive cultural forms—stories, songs, art, ritual, and the like—the mythopoetics through which Tlingits articulate their relationships to the land. For example, chapter 3 examines Huna Tlingits' continuing ties to Glacier Bay as expressed through clan legends, names, and iconography. As the discussion shall show, these cultural forms represent the foundation of Huna clans' identification with and sense of belonging to Glacier Bay, as well as their legal "title" to it.

Changes in material production have been more varied. While fish and wildlife harvests remain an integral part of rural economies, other aspects of production, such as the manufacturing of tools, have been largely abandoned in favor of imported technologies. Modern transportation and extractive technologies in particular have often profoundly altered the relations of production and, hence, the nature of interactions with places. For example, a shift in transportation from canoes and hand-powered boats to powerboats with room to dwell and carry cargo allowed people to exploit resources in areas more remote from their permanent homes without establishing seasonal camps or settlements. Similarly, the development of roads and use of motor vehicles on the archipelago have altered patterns of engagement with upland resources, such as deer. These shifts have affected not only the way that places are inhabited and utilized but also the way they are conceptualized.

Economic production and relations to place have been affected greatly by changes in social organization, specifically the transformation from a localized matrilineal clan structure to a community and regional tribal structure more consistent with non-Native socioeconomic organizations and subject to American law. These socioeconomic changes have severely undermined traditional Tlingit land and resource tenure systems, displacing the traditional *communal* systems with alien structures for managing *common* property resources (Langdon 1989). At the same time, among Tlingits there remains a strong allegiance to some aspects of traditional social organization and an implicit belief that Native management of their own places is in the best interest of both the resources and the people.

Similarly, despite more than a century of Christian missionizing, the ritual life of Tlingits remains strong (though not unchanged), especially the memorial *ku.éex'* (literally "to invite"), or potlatch, the central ritual in Tlingit ceremonial life (Kan 1989). Each fall and winter, dozens of memorial potlatches are mounted, involving thousands of Tlingits in lavish ceremonial feasts and exchanges to honor recently deceased relatives, while at the same time celebrating Tlingit personhood, social identity, and sense of place.

While the cultural means by which Tlingits experience place have undergone considerable change, they continue to invest themselves in the land and to bind places to their identity and sense of being in very distinctive ways. It is tempting and all too common for observers to overestimate the impacts of technological change and overlook the ways Tlingits continue to relate themselves to places. "The most effective technology for nomadic people is one that can be carried around in their minds," Robin Ridington (1990:12) reminds us; I term this cognitive technology "place intelligence." Unfortunately, technology has too often been reduced to artifact, when it also involves artifice—place-based strategies and ways of knowing—that endure despite the adoption of new material technologies (see also Goulet 1998; Sharp 2001).

DEFINING PLACE

It is surprising how many studies of place proceed without a definition of the central term, leaving *place* itself a rather "unclarified notion" (Casey 1997:xii). Admittedly, defining what philosophers have described as "the first of all things" can be difficult. The primary, phenomenal, and processual character of place seems to defy essentialist definitions. With these caveats in mind, I offer the following definition: *A place is a framed space that is meaningful to a person or group over time.* In some ways this definition is deceptively simple. But in analyzing it one finds that it contains three critical elements: space, time, and experience. Each element is itself a phenomenon and a process requiring some explication.

Space

It is common for people to confound *space* and *place*. Elemental space is an abstract physical concept that can be intuited but not experienced. As Walter (1988:142–43) observes, "Modern 'space' is universal and abstract, whereas a 'place' is concrete and particular. People do not experience abstract space; they experience places." As Clifford Geertz (1996:262) puts it, "No one lives in the world in general. Everybody, even the exiled, the drifting, the diasporic, or the perpetually moving, lives in some confined, limited stretch of it—the world around here." This is not to say that places are neatly confined or bounded, for indeed they are not. Rather, places are spaces that are framed through salient natural and social frameworks that individuals develop through experiences in nature and as members of a society to render "what would otherwise be a meaningless aspect of the scene into something that is meaningful" (Goffman 1974:21). Without our individual and collective frames of experience, space would remain boundless and indeterminate.

For this reason many philosophers have argued for the ontological priority of place over space and other environmental elements. To exist at all, according to the phenomenologist philosopher Edward Casey (1993), is *"to be implaced,"* that is to say, put in a space that is concrete and particular. Casey shows how this proposition has deep roots in philosophy going back to the Pythagorean Archtas of Tarentum (428–347 BC), who reasoned, "Since everything that is in motion is moved in some place, it is obvious that one has to grant priority to place, in which that which causes motion or is acted upon will be. Perhaps, thus it is the first of all things, since all existing things are either in place or not without place" (in Casey 1993:14). It is impossible, then, to conceive of a space completely devoid of objects or boundaries without first envisioning concrete places as parameters for the "between-ness" of empty space. In human consciousness, space is preceded by place. Place is our most basic geographic unit.

Phenomenologists argue that our concepts of space, time, and place must begin with our own physical constitution as embodied beings with certain corporeal orientations and sensory capacities. In his *Critique of Pure Reason* Immanuel Kant (1956:71) acknowledged that "it is . . . solely from a human standpoint that we can speak of space." All space is therefore embodied (cf. Low 2003), and the same is true of time. As the anthropologist Nancy Munn (1996:449) argues, space-time is best considered as "a symbolic nexus of relations produced out of of interactions between bodily actors and terrestrial spaces." The importance of body in the experience and conceptualization of place is examined further below.

One of the earliest social theorists to emphasize the human dimension of space was Émile Durkheim, who argued in *The Elementary Forms of Religious Life* that

> space is not the vague and indetermined medium which Kant imagined; if purely and absolutely homogenous, it would be of no use, and could not be grasped by the mind. Spatial representation consists essentially in a primary co-ordination of the data of sensuous experience. . . . To dispose things spatially there must be the possibility of *placing* them differently. . . . That is to say space could not be what it is if it were not, like time, divided and differentiated. But whence come these divisions which are so essential? All these distinctions evidently come from the fact that different sympathetic values have been attributed to various regions. ([1915] 1965:23; emphasis added)

For Durkheim the perception of space relied on more than just the phenomenology of perception and humans' "organo-physical constitution"; spatial concepts were a reflection of society and a product of the individual's experience within a particular social context.[2] Both the phenomenological and cultural perspectives, I will argue, are critical to an understanding of the nature of place in Tlingit society.

While Durkheim and others were moving toward a more humanistic geography, geography and the spatial sciences generally were moving in the opposite direction, one that de-emphasized the human dimension of space in favor of its more easily objectified elements, such as geometric coordinates and material resources. This rationalization of space also led to its being objectified in representational forms, like maps. As Michel Foucault (1980:70) has remarked, this objectification led to changes in the interpretation of space as a medium: "Space was treated as the dead, the fixed, the undialectical, the immobile," and carried an air of "anti-history. Time, in contrast, was richness, fecundity, life, dialectic." "To speak of 'social space'" in this context, remarks philosopher Henri Lefebvre (1991:1), "sounded strange." The subordination of space to time has been traced to the development of certain navigational technologies in the seventeenth century (Casey 1993:8) and was boosted significantly by positivist developments in capitalist-industrial modes of production in the modernist era (Harvey 1989).

Whatever its source, the movement to objectify and subordinate the spatial element in social life severely weakened social analyses because this important and constitutive element of social relations was taken for granted and underanalyzed. Echoing Durkheim, Foucault (1984:252, 246) points out the inherent problem with the objectivist perspective: "Space is fundamental in any form of communal life; space is fundamental in any exercise of power. . . . I think it is somewhat arbitrary to try to dissociate the effective practice of freedom by people, the practice of social relations and the spatial distributions in which they find themselves. If they are separated, they become impossible to understand. Each can only be understood through the other." Once the human and cultural dimensions of space are recognized, it is possible to analyze sociocultural phenomena, including the exercise of power, emotion, symbol, and social relations within this dynamic medium of space. Similarly, with the realization that space is a product of cultural and environmental processes, one can begin to better understand the unity and diversity among human senses of place.

The most important institution in the construction and maintenance of sociological space is social structure. Durkheim recognized the constitutive power of society in defining concepts of space. Others, such as Evans-Pritchard (1940) in his classic study of the Nuer, have explored how the sociological environment—social structure and the ebb and flow of social relations within this structure—can lead to the conceptualization of a sociological space and distance that is quite distinct from physical space and varies independently of physical distance. At the architectural level, Pierre Bourdieu (1973) and others have employed structuralist frames to analyze built environments, such as the Berber house, as microcosms of key symbolic relations between nature and culture, male and female, and other dichotomous forces. But Bourdieu (1977) and the praxis theorists, who have explored the relationship between habitus (culturally derived cognitive and behavior patterns and dispositions) and practice (self-interested manipulation of those patterns and dispositions), also have convincingly shown how space and other basic cultural concepts are not simply determined by a sui generis culture, as Durkheim would have it, or sprung from deep-seated, universally dichotomizing cognitive structures, as Claude Lévi-Strauss (1966; see also Descola and Pálsson 1996) suggests, but rather are subject to strategic manipulation by self-conscious and self-interested individuals within that culture. Thus, the social environment becomes a strategic context for defining both space and place. Spaces are not simply reproduced by cognitive and social structures but are also contested, refined, and reshaped by individuals through the practical experiences of living.

Among the Tlingit, the relationship between sociological space and physical space has not been studied in detail. In her study of the Angoon Tlingit, however, Frederica de Laguna (1960:17–18) made an important observation on the role of social structure in shaping the individual Tlingit's sense of history and geography:

> I believe it would be possible to show that the individual Tlingit's sense of history and geography is strongly affected by the dominance of the sib [local clan or house group] which controls the social, political, and ceremonial aspects of his life. Tlingit histories are concerned with the origin of lineages or sibs, the quarrels or other events that caused such family groups to break away from their parent bodies or to leave their original homes, and the subsequent wanderings of these groups until they reached their present locations. The stories deal also with the supernatural occurrences upon which the claims to lineage and sib totemic crests are based, and lastly they tell of encounters with other sib groups. . . . The reality of this history is kept vivid because personal names, especially those that are assumed as titles, are derived from legendary or historic events, and those who bear them are reincarnations of the dead ancestors who took part in these events. Similarly certain localities, even though they may lie beyond the present boundaries of Tlin-

git country, must have special meaning, a special quality of reality for the sib members, because these places are the scenes of sib history. It is the sib that provides a sort of unity to geography and history, a "logic" which may prove to be more important than a purely spatial and temporal framework.

Following de Laguna's lead, in chapter 2 I explore the logic of Tlingit social geography and how it functions to coordinate individual experience and relationships to place.

While social structures organize people in space-time, ecological conditions also shape how people live there. The ecological environment includes the physical geography of space and place as well as human ecological variables, such as economic patterns, which structure how people make a living in a particular region. While the physical environment does not dictate conceptions of space and place, as the vulgar environmental determinism would have it, it does constrain them. As opposed to the strategic context of the social environment, the physical environment is a parametric context, meaning that its constraining influence typically functions independently of other variables, such as the social context.[3] Thus, for example, although a great deal of variety is seen among the peoples of the Northwest Coast, all of them display a maritime or riverine orientation because the rugged upland environment all but prohibits other means of existence. However, much of human ecology, like the social environment, can be viewed as a strategic context where variables are dependent on one another. Thus, a particular mode of subsistence may be facilitated by a certain social structure (or structures) or vice versa. As an illustration of this, Allan Richardson (1982) shows how different types of social organization among Northwest Coast Indians can be correlated with variations of the spatiotemporal distribution of resources within this coastal rainforest ecosystem. The parametric constraints of the physical environment, combined with the strategic contexts of the social and ecological environments, serve to define the interrelationships between people and places.

In summing up this discussion, it is worth noting that in defining the word *place* dictionaries typically refer to both the physical and social contexts of the environment. The most common definition of *place*, of course, refers to its being "a portion of space" or the physical envi-

ronment. But other definitions invoke the idea of a sociological ordering, as expressed, for example, in the phrase "to take one's place." Both
of these orderings are vital to understanding the concept and role of
place in human society.

Time

Dictionary definitions of *place* also include the verb phrase "took place,"
which denotes a temporal ordering. Just as space is basic to the concept of place, so, too, is time. Part of the postmodern critique of anthropology has focused on traditional ethnology's reification of the
ethnographic present and consequent neglect of historical contingencies that define particular groups in particular settings at particular times
(e.g., Fabian 1983; Wolf 1982). Places are products of history; to ignore
this fact is to risk missing a good deal of their nuance and meaning.
Even the functionalist Bronislaw Malinowski (1922:330) was sensitive
to this, pointing out long ago that named places often serve as historical markers on the landscape, symbolizing and bringing forth events
of the past and making them "tangible and permanent" through the
enduring features of the landscape. It is impossible to comprehend the
meaning of such places without knowing something of their history.

But there is even more to it than this. In distilling events of the past
into a geographic present, places also reach *across* time, making elements of the past accessible to those who have not experienced them
directly. In this sense, places are not only situated in historical time and
space, but they also situate time and space through their symbolism, be
it in place-names or other associations that succinctly reference events
of the past. Time is thus "part of our experiences of places, for these
experiences must be bound up with flux or continuity. And places themselves are the present expressions of past experiences and events and of
hopes for the future" (Relph 1976:33).

One social theorist who has shed considerable light on the relationship between time, space, and place is Anthony Giddens, whose structuration theory parallels in many respects Bourdieu's theory of practice.
Giddens (1984:127) argues that all social interaction is contextual—
"situated" in time and space—yet stretches across time-space "dis-

tances," and that it is the business of social theory "to try to grasp how it comes about that the situated action which is the 'materiality' of social life intersects with the form of institutions which span large 'stretches' of time-space." In an effort to remake a social theory that is sensitive not only to social structures and space but also to human agency and time, Giddens and others (e.g., Pred 1990) have drawn on concepts of temporality from the philosophy of Heidegger, the history of Fernand Braudel, and the time-geography of Torsten Hägerstrand.

In his existential philosophy of Being and time, Heidegger introduces the concept of *Dasein*, usually translated as "Being-in-the-world" (Heidegger 1962). *Dasein* emphasizes the phenomenological experience of place and the "presencing" (or becoming "present-at-hand") that occurs in encounters with place. Presencing involves, among other things, the transcendence of time in place, a gathering and uniting of time(s) and space(s) in a unique ensemble. This transcendental quality of place enables places to fuse elements of history and the landscape in the human consciousness. Places, then, may serve as "mnemonic pegs" (Basso 1984a:43), or what Mikhail Bakhtin (1981:84–85) calls "chronotopes," for the collective memory. Chronotopes are "points in the geography of a community where time and space intersect and fuse. Time takes on flesh and becomes visible for human contemplation; likewise, space becomes charged and responsive to the movements of time and history and the enduring character of a people. . . . Chronotopes thus stand as monuments to the community itself, as symbols of it, as forces operating to shape its members' images of themselves" (cited in Basso 1984a:43–44). Like Heidegger's *Dasein*, Bahktin's concept of the chronotope, perhaps best translated as space-time or place-time, represents the merging of temporal and spatial sequences, where neither space nor time can be understood without reference to the other. As poignant means of materializing time in space, places and their referents (place-names, images, and the like) become important and powerful chronotopes for orienting and shaping audiences' "images of themselves" in narrative, song, and other media.

Among the Tlingit, as with Keith Basso's Western Apache, the landscape helps not only to make history but also to hold it in place, "as a repository of distilled wisdom, a stern but benevolent keeper of tradition" (1996:63). As de Laguna (1972, 1:58) points out,

The human meanings of the landscape are more than the mythological dimension recognized by Malinowski. . . . They involve not simply places visited and transformed by Raven in the mythical past, but places hallowed by human ancestors. For individuals, of course, the world has special meanings, for there are places about which their grandparents and parents have told them, spots they have visited in their youth, or where they still go. None of these personal associations are completely private; all are intermeshed through anecdote or shared experiences.

It is one of the unique features of places that they gather, intermesh, and crystallize time in this way.

Another method to analyze the temporal dimension of place in personal terms is through time-geography. Developed by the Swedish geographer Hägerstrand (cf. 1975) time-geography involves plotting the spatial course of daily life on a three-dimensional plane showing time, space, path (time-space sequencing), and project. Hägerstrand seeks to spatialize time, giving separation as distance to separation as time. Using his spatial notation to track individuals' time-geographies, it is possible to analyze the spatial contexts and time-space routines that constitute daily life in particular places. When individual map "biographies" are aggregated or superimposed, intersections between individuals' paths and projects are given geometric form, and the important "stations" or locales of human interaction can be viewed. As Giddens (1985:266) observes, Hägerstrand's time-geography is important because it highlights five facets of "time-geographic reality" that "express the material axes of human existence and underlie all contexts of association in conditions of co-presence." These facets are (1) the indivisibility of the body and the limitations corporeality imposes on movement and perception; (2) the finite life span of humans across space and time; (3) the limited capacity of humans to participate in more than one activity (multitasking aside) and the recognition that every task has a duration; (4) the fact that movement in space is also movement in time; and (5) the limited "packing capacity" of time-space, such that two persons cannot occupy precisely the same space at the same time. Through his system of notation representing the physical ontology of beings in time-space, Hägerstrand seeks to elucidate the "'fundamental bonds' among life, time, and space" and to provide a "situational ecology," or schema for demonstrating how commitment to any precisely situated activity constrains subsequent daily activity participation" (Pred 1990:20). By charting the competitive flow of "interrelated presences and absences" between people and spaces, Hägerstrand's spatialized biographies provide a basis for a phenomenological understanding of individuals' relationships with places. It also underscores the unique system of cognitive maps, or what anthropologist Anthony F. C. Wallace (see 2003) terms "mazeways," possessed by any individual within a (necessarily heterogeneous) culture.

Giddens appropriates Hägerstrand's muscular geography but faults him for a weak sociology. To compensate, he combines Hägerstrand's emphasis on tracking the individual corporeal being in time-space with two sociogeographical concepts from his theory of structuration, locale and regionalization, which emphasize the organization of the settings of interaction and their relation to human agency and individual paths and projects in space. "Locales refer to the use of space to provide the settings of interaction in turn being essential to specifying its contextuality" (Giddens 1985:271). Thus, locales are more than simply points in space. They are places defined by the predictable human interactions and activities that occur there as much as by the physical setting itself. They may be as small as a street corner or as large as a nation-state. Correlatively, regionalization is the "zoning of time-space in relation to routinised practices" (272). For example, rooms or floors of a house, whether it be a Tlingit clan house or an American nuclear family home, may be zoned for certain activities in space, and certain parts of the day may be reserved expressly for some activities while others are considered taboo. For Giddens space and time are strategic components of social action, not simply containers for it. As David Harvey (1989:211–12) and Foucault stress, from a political economy perspective, they are also strategic components of hegemony and domination.

Giddens also offers a more general evaluation of changes in the construction of time-space that have come as a result of modernity. Since the eighteenth century, he argues, face-to-face interactions have become less central to social integration because of technological and organizational innovations. As a consequence, the everyday spheres of social life have become "disembedded" from the here and now, although they still exist at the abstract level, through what he calls "time-space distanciation." By recognizing these processes of disembedding and time-space distanciation, Giddens attempts to account for the absences as well as presences in modern social life. This concept is closely related to Harvey's (1989) concept of "time-space compression," a phenomenon he traces to changes in material production, specifically the move from conventional "Fordist" assembly line–style industrial production, which was rigidly organized and spatially centered, to the present-day "flexible accumulation" mode of production, epitomized by its fluidity in time and space and flexibility in exploiting labor and markets. Flexible accumulation has led to a compression of time-space because "time horizons of both public and private decision-making have shrunk, while satellite communication and declining transport costs have made it increasingly possible to spread those decisions immediately over an ever wider and variegated space" (1989:147). As shall be seen, the time-space distanciation and time-space compression that have accompanied modernization and development in Southeast Alaska have had a profound effect on Tlingit person-place relations.

Another concept of temporality that has informed modern place theory is historian Fernand Braudel's notion of a spatialized time. Braudel and the French Annales school helped to launch a paradigmatic shift in historical writing, moving away from chronicling the major events and figures of a particular era and toward a focus on the activities of ordinary people over long periods of time (*la longue durée*). Braudel viewed time from three perspectives, which he outlines in the introduction to *The Mediterranean and the Mediterranean World in the Age of Philip II* (1972:20–21).

The first and most basic temporality, according to Braudel, is that of natural time, or "geographical history." Geographical history is one "whose passage is almost imperceptible, that of man in his relationship to the environment, a history in which all change is slow, a history of constant repetition, ever-recurring cycles" (1972:20). Braudel was critical of the lack of deference typically given to the natural setting in historical writing, believing it was myopic to view natural history merely as a backdrop rather than a major, continuous constraint on human activity.

Social time, "the history of groups and groupings," is Braudel's second temporal perspective. From this perspective one can track the *durée* of sociocultural institutions, of demographic fluctuations, and of other dimensions of social life that carry on well beyond the life span of an individual or generation.

Braudel's third frame is the *durée* of daily life, filled with remembrances of specific events and personalities. This is the perspective that is richest in human interest and, as a consequence, tends to draw the most attention from historians. But for Braudel these events and personalities are only "surface disturbances, crests of foam that the tides of history carry on their strong backs" (21). In contrast, for Giddens and Hägerstrand the events of daily life and how they reproduce or reconfigure time-space routines and other aspects of social structure (and social time) represent an important temporal frame of analysis. Undoubtedly, all three dimensions of time converge in the individual's experience of place, making history a key component of place.

It is worth noting that Braudel's three temporalities correspond in some ways to Tlingits' own spatialized sense of time. An analog to Braudel's natural time is the Tlingit notion of "mythic" time (*tlakw*, "eternal"), the primordial (but not temporally fixed) era in which the formation of the world took shape, including elements of the physical and social worlds that continue to structure human life. Although the events of mythic time are rooted deep in the past, this history is ongoing and recurring in the sense that Tlingits continually make reference to their existence and being in relation to these events and their settings. Thus the Old Woman of the Tides is not merely a remote mythical figure but a continuing phenomenal presence in the ebb and flow of daily sea tides. This temporality is also embodied in the Tlingit concept of *shagóon*, often translated as "heritage and destiny." As I shall demonstrate in chapter 2, this construction of identity fuses spatial and temporal dimensions in powerful ways.

Tlingits also give high priority to social history, including clan histories, historical relations between social groups, and interactions with non-Tlingit peoples and institutions. And finally, Tlingits have a category of historic time, akin to Braudel's *durée* of daily life, which is largely contained within the past century or several generations and includes remembrances of daily life, events, personalities, and, of course, places.

In sum, *Dasein*, time-geography and structuration, and notions of historical temporality and *durée* are all important analytical tools for defining the phenomenon of place. Although different cultures may conceptualize time in different ways, time is everywhere inseparable from place because it is through temporally situated interactions with specific locales that cultural and individual conceptions of place are formed. Thus, as Casey (1993:21) observes,

> place proves to be a deeply constitutive, indeed an irreplaceable, factor in the phenomenon of time and its understanding. There is *no (grasping of) time* without place. . . . Place situates time by giving it a local habitation. Time arises from places and passes (away) *between* them. It also vanishes *into* places at its edges and *as* its edges. For the "positions" of time are its effective limits, without which . . . time would not be able to present itself to us, would not be timelike or temporal in the first place.

As I shall discuss in more detail, Tlingits have their own temporalities and distinctive linguistic and cultural means of transcending and otherwise reckoning time with place.

Experience

The third key element in defining place is experience. Unlike abstract spaces, places are infused with meaning and value through the process of human experience. "Every event happens somewhere," writes Walter (1988:117), "but we don't often locate it by its longitude and latitude. We say this experience happened to me in Manchester, or I felt this way in New York, or I did such and such in Boston." The episodes, feelings, and activities that characterize experience serve to construct places in our minds. The boundaries and scale of place are likewise framed by experience. The "fireplace and the home are both places; a distinctive region is a place, and so is a nation" (Tuan 1975:153). Each setting is meaningful as a place because it is the locus of experience.

Geographer Yi-Fu Tuan (1977:6) suggests experiences with places can be "direct and intimate" or "indirect and conceptual." Thus, places acquire meaning both from primary apperception of the landscape through sensual experience and through indirect experiences of place conveyed exclusively by symbols encoded in language and other cultural forms, such as songs, stories, poems, names, recipes, games, festivals, tools, crafts, and art.[4] These cultural forms codify not only knowledge and conceptions of place but also feelings toward place. Folklorist Mary T. Hufford (1986:49) has suggested that cultural forms that are inextricably "bound to their locales," indeed "all things that are crafted out of the imagination's encounter with the land and its resources," can be considered "genres of place." Genres of place reveal not only human adaptation to and integration with local environments but also broader aspects of an ecological consciousness based on sensuous experience, or as Hufford puts it, "an ability to make sense of the environment, not only to tell what is there, but to understand the relationships between environmental elements" (1987:16; see also Hufford 1992, Ryden 1993).

The physical experience of the environment is mediated not only by the senses but by the body itself. As Tuan (1977:34) points out, drawing on cultural and phenomenological theory:

> Space is an abstract term for a complex set of ideas. People of different cultures differ in how they divide up their world, assign value to its parts, and measure them. . . . Nonetheless certain cross-cultural similarities exist, and they rest ultimately on the fact that man is the measure of all things. That is to say, if we look for fundamental principles of spatial organization, we find them in two facts: the posture and structure of the human body, and the relations (whether close or distant) between human beings.

Citing examples from around the world, Tuan goes on to show how, "in a literal sense, the human body is the measure of direction, location, and distance" (1977:44).

Why should such a pattern exist? According to the French phenomenologist philosopher Maurice Merleau-Ponty (1962), spatial terms are necessarily anthropocentric because the body is not only a universal standard of measure for humans, but it is also the ultimate mediator of their perception. When the body is viewed as the first and most essential environment one inhabits and possesses a priori, before enculturation, it is easy to see why it is commonly referenced in descriptions of the larger physical environment. As Marcel Mauss asserts, "The body is man's first and most natural instrument . . . man's first and most natural technical object, and at the same time [his] technical means"

(1979:104). To posit this is not to deny that different cultures conceive of the body differently; rather, it is to suggest that the body is the ultimate arbiter of human interaction with the environment:

> My body continually *takes me into place*. It is at once agent and vehicle, articulator and witness of being-in-place. Although we rarely attend to its exact role, once we do we cannot help but notice its importance. Without . . . our bodies, not only would we be lost in place—acutely disoriented and confused—we would have no coherent sense of place itself. Nor could there be any such thing as *lived* places, i.e., places in which we live and move and have our being. Our living-moving bodies serve to structure and configurate entire scenarios of place. (Casey 1993:48)

Our precognitive embodiment of place affects both our direct and indirect experiences of place. It not only mediates our physical interaction with places but, as a metaphor and schema, structures how we conceptualize and talk about place (Lakoff and Johnson 1980; M. Johnson 1987). Thus, anatomical references are common in place-names, and allusions to bodily movement, hazards, sustenance, and so on are necessarily employed in geographic narratives to orient the listener.

This view is very much in keeping with the "experiential realist" school of thought that has emerged in the cognitive sciences (Lakoff and Johnson 1999; see also Varela, Thompson, and Rosch 1991). According to George Lakoff (1987:xiv), one of the school's main proponents, "Thought is embodied, that is, the structures used to put together our conceptual systems grow out of bodily experience and make sense in terms of it; moreover, the core of our conceptual systems is directly grounded in perception, body movement, and experience of a physical and social character." Thus, the body, as prototypical environment, becomes a preconceptual cognitive tool for classifying natural phenomena as well as a key metaphor for interpreting experience. The experiential realist school offers itself as an alternative to the objectivist "mind-as-machine" view, spawned by René Descartes' notion of thought as abstract and disembodied, and the extreme form of linguistic relativism, which posits that the nature of experience is determined not by cognitive universals such as embodiment but by the arbitrary and varying linguistic and cognitive structures possessed by different cultures.

Another important set of constraints in defining the experience of place is what Franz Boas (1934:14) broadly defines as "cultural interests." Cultural interests involve not only basic subsistence and economic needs but also such things as orientation, safety, and recreation. For the Kwakiutl (Kwakwaka'wakw) whom Boas studied and other groups such interests help to differentiate places and to structure interactions with specific locales. Boas noted in particular how cultural interests are reflected in place naming. Thus, a narrow marine pass between two islands might be labeled not explicitly for its topography but rather as a "place where you harpoon seals," citing the cultural phenomenon that occurs there. The human activity, the cultural interest, comes to stand for the place itself through the principle of metonymic association.

The experience of making a living in an environment is central to what it means to "inhabit" a place as opposed to simply observing or passing through it. Dwelling is what transforms space into a lebensraum (living space). As the writer Wendell Berry (1977:22) explains:

> The concept of country, homeland, dwelling place becomes simplified as "the environment"—that is, what surrounds us. Once we see our place, our part of the world, as *surrounding* us, we have already made a profound division between it and ourselves. We have given up the understanding—dropped it out of our language and so out of our thought—that we and our country create one another, depend on one another; that our land passes in and out of our bodies just as our bodies pass in and out of our land; that we and our land are part of one another, so all who are living as neighbors here, human and plant and animal, are part of one another, and so cannot possibly flourish alone; that, therefore, our culture must be our response to our place, our culture and our places are images of each other and inseparable from each other, and so neither can be better than the other.

These sentiments are echoed in Heidegger's (1971) seminal essay, "Building Dwelling Thinking," in which he traces the concepts "to dwell" and "to build" back to the same German verb, *bauen*. *Dwelling*, Heidegger observes, implies such things as "sparing" and "preserving" places as well as "cultivating" them, while *building* merely denotes constructing things. Unfortunately, in modern usage, the "dwelling" nuance of *bauen* has been eclipsed by the notion of "building" or constructing, despite the centrality of the concept of dwelling to place, experience, and sense of being.

Dwelling breeds a certain intimacy through everyday experience that is often profoundly different from the peak experiences that may accompany a fleeting encounter with place. As Tim Ingold (2000:192) stresses: "A place owes its character to the experiences it affords to those who spend time there—to the sights, sounds and indeed smells that constitute its specific ambience. And these, in turn, depend on the kinds of activities in which its inhabitants engage. It is from this relational context of people's engagement with the world, in the business of dwelling, that each place draws its unique significance." In Southeast Alaska this contrast is evident in the way that Alaska Natives and tourists encounter the same landscapes. While tourists tend to marvel in Muir-like mystical terms at the fabulous peaks, glaciers, fjords, and other physical features of grandeur, Tlingits, at least in their own locales, are more likely to perceive and characterize places in terms of the practical activities that engage them, what ecological psychologists (J. J. Gibson 1979; see also Ingold 2000) term "affordances" (e.g., "a good fishing hole," "egg gathering country," or "dangerous rapids"), or in terms of their social geography and history (e.g., "That's Coho [clan] country," or "That's where Raven made his swing"). Of course, Tlingits have peak landscape experiences too, and extraordinary onetime encounters with place—both good and bad—comprise an important genre of their oral traditions. But the negotiation of mundane affordances in the process of dwelling is more central to Tlingit place making than the extreme geographies produced and consumed through tourism.

In his innovative work *The Experience of Landscape*, Jay Appleton (1975) suggests that one's reactions to particular landscapes are in fact conditioned by basic human needs such as finding resources (prospect) and shelter (refuge) and avoiding "hazards," the fulfillment of which is critical to survival and evolutionary success. Combining the experientialist philosophy of John Dewey with insights of nineteenth-century British landscape and aesthetics philosophers, such as John Ruskin, Appleton fashions a "habitat theory" in order to explain how experience has informed human aesthetic responses: "Aesthetic satisfaction, experienced in the contemplation of landscape, stems from the spontaneous perception of landscape features which, in their shapes, colours, spatial arrangements and other visible attributes, act as sign stimuli indicative of environmental conditions favourable to survival, whether they *are* favourable or not. This proposition we call *habitat theory*" (69). A corollary to this is *prospect-refuge* theory, which "postulates that, because the ability to see without being seen is an intermediate step in the satisfaction of many of those [biological] needs, the capacity of an environment to ensure the achievement of this becomes a more immediate source of aesthetic satisfaction" (73). Using the principles of prospect, refuge, and hazard, Appleton develops a framework for classifying landscape imagery and symbolism in evolutionary ecological terms. In this scheme, well-illuminated vistas and panoramas symbolize prospect and are pleasing because they provide a vantage point for the hunter in pursuit of food. Similarly, refuges are attractive because these landscapes provide cover and defensible shelter necessary for survival. Those features of the landscape that block or prevent human survival are classified as hazards. Appleton contends that these associative principles inform all humans' intellectual and emotional responses to landscapes and thus help to define the human experience of landscape.

Appleton even marshals ethnographic data from the Tlingit—Aurel Krause's (1956:125) nineteenth-century descriptions of Chilkat hunters patiently waiting in blinds for hours until game approaches—in support of his notion that the combination of searching (prospect) and hiding (refuge) is fundamental to human survival and thus the key to aesthetics (Appleton 1975:72–73). However, he makes no attempt to apply his aesthetics response theory to Tlingit or other Northwest Coast art. Indeed such a task would seem problematic, as Northwest Coast art is highly stylized and typically represents the landscape in rather abstract terms having little resemblance to what one might conceive of as natural prospects, refuges, or hazards, but everything to do with Tlingits' sense of being in relation to those sites (a point I shall return to later). Thus, despite the elegance and utility of his prospect-refuge theory, Appleton's aesthetics, which continue to influence evolutionary theorists (cf. Pinker 1997:374–78), provide little explanation for the vast differences found in the art and landscape representations of different cultures, or how Northwest Coast art in particular gives complex "voice to the many forms of interconnecting life and consciousness that cooperate to manifest the world" (S. Brown 2000:112) as experienced by emplaced individuals.

Along with these biological and materialist concerns that mediate experience in and responses to environments in direct and—if one accepts Appleton's thesis—uniform ways are the more indirect experiences of place through other expressive cultural forms or genres. As A. Irving Hallowell (1967:7) long ago pointed out:

> The representations of objects and events of all kinds play as characteristic a role in man's total behavior as does the direct presentation of objects and events in perception. Thus skill in the manipulation of symbols is directly involved with the development of man's rational capacities. But symbolization is likewise involved with all other psychic functions—attention, perception, interest, memory, dreams, imagination, etc. Representative processes are at the root of man's capacity to deal with the abstract qualities of objects and events, his ability to deal with the possible or conceivable, the ideal as well as the actual, the intangible along with the tangible, the absent as well as the present object or event, with fantasy and with reality.

While some theorists, such as cultural materialists, tend to regard these "indirect" representational processes as subordinate to ecological variables when it comes to place making, others have shown convincingly that they are central to the construction of landscape and memory (cf. Schama 1995). Basso (1984a:48) argues that materialist models of the landscape "ignore the fact that American Indians, like groups of people everywhere, maintain a complex array of symbolic relationships with their physical surroundings, and that those relationships, which may have little to do with the serious business of making a living, play a fundamental role in shaping other forms of social activity." He goes on to outline his vision of a "cultural ecology that is cultural in the fullest sense, a broader and more flexible approach to the study of man-land relationships in which the symbolic properties of environmental phenomena receive the same kind of care and attention that has traditionally been given to their material counterparts" (49).

In fact the distinction between direct and indirect experience, between the material and the symbolic worlds, is impossible to make in these Native American ontologies. Among Tlingits, as among Basso's Apaches and Hallowell's Objiwa (see Black 1977:101–2), indigenous ways of knowing and modes of perception allow for "the expectation that individuals will 'see' different objects in the same landscape, will 'hear' different sounds . . . [and] that the same entity may appear in different forms from one time to another." And yet these different ways of seeing are accommodated within broader cultural frames that are held in common. A great virtue of looking at culture through the perspective and experience of place is that both individual and collective perceptions are embraced, and material and symbolic components of the environment are not artificially separated but rather inextricably intertwined. Similarly, in studying place feelings need not be subordinated or divorced from cognition, for emotion is basic to the way we sense and think about our world (Milton 2002).

Perhaps nowhere is this more evident in Tlingit than in the processes of place making through expressive cultural forms, or genres of place, which are at once representations of places and ways of sensing them. They constitute what Ingold (2000) terms the "poetics of dwelling."

EXPRESSIVE CULTURE, MULTIMEDIACY, AND GENRES OF PLACE

The phenomenal experience of place forges complex symbolic and material relationships with the landscape, which emphasize "dwelling" in the Heideggerian sense. As I have suggested, these complex relationships can be understood not only by examining key cultural structures that forge them but also through the uniquely expressive cultural forms, or "genres" of place, that represent them. Tlingits have a term for genres of place that take on sacred status as possessions: *at.óow* (literally "owned things"). *At.óow* include not only geographic sites themselves but also material and symbolic resources that Tlingit matrilineages identify with as emblematic (and chronotopic) of their being and relations to specific environs. *At.óow* are deployed, most poignantly in ritual, to bolster individual and collective claims about identity, being, place, and other prerogatives.

At.óow are both representations and tools of emplacement. In the absence of being there, they give to place a sense of tangibility through their immediacy and multimediacy. As Angoon elder Lydia George explained to me, the places Tlingits hold sacred tend to have four ingredients: a name, a story, a song (typically accompanied by a dance), and a design (or crest). Each of these ingredients is itself an *at.óow*, a chrono-tope, and a genre of place. Together they constitute a cultural nexus of sacredness that endows places, and the people who possess them, with profound webs of significance. In the potent context of ritual, *at.óow* may go beyond multimediacy and take on a spiritual agency such that participants sense they have been literally transported to ancestral places (see chap. 5).

Stories and songs are components of oral tradition, which may contain just about any enduring notion, belief, or narrative of place that is consciously transmitted from one generation to the next. Through the plots and settings of story and song societies define themselves in time and space. While not all myths are explicitly explanatory or didactic in nature, through their settings, characters, and tropes these narratives chronicle human relations with the landscape over time. When discussing native place-names in an area, Tlingits often make the general comment that "all these places have stories behind them," the implication being that vital parts of Tlingit history, and thus their own history and identity, are, to quote Munn ([1973] 1986:214–15) on the Walbiri, "carried in the experience of the country as a network of objectifiable places, the prime givens of the external environment."

For groups that stress oral tradition, "excursions into the past are meticulously marked onto the landscape" rather than a calendar (Rosaldo 1980:48). In Tlingit oral tradition, time is reckoned by era, as suggested above, but precise dates are not often important. In contrast, place and setting are usually reckoned with precision. For the Tlingit, like the Western Apache (Basso 1988:110), "nothing is considered more basic to the effective telling of a . . . 'story' or 'narrative' . . . than identifying the geographical locations at which events in the story unfold." This is not because the settings are obscure; on the contrary, it is because they are well known as physical and symbolic landmarks.

> For unless Apache listeners are able to picture a physical setting for narrative events (unless, as one of my consultants said, "your mind can travel to the place and really see it"), the events themselves will be difficult to imagine. This is because events in the narrative will seem to "happen nowhere" (*dohwaa'agodzaa da*), and such an idea, Apaches assert, is both

preposterous and disquieting. Placeless events are an impossibility; everything that happens must happen somewhere. The location of an event is an integral aspect of the event itself, and therefore identifying the event's location is essential to properly depicting—and effectively picturing—the event's occurrence. (10)

As Leslie Marmon Silko (1990:888) observes for the Pueblo, this depicting and picturing is also critical in that "often . . . the turning point in the narrative [involves] a peculiarity or special quality of a rock or tree or plant found only at that place."

Because place is so central to oral tradition, place-names are often key elements of narrative and history. But they also stand on their own as a domain of knowledge, identity, and *at.óow* and therefore as a genre of place. As linguistic artifacts on the land, place-names function not only to define places but also to re-present them in human knowledge, thought, and speech. Naming, of course, is a ubiquitous cultural trait born of the need to communicate distinctions between persons, places, and things. Place naming in particular is motivated by the desire to distinguish meaningful spaces from space in general. Some philosophers maintain that a place cannot exist unless it has a name. While this may be going too far, there is no denying that place-names are "richly evocative symbols" (Basso 1988) conveying a wealth of information about the spaces they signify and the cultures that speak them. As icons, indexes, and symbols of place phenomena, place-names have enormous referential power. They evoke not only material aspects of the landscape but also human tasks, events, emotions, and other mental associations tied to those locales. As Lévi-Strauss (1966:168) rightly observes, "Space is a society of named places, just as people are landmarks within the group." Thus, "both are designated by proper names, which can be substituted for each other in many circumstances common to many societies." This pattern is strongly evident in Tlingit naming, as illustrated in chapter 2.[5]

Visual iconography, the *at.óow* of design, comprises another important expressive medium though which people represent sacred relationships to place. Tlingit icons and motifs in visual art work on a number of different levels. They reference events, emotions, kin, places, and other themes that are fundamental to individual and social group identity.

The most sacred icons are clan crests, manifestations of animals, places, and other entities, which are incorporated into artistic designs, regalia, and other cultural forms. Crests, observed de Laguna (1972, 1:451), "are, from the native point of view, the most important feature of the matrilineal sib or lineage, acquired in the remote past by the ancestors and determining the nature and destiny of their descendants." This combination of heritage and destiny, or *shagóon*, is believed to be embodied in the sacred property of the matrilineage and also in the social group members themselves. Each crest, too, has a story "behind it" that evokes elements of the present landscape in relation to the distant past.

Animals were taken as crests typically because of specific events that occurred at particular places involving them and members of the social group. In other cases geographic places, themselves animate, were adopted as crests. When a place was appropriated as a crest, its image served to link indelibly particular social groups to particular terrains. In many cases, as I shall show, the social groups actually derive their names from these locales, and thus the crests serve to fuse members' identities, origins, and history. In this way, crests and other visual art, as representations of places, endow portions of the landscape with multiple layers of meaning and identify them as the property and heritage of specific social groups, and the landscape itself is continuously defined and redefined through iconography. Thus, although Tlingit art differs markedly in style from most Euro-American landscape art, both constitute genres of place because they explicitly appropriate and idealize places and therefore shape the perception and experience of those landscapes.

Names, stories, songs, and crest designs represent genres of place that have been ritually sanctified as *at.óow*. But more mundane aspects of culture, such as local technologies, can also be considered genres of place. A good example of this is the Barnegat Bay sneakbox, a small boat developed by inhabitants of the New Jersey Pine Barrens for hunting and fishing.

It was custom made for the marshes of estuaries of South Jersey. In its form we see every contingency neatly anticipated. Its spoon-shaped hull enables it to glide through areas marked as land on coastal maps. . . . [It] is light enough for one man to haul over land between channels. It is equipped with a mast-hole, centerboard well, and detachable rudder for sailing; winter and summer sails; folding oarlocks and a removable decoy rack to suppress its profile; runners for traveling on ice; and two kinds of accessory ice hooks for breaking up slushy ("porridge") and hard ("pane") ice. Its sloping transom allows a hunter to row backward in channels that are too narrow to turn around in. . . . In the sneakbox the shapes of men and meadows are fused. (Hufford 1987:32)

For Hufford, this technology "comprises a distinctive response to distinctively regional conditions, a tool whereby local men distinguish themselves as inhabitants of a singular region" (1990:50). Its form and function also reveal a deep understanding and experience of place, and the technology itself "synthesizes the observations of generations of baymen of water, land, air, man, and mud." In this way the material technology not only comes to symbolize the place itself and but also serves as a unique extension of the body and the senses in experiencing place. What is more, objects of material culture take on emplaced "biographies" within communities, as they are passed on from generation to generation. For this reason, material culture provides an ideal frame for evaluating what Peter Jordan (2003:306) terms "landscape enculturation," because it is through the manufacture, use, transmission, and deposition of material artifacts that "communities bring rich symbolic meanings to the landscapes they inhabit, and at the same time transform the physical terrain."

The same sense of place is evident in the Tlingit *gudiyé,* a specialized seal hunting canoe apparently first developed for use among the ice floes of Icy Bay by its Eyak and Tlingit inhabitants. These nimble craft were built with a heavy prow and equipped with a special wooden protuberance off the bow designed to quietly push aside the glacial ice as hunters stalked their prey. They were so well adapted to the ice-filled bays of the Gulf of Alaska that their inventors reportedly kept them hidden in a secret lake called *Ligaas.aa,* "Tabooed Lake," above Icy Bay (de Laguna 1972, 1:97). Protected and celebrated, these marvels of marine technology seem to have attained the status of *at.óow* for their Yakutat possessors. Yet, in Glacier Bay, just one hundred miles to the south, Huna Tlingits developed a very different but equally adaptive technological genre of place to aid in seal hunting in this larger, less ice-choked bay: glacier-white camouflage clothing and outrigged white blinders for canoes. Here, visual cover, as opposed to auditory cover or tight maneuverability, was critical to successful sealing, and so the processes of landscape enculturation differed.

Finally, in addition to producing rich material and symbolic genres of place, the human experience of place engenders profound feelings toward the landscape. These affective ties may be strongly positive, indicative of what Tuan (1974:93) and others call "topophilia," or they may also be profoundly negative, engendering "topophobia," especially when associated with danger or tragedy. Either way, affective ties to place are derived from individual and collective experience of the landscape rather than the physical environment itself. Cultural structures mediate our interactions and experiences with a particular place and consequently help to define our sense of place. Through bodily engagement, inhabitation, dwelling, and cultural frames we become familiar and intimate with many places, find security in some, and ultimately come to identify with them. In this way "places become a point of departure from which we orient ourselves in the world" (Relph 1976:43).

CONCLUSION

The power and dynamics of place have received expanded attention in recent years. In this chapter I have laid out an operational definition of place and an ethnographic means of exploring humans' senses of place across cultures. I have defined place not as an object or geographic given but as a set of phenomenal and cultural processes consisting of three elemental dimensions—space, time, and experience. These dimensions are culturally and environmentally mediated and exist in synergistic and synesthetic webs of interanimation. Unfortunately, past analyses of place have often tended to emphasize one dimension of place to the neglect or exclusion of the other two. In contrast, a holistic anthropological perspective of place contributes to the knowledge of both culture and geography and the dynamic, organic ties that link them. Through such a perspective, a foundation is laid for understanding Tlingits' senses of place and being, and those of other societies, as cultural processes.

Among the Tlingit and other indigenous groups there are at least four key cultural structures that mediate relationships between people and place: social organization, language and cognitive structures, material production, and ritual. In the remaining chapters I examine in detail each of these cultural structures in action—through Tlingit processes of dwelling—to show how individual and collective Tlingit notions of place, being, and identity are forged.

2 KNOW YOUR PLACE

The Social Organization of Geographic Knowledge

Aadooséi yee xoo gunei yakwáan (Who is an outsider among us)? [A Tlingit rhetorical expression of belonging, sometimes used to punctuate the recounting of a social history weaving various social groups together in time and space]. —HERMAN KITKA SR.

"How is it that you know about all of these places so far from your homeland?" I asked Sitka Kaagwaantaan elder Herman Kitka Sr., after one of our early work sessions documenting his extensive knowledge of indigenous place-names outside of the Sitka area where he lives. "I guess you could say that's my family background," he replied. "My relatives told me about these places as part of our history, and they always referred to them by their Tlingit names," he added. "I got to know a lot of them firsthand, too, because I fished pretty near all over southeastern Alaska, even down to Puget Sound and on up to Prince William Sound."

For Herman Kitka and the Tlingit, indeed all indigenous peoples, social organization is both a response to place and a constitutive force in shaping individual and collective senses of place. This chapter first explores the ways in which the fundamental units of Tlingit social structure evolved in relation to Southeast Alaskan geography and what this means for the production and maintenance of geographic knowledge. Second, it examines the power of Tlingit social geography in organizing ethnogeographic knowledge and shaping individual consciousness of place. The role of fishing and other practical activities in the development of place consciousness, also alluded to by Mr. Kitka, is taken up in chapter 4.

The key role of social structure in the formation of Tlingit geographic knowledge was first remarked on by de Laguna (1960:17–18), who spec-

36

ulated on the strong force that the matrilineal sib (or clan) exerts over a Tlingit individual's "sense of history and geography." De Laguna also recognized that Tlingit territory at the most fundamental level was conceptualized not in terms of large swaths of land but rather as constellations of points or locales. These named locales typically marked sites of importance to the social history of the group and were enlivened and enriched by experience on the land, tutelage by elders, and two distinctive animating features of Tlingit social structure: *at.óow* (owned things) and *shagóon* (heritage or destiny). By examining these features of social structure from an evolutionary, ethnogeographic perspective one can understand how Tlingit social structure integrates personhood and place.

In analyzing the evolution of Tlingit social structure in relation to place, I am most interested in the period prior to the effects of extensive contact with non-Natives beginning in the mid-nineteenth century. The "traditional" portrait is, of course, an idealized temporal composite in the sense that Tlingit territorial boundaries were in a constant state of maintenance and flux as a result of the abundance and distribution of resources, intra- and interethnic conflicts and tensions, and other variables. This record of shifting territoriality in relation to such factors as migration, war, population growth and decline, natural disasters, trade, and so on is significant and well documented in the Tlingit historical record.

Still, evolutionary changes in precontact Tlingit sociogeographic organization were gradual compared to the cataclysm wrought by Euro-American contacts. In contrast to precontact fluctuations, which were mainly dispersions of Tlingit groups—clans or sibs hiving off from established settlements and founding new settlements or new houses in existing settlements—postcontact change has been a process of considerable geographic (but not sociological) consolidation. Instead of ḵwáan (dwelling area) settlements consisting of one or more winter villages and perhaps a dozen or more seasonal camps, today most ḵwáans consist of a single permanent town or city and perhaps a few seasonal habitation sites. This geographic consolidation of settlements has had a number of effects, but as far as relations with place are concerned it has often meant that areas peripheral to the present villages are less visited because of the time and costs involved in reaching them.

At the same time, sociologically, clans have become more and more dispersed as individual clan members have chosen to settle outside of their traditional villages, particularly in cities, such as Juneau, Ketchikan, Anchorage, Seattle, and beyond. These changes in social geography are part of the wider trend of time-space distanciation discussed in the previous chapter. Whatever the reasons for migrating out of the villages, be it employment, marriage, or services, the effects are the same: people become alienated from their homelands, as direct physical and material ties to place diminish.

In addition to changes in settlement patterns, regulatory restrictions on habitation and use of traditional Tlingit country also have attenuated physical and material ties to place. For example, settlement is prohibited on most federal lands, including National Park Service and Tongass National Forest lands, which together make up more than three-quarters of the land base in Southeast Alaska. In parks and other restricted areas, hunting, fishing, gathering, and other activities may be limited or banned. These constraints, too, have contributed to the alienation of Tlingits from landscapes they historically inhabited and utilized.

The loss of connection to places through dwelling has made it more incumbent on people to continue their identification with lands through symbolic means. Among the most important of these symbolic means, as noted in the previous chapter, are clan *at.óow*, or "owned things." *At.óow* consist of material and symbolic property claimed by the matrilineal clan or house group (a sublineage of the clan) as part of their ancestry, heritage, and destiny (*shuká*; literally "that which lies before us").[1] This property includes geographic sites, such as salmon streams, halibut banks, shellfish beds, fort sites, and prominent mountains, as well as symbolic capital, such as ceremonial regalia, stories, songs, spirits, and names. As with *shuká*, there is a collective and individual element to *at.óow*. Clan and house-group members may share much *at.óow* (territory, songs, and stories, for example), but within the same lifetime, two individuals never claim exactly the same *at.óow* (their names, for example, differ). As such, the sum total of a person's *at.óow* serves to mark that individual as a distinct member of the community and constitutes a pillar of personal identity. In summing up the foundational role that these possessions play in identity and being, both past and future, one elder simply declared, "Our *at.óow* are our life" (Emma Marks in Dauenhauer and Dauenhauer 1994:v).

The life-sustaining role of material resources, such as productive salmon streams, is readily apparent, but the importance of the symbolic property in defining one's existence requires a deeper understanding of the production, meanings, and roles of *at.óow* in defining the individual's and the social group's existence in the world. *At.óow* are important precisely because they reference and encapsulate key elements of Tlingit social group history. Events, beings, objects, and places typically become *at.óow* when they are crystallized as encapsulating images—usually in artistic designs—and consecrated through ceremonial use and formal dedication within the context of the *ḵu.éex'* (potlatch or party; literally "to invite"). Only after these representations or simulacrum become publicly invested with meaning and value through ritual is the prerogative of ownership recognized and the status of *at.óow* achieved. Additionally, in the sacred context of ritual, *at.óow* become more than mere images or representations. Through mediation in expressive ritual forms such as oratory, song, and dance, *at.óow* have the power to evoke and make present the spirits of those things they resemble and encapsulate.

Another important means by which symbolic connections to place are reproduced is through *shagóon*. This term, also subsidiary to *shuká*, may be translated as "heritage" or "destiny," and it is often used to reference the collective ancestry, history, and geography of a clan. According to de Laguna (1972, 2:813), *shagóon* means or implies "the destiny of a people (or individual), established in the past by the ancestors and extending to the descendants. It is one way of expressing 'the way things are.'" The concept is especially important in ritual, where a clan's history and prerogatives, including territorial rights, are negotiated and validated by the opposite moiety. *Shagóon* also is embodied in Tlingit naming practices. Clans are named for ancestral territories, and individuals are named after clan ancestors. In these and other ways the concept of *shagóon* merges place and being. Thus, as one elder put it, "if you sell our land, you sell our ancestors."[2]

PLACE AND THE EVOLUTION OF TLINGIT
SOCIOPOLITICAL ORGANIZATION

The links between the evolution of indigenous political systems and ecological factors of place have long been recognized in anthropology (Steward 1955; Service 1962). In the Native North American culture area known as the Northwest Coast, stretching from northern California to the rugged, mountainous coniferous rainforests and archipelagos of Southeast Alaska, researchers have posited a strong correlation between abundant natural resources and complex forms of sociopolitical organization (Kroeber 1939; Drucker 1951, 1983). Ethnologists proposed that large quantities of localized resources, particularly salmon, allowed Northwest Coast societies to support higher populations and sedentism and that this, in turn, led to the development of more complex social and political institutions. These features helped to define the Northwest Coast groups as unique among hunting and gathering peoples. In contrast to many of the world's foragers, whose politics were characterized by small-scale, flexible, and relatively egalitarian institutions, Northwest Coast groups boasted formal local and regional sociopolitical structures and a high degree of social stratification, including slavery.

Yet, while the basic assumption about the relationship between Northwest Coast ecological abundance and sociopolitical complexity is ultimately valid, it does not go very far toward explaining the proximate causes for the evolution of very diverse political systems within the culture area over time. More recently, Northwest Coast scholars have begun to consider these issues in detail, and a range of important socioecological factors have been emphasized as contributing to the unity and diversity of political development among various Northwest groups (see Suttles 1968; Fladmark 1975; Schalk 1977; Richardson 1982; Drucker 1983; Ames 1994; Matson and Coupland 1995; Moss 1998; Thornton 1999b, 2002; Ames and Maschner 1999). Key factors include (1) macro-environmental changes; (2) spatial and temporal variation in resources; (3) increased availability of and reliance on marine resources, especially salmon; (4) the advent of preservation and storage techniques; (5) the production of surpluses for trade; and (6) conflict and stresses related to sedentism, population growth, environmental circumscription, and resource competition. These factors combined in different ways at different times to produce a variety of complex foraging societies on the Northwest Coast.

Even within Tlingit country, there are important ecological distinctions that relate to social geography and cultural differentiation. Three important microenvironments comprise Southeast Alaska: the southern, northern, and Gulf Coast regions. Frederick Sound is the dividing line between the northern and southern regions, while the Gulf Coast commences north of Cross Sound. Frederick Sound also serves as the dividing line for migrating salmon stocks and the availability of important plants, such as red cedar (present in the milder southern region). These ecological regions correlate with important cultural variations, such as the northern and southern dialects of the Tlingit language.

A similar gross distinction can be made between the island and mainland environments. The largest mainland rivers, including the Stikine, Taku, Chilkat, and Alsek, supported large multispecies salmon runs and provided access to the interior through the coastal mountain barrier. Accordingly, these rivers played host to large, often more sedentary, population settlements. However, while fish, game, and plants abounded throughout the coast, some resources, such as marine mammals and edible seaweeds, were more plentiful on the islands (and Gulf Coast), while others, such as eulachon, soapberries, and mountain goat, were found almost exclusively on the mainland. These variations in natural resources distribution contributed to cultural differences in production and the establishment of complementary trade networks between various mainland and island Tlingit groups. For example, people from mainland settlements at Chilkoot or Chilkat might trade eulachon oil for herring eggs from the island settlement at Sitka. The same principles provided the impetus for trade with foreign groups in the interior and elsewhere on the Pacific coast.

Strictly speaking, then, there is no such thing as a pure aboriginal or "traditional" form of social structure or governance among the Tlingit. Rather, their sociopolitical organization has been evolving continuously over the past five thousand to ten thousand years. What is more, it continues to evolve in response to the current environment, a landscape in which valuable resources are gained not just through the domestic production of natural resources and regional trade and ceremonial networks but also from state and federal governments and participation in the global economy and international social movements. Thus, I have argued elsewhere (Thornton 2002) that the new layers of sociopolitical organization, including Alaska Native Brotherhood and Sisterhood Camps and Grand Camps (founded in 1912), Indian Reorganization Act tribal governments (post-1936), Alaska Native Regional and Village Corporations (a product of the 1971 Alaska Native Claims Settlement Act), among others, are important evolutionary responses to the political ecology of the modern era and have made an already complex Tlingit social organization even more byzantine.

The earliest recorded encounters with the coastal Tlingit occurred in the mid-eighteenth century when Russian and other European explorers began to journey along the northwest coast of America. They were followed by European and American traders, who tended to interact with their Tlingit business partners in relatively instrumental and coequal ways. Until the Russian American Company's colonization of Sitka in the early nineteenth century, contacts were largely limited to trading encounters. Even so, whites were quick to recognize the complexity of Tlingit social structure, which included nobles or elites (often assumed to be "chiefs"), commoners, and slaves and powerful roles for women (see de Laguna 1983). At the same time, there was a great deal of ethnocentric misrecognition on the part of the newcomers as to the degree of division, relationships, and prerogatives among the various levels of Tlingit sociopolitical organization. Thus, early visitors often erroneously assumed that each Tlingit village had a single, paramount chief rather than a host of clan leaders.

At the time of contact there were in fact six major levels of political organization (see table 2.1), which can be ranked from broadest to narrowest as follows: nation (Lingít); moiety (naa, from the term for "clan"); ḵwáan; clan (naa); house (hít); and person (ḵáa).[3] Some might object to "person" being classified as a sociopolitical unit, but considering that persons were ranked within Tlingit society and bestowed with hereditary names and titles of political significance that essentialized and publicized political identity as an element of personhood, it is logical to include it.

1. *Nation.* Tlingits can be said to have constituted a nation only in the sense of cultural geography. They recognized a certain degree of unity among themselves, including a distinct language (*Lingít*), lebensraum (*Lingít Aaní*), and culture (*Lingít Ḵusteeyí*), but they were not overseen by a single leader or government. Indeed, at the time of contact, Tlingit culture was in a period of northern expansion, and, with few exceptions, villages and social groups were becoming increasingly scattered and fragmented rather than unified. Consider that the village of Yakutat, at the

TABLE 2.1. Tlingit Sociopolitcal Organization (1750–1912)

Level	Sociopolitical Unit	Political Status	No. of Units
1	Nation	Weak political status based primarily on common language and culture	1
2	Moiety	Important for organizing reciprocal exchange in ritual politics	2
3	K̲wáan	Weak political status based on common habitation, usually of a single winter village	13–18
4	Clan	Central sociopolitical unit based on matrilineage	70+
5	House	Based originally on the segment of a matrilineage residing in one house	200+
6	Person	Sociopolitical status acquired by birth, but big names/titles also reserved for high born Tlingits who distinguish themselves	10,000+

NOTE: For analysis of seven additional layers added between 1912 and the present, see Thornton (2002).

northern frontier, stood several hundred miles and many days' canoe journey from Cape Fox, at the southern boundary of *Lingít Aaní*. Such expansion and distancing favored differentiation over unification. Significantly, there is no generic term for nation in Tlingit, and foreign nations, such as the Tagish, typically were conceptualized as k̲wáans or clans.

   2. *Moiety.* Moieties formed a vital component of Tlingit identity but played only a minor role in politics and governance. Just as k̲wáans categorized people as inhabitants of certain regions, moieties (from the French term for "half") identified Tlingits as members of two major

super matrilineages, Raven (Yéil, also known among interior Tlingits as Crow) or Eagle/Wolf (Ch'áak'/Gooch), under which the approximately seventy major clans were grouped.[4] There is evidence to suggest that the moieties evolved from two ancient clans, the Laayineidí of the Raven side and the Shangukeidí of the Wolf side, as the Tlingit, lacking a generic term for moiety, used these clan names to label the two superlineages (Swanton 1908:423; Shotridge 1920; de Laguna 1972, 1:450). Undoubtedly, moieties evolved subsequent to the more basic unit of the clan, probably as the number of clans proliferated and became geographically dispersed in a hodgepodge, and thus more difficult to organize practically and conceptually.

While politically weak, moieties were nevertheless important strands that linked and organized members of disparate communities and clans into exogamous, reciprocating "sides" to carry out major production and exchanges through rituals such as potlatches. Although they had the advantage of providing a vast network of relatives, moieties had no singular leaders or governing authority beyond that of their constituent clans. Of all levels of Tlingit social organization, moieties were the least geographic. The Raven/Crow and Eagle/Wolf moieties situate people in an abstract, binary-oppositional genealogical and ritual space, but not a geographic one. In fact the evolution of moieties might be best explained as a tool to overcome or transcend the limitations of geography in order to organize effectively Tlingits dwelling in increasingly dispersed places.

3. _Kwáan._ Unlike the moiety, the kwáan is quintessentially a unit of social geography. Europeans sometimes mistakenly assumed that Tlingit villages, or kwáans, were governed by autonomous political units like those found in Western towns and villages. And in modern times the federal government has sought to make Tlingits more governable by constituting tribal governments along village-kwáan lines through the Indian Reorganization Act and other measures (Thornton 2002). But historically kwáans were not governed like villages. The term _kwáan,_ derived from the Tlingit verb "to dwell," simply marks Tlingit individuals as inhabitants of a certain living space consisting of the total lands and waters used and controlled by clans residing in a particular winter village. A list of contemporary and historical Tlingit kwáans can be found in table 2.2. In addition, the term _kwáan_ might be extended to refer-

TABLE 2.2. Major Ḵwáans in Tlingit Territory from North to South

Ḵwáan	Translation	Modern Village Area
Galyáx Ḵwáan	Inhabitants of Galyáx (Kaliakh River) Area	Kaliakh River
Laaxaayík (a.k.a. Yakwdaat) Ḵwáan	Inhabitants of the Area with Ice Inside	Yakutat
Gunaaxoo Ḵwáan	Among the Interior Athabascans	Dry Bay
Jilḵaat Ḵwáan	Inhabitants of the Chilkat River	Klukwan / Chilkat River
Jilḵoot Ḵwáan	Inhabitants of the Chilkoot River Area	Haines / Chilkoot River
Xunaa Káawu (Ḵwáan)	Inhabitants of the Area under Cover from the North Wind	Hoonah
T'aaḵu Ḵwáan	Inhabitants of the Area Where the Geese Flood Into	Juneau / Taku River
Aak'w Ḵwáan	Inhabitants of Auke Lake Area	Juneau / Auke Bay
S'awdaan Ḵwáan	Inhabitants of the Dungeness Crab Area	Sumdum / Holkam Bay
Xutsnoowú (a.k.a. Xudzidaa) Ḵwáan	Inhabitants of the Brown Bear Fort (a.k.a Burned Wood) Area	Angoon
Sheet'ká (a.k.a. Sheey At'iká) Ḵwáan	Inhabitants of the Oceanside of Shee (Baranof Island)	Sitka
Kéex' Ḵwáan	Opening of the Day (Sunlight through Rocky Pass) People	Kake
Kooyu Ḵwáan	Inhabitants of Kooyu (Going into the Stomach [Tebenkof Bay])	Kuiu Island Tebenkof Bay
Shtax'héen Ḵwáan	Inhabitants of Shtax'héen (Water Biting Itself [Stikine River]) Area	Wrangell / Stikine River
Taant'a Ḵwáan	Inhabitants of the Sea Lion [Island] Area	Ketchikan
Taḵjik'aan Ḵwáan	Inhabitants of the Taḵjik'aan [a village] Area	Tuxekan
Hinyaa Ḵwáan	Inhabitants of the Area across the Water	Klawock
Sanyaa Ḵwáan	Inhabitants of the Area Secure in Retreat	Saxman

ence a people dwelling beyond the boundaries of Tlingit ethnicity or territory. Thus, white men in Southeast Alaska became known as Gus'k'i Kwáan (People Dwelling at the Base of the Clouds), while the Tagish Athabascans were known as Tagish Kwáan.

The term *kwáan* also was applied to nonhuman beings, including spirits, which were believed to dwell in localized communities in nature. These communities of spirits were referred to as kwáani, always with the possessive suffix *i* to indicate that they "belong to" (or are "possessed by") something. Thus the Kóoshdaakaa Kwáani, or spirits of the land-otter men—powerful beings capable of capturing and transforming human beings—were conceived of as dwelling in land-otter-like beings that resided in communities. These communities, in turn, were believed to be centered in certain places, though land-otter men could manifest themselves almost anywhere, particularly in certain socio-environmental contexts, such as a human drowning or premature death due to exposure (cf. de Laguna 1972; Emmons 1991). Like human kwáans, spirit kwáans inhabited both cosmological and social spaces.

Interestingly, when referencing human communities, the possessive suffix *i* is omitted in accordance with Tlingit grammatical rules for embodied entities, such as body parts and kinship terms (Dauenhauer and Dauenhauer 1990:127). This suggests that, unlike noncorporeal objects, which are disembodied and may be possessed or dispossessed, a person's kwáan, or homeland, is, according to Tlingit ideology, an organic part of his or her makeup and thus inalienable. The linguistic construction mirrors the social reality. Consequently, if a child is born in Sitka and the parents are of clans localized there, that child is forever Sitka Kwáan regardless of where he or she may eventually reside. Like personal and clan names, a person's residential kwáan is a basic component of his or her identity.

Kwáans themselves typically did not act as political entities; unlike Western town and village governments, there were no kwáan councils or assemblies to issue ordinances, mete out punishments, or raise revenues. All of these activities were carried out at the clan level, prior to the reprioritization of the kwáan as a major political entity (i.e., the federally recognized tribe) in the modern American era.

4. *Clan.* The exogamous, matrilineal clan (also termed sib) is the oldest and most basic unit of Tlingit social structure and the foundation

of both individual and group identity. Tlingits consider a person to be a member of his or her mother's clan, a child of the father's clan, and a grandchild of other clans. Traditionally, this identity formed the basis for nearly all forms of social action. Clans or their localized segments, known as house groups, owned and maintained use rights to physical property, including salmon streams, halibut banks, hunting grounds, sealing rocks, berrying grounds, shellfish beds, canoe-landing beaches, and other landmarks, as well as symbolic property, such as names, stories, songs, regalia, crests, and other cultural icons, including clan ancestors. These possessions, or *at.óow*, comprised the foundation of Tlingit identity, and each clan was conceived of as having not only its exclusive property but also its own unique "personality" and ways of being (de Laguna 1972, 1:451). Virtually all legal and political authority was vested in the clan. Clans or their localized segments, rather than regional "tribes" or ḵwáans, made war and peace, conducted rituals, and organized material production. Traditionally, in times of conflict, loyalty and "patriotism" were with the clan, a reality that created inherent structural tensions in interclan contexts, such as marriage, residence, and ritual (de Laguna 1983). The centrality of the clan is further reflected in the fact that closely associated foreign groups, like the Haida (Deikinaa, "Way Outside Clan") and Southern Tutchone Athabascans (Gunanaa, "Interior Clan"), were conceived of as clans.

An important but often overlooked aspect of clans is their geographical basis. Two aspects of clan geography are particularly significant: origin and distribution. Origin refers to the location where the clan was founded as a distinct social group and is typically from where it derives its name. The majority of Tlingit clans adopted their names from the geographic areas they inhabited, and the linguistic construction of such clan names invoked a sense of belonging or being possessed by the named place (see table 2.3). For example, *Gaanaẖ*, the Tlingit name for Port Stewart in Behm Canal, was settled by a Tlingit group who then became the Gaanaẖ.ádi, literally the "beings of" (or "possessed by") Port Stewart. An offshoot of this group, the Gaanaẖteidí, settled at the head of the same bay (*Gaanaẖ Tahéen*) and later migrated north, eventually establishing the famous Whale House of Chilkat. These origin sites were often taken as crests by the clan and, as such, were considered sacred property (*at.óow*). Clans not named for natural sites

TABLE 2.3. Some Tlingit Clans Named For Places and Their Distribution

Clan	Translation	Place Affiliation (Origin)	Translation	Kwáan Distribution
Chookaneidí	People of Chookanhéeni	Chookanhéen (Berg Bay / Creek)	Straw Grass Creek	Xunaa, Sheet'ká
Dagisdinaa	Clan of Dagis [a creek]	Dagis (near Alsek River)	?	Gunaax̱oo, Jilḵaat, and Interior
Daḵl'aweidí	People of Daḵl'eiw	Daḵl'eiw (Sandbar on Stikine River)	Back of the Sand	Jilḵaat, Xutsnoowú, Taant'a, and Interior
Deisheetaan	Residents of Deishu[hít]	Deishu[hít] (Angoon)	End of the Trail [House]	Xutsnoowú and Interior
G̱aanax̱.ádi	People of G̱aanax̱	G̱aanax̱ (Port Stewart)	Sheltered [Harbor]	Jilḵaat, Aak'w, T'aaḵu, S'awdaan, Taant'a
G̱aanax̱teidí	People of G̱aanax̱ ta	G̱aanax̱ ta (Head of Port Stewart)	Head of Sheltered [Harbor]	Jilḵaat
Ḵaach.ádi	People of Ḵáach	Ḵáach (Little Pybus Bay)	Mat	Keex̱', Shtax'héen

Clan	Translation	Place name	Meaning	Locations
Kaagwaantaan	Charred House People	*Kax'noowú*	Female Grouse Fort	Galyáx, Laaxaayík, Xunaa, Jilḵaat, Sheet'ká, Gunaaxoo
Kiks.ádi	People of Kiks	*Kiks* (Helm Bay)	?	Sanyaa, Sheet'ká, Shtax'héen
Kwáashk'i Ḵwáan	Inhabitants of Kwáashk'	*Kwáashk'* (Humpback Salmon Creek)	Humpback Salmon (Eyak)	Galyáx, Laaxaayík
L'uknax.ádi*	People of L'ukanáx	*L'ukanáx* (Deep Bay)	Coho Community	Xunaa, Sheet'ká, Laaxaayík, Gunaaxoo
Lukaax.ádi	People of Lukaax	*Lukaax* (Duncan Canal)	Off the Point	Jilḵóot, Gunaaxoo and Interior
Naanya.aayí	People of the Uppermost Stream	Tributary to Stikine River	Uppermost Stream	Shtax'héen, T'aaku
Neix.ádi	People of Neix	*Neix* (Naha Bay)	?	Sanyaa
S'iknax.ádi	People of S'iknax	*S'iknax* (Limestone Inlet)	Whetstone Place?	Shtax'héen
Shangukeidí	People of Shánkw	*Shánkw* (Saint Philip Island?)	Little ?	Taant'a, Hinyaa, Ḵéex', Jilḵóot, Gunaaxoo

TABLE 2.3. *(continued)*

Clan	Translation	Place Affiliation (Origin)	Translation	Kwáan Distribution
Skanax.ádi	People of Skanáx	*Skanáx* (Saginaw Bay)	Noisy Beach?	Kéex'
Sit'kweidí	People of Sít'koh	*Sít'koh* (Port Snettisham)	Glacier Cove	S'awdaan, T'aaku
Sukteeneidí	People of S'uktuhéen	*S'uktuhéen* (Big John Creek)	Wide Grass Stream	Kéex'
T'akdeintaan*	Residents of T'akdeinx'áat	*Takdeinx'áat'* (Island in Lituya Bay)	Toward the Side Island	Xunaa
Taalkweidí	People of Taalkw	*Taalkw* (Thomas Bay)	Basket?	Shtax'héen
Taneidí	People of Tanahéen	*Tanahéen* (Tunehean Creek)	Jumping Fish Creek	Shtax'héen, Kéex'
Teikweidí	People of Teikw	*Teikw* (Dall Island?)	?	Taant'a, Sanyaa, Xutsnoowú, Laaxaayík

Tsaagweidí	People of Tsaagwáa	Tsaagwáa (South Arm, Hood Bay)	Harbor Seal Ice Floes	Kéex'
Tsaat'ineidí	People of Tsaat'ehéen	Tsaat'ehéen (Young Bay)	Behind the Seal Water	T'aaku
Tukyeidí	People of Tukyee	Tukyee (Mitchell Bay?)	Outlet of a Lake	Xutsnoowú, Carcross
Was'ineidí	People of Was'héeni	Was'héeni (Creek near Hamilton Bay)	Water Lice [Wéis'] Creek	Keex'
X'at'ka.aayí*	'Those on the Island	X'at'ká (Island in Dry Bay)	Island On	Xunaa, Gunaaxoo
Yanyeidí	People of Yán	People of Yán (a hemlock house built on Taku River)	Hemlock [House]	T'aaku, and Interior

NOTE: For source information, see Hope and Thornton 2000:150–51; Emmons 1991; McClellan 1975; and Leer n.d.
* All considered to be "Coho Tribe" clans.

often took their identity from some aspect of the village geography, such as an architectural feature of their clan house (e.g., the Kaagwaantaan, "Charred House People") or its location within the village (e.g., the Deisheetaan, "End of the Trail House People"). The linguistic homology between clan names and sacred geography served to reinforce strong material, social, and spiritual ties to place among clan members, and the understanding of these ties was considered to be an essential component of one's heritage and identity (*shagóon*).

The geographic distributions of clans are noteworthy because of their discontinuity in space. Segments of a single clan are typically dispersed in several, often nonadjacent, communities or ḵwáans. For example, the Shangukeidí are found in the northern ḵwáans of *Jilḵóot* (Chilkoot) and *Gunaaxoo* (Dry Bay) and the southernmost ḵwáans of *Taant'a* (Tongass) and *Hinyaa* (Klawock), but nowhere in between except *Ḵéex'* (Kake). This dispersed network of multilocal clans, which evolved through the twin processes of fission and migration (and perhaps confederation in the case of Shangukeidí), contributes to a social geography with its own spatial logic and unity. This logic, in turn, shapes the Tlingit individual's basic knowledge of physical, social, and historical geography. Thus, through his clan's oral traditions, a northern Chilkoot Shangukeidí may possess a strong sense of his clan's historical roots in southern Southeast Alaska, despite the fact that these sites lie hundreds of miles away, and he personally may have never traveled to these places (cf. de Laguna 1972, 1:225–26). Similarly, a Deisheetaan living in the interior of Canada (e.g., Carcross, Tagish, or Teslin) may gain knowledge of her group's historical ties to the distant island Alaskan village of Angoon, as evidenced in this statement by Carcross-Tagish elder Angela Sidney:

> One time, long ago, a chief of the Deisheetaan nation [clan]—that's us— came in from Angoon. That chief's family sailed up the Chilkat River; they stayed there with the Chilkat people . . . maybe for two months. When they're going to head back, here that Chilkat chief's son has fallen in love with that Deisheetaan's chief's daughter! Well they got married . . . her children grew up around Taku River. [When they were grown] her three girls married [inland] to Tagish, to Teslin, to Telegraph Creek.
>
> It was the women who came up here, who married up here, but it has to

be a man who claims the country. . . . To tell the truth of it, I met someone last summer [1980] from coast people. I told him that I'm Deisheetaan sháa [woman] from Angoon. "Oh my," he said. "My great-grandmother told me, 'Two women went that way, inland. Two or three. They got married inland!' Now I'm glad to meet you." He shakes hands with me. I know now that coast people are our relations. (In Cruikshank 1990b:37–39)

Because the social body of the clan has ties to certain places, as this example illustrates, so too do its individual members, despite their relocation, segmentation, or other distanciations in space. These multiple ties to place are embodied in the clan's *at.óow* and *shagóon*, including names, ancestors, regalia, songs, stories, and the like. Tlingit history and geography, then, must be read through the clans.

The symbolic effects of this linguistic grafting of social bodies onto physical places have a profound influence on the identity of each. In Charles Peirce's (1960) semiotic terms, each becomes an indexical icon of the other. Every time the clan name is spoken, the geographic associations are invoked in a way that merges the social group with the place. Thus, one cannot speak of the Kiks.ádi without implicitly invoking their ties to Kiks Bay (near the Nass River), the distant place for which they are named. The converse is also true: when the place-name is mentioned, the people and their history are naturally alluded to. These associations remain poignant even after the clan's place of origin has been abandoned, provided that the clan itself remains a vital social group and continues to maintain its heritage (*shagóon*). As the clans' places of birth (or rebirth), these geographic sites are particularly sacrosanct and may serve as crests (*at.óow*), vital sources of symbolic capital.

The formation (or reformation) and naming of a clan is often associated with cataclysmic events in antiquity (cf. Allaire 1984:97). The epic Flood is a case in point. This ancient and catastrophic deluge washed away early Native villages, forcing people to seek refuge in the liminal space of rafts, "stone nests" on mountaintops, and other temporary shelters. When the floodwaters subsided, both the social group and the landscape itself were in a sense reborn. While the events surrounding clan origins date back to time immemorial, clan histories are performed and alluded to again and again in narrative, song, dance, visual art, and other symbolic forms in which the deep and powerful social, emotional, and material ties of specific social groups to specific places are reproduced. Place-names and clan names embody these associations profoundly and succinctly.

The linguistic homology between *clan* and *place* leads to other metaphoric associations, too. Two images are especially poignant: place/clan as *protector* and place/clan as *provider*. Port Stewart (Gaanax̱, "Sheltered"), is bay recognized and named for its protective capacities to shelter people from wind and weather; likewise, the Gaanax̱.ádi clan may be conceptualized as a kind of protective container for its individual members. Similarly, in a metaphor of sustenance, the Tsaagweidí can allude to their connection with the key resource, harbor seal (*tsaa*), found in their place of origin, Hood Bay (*Tsaagwáa*, "Seal Ice Floes"). Such metaphors are skillfully blended in the context of visual and verbal art.[5]

Both male and female clan leaders carried special authority and titles and to this day are referred to in Tlingit as *Naashádaháni* (clan head) and *Naa Tláa* (clan mother), respectively. Since descent was reckoned through the mother, but males were largely responsible for laying claim to territory and public offices such as *hít s'áati* (house leader), the mother's brother, or maternal uncle (*káak*), played an important role in training her children, the future leaders of the matrilineage. As one Deisheetaan elder put it: "Long time ago the uncles, they used to be responsible for their nephews; they have to train them because the Tlingits believe that a father is not very stern with his own children . . . so his [wife's] brother is always responsible for training the boys" (Greer 1995:18).

Clans also were measured in relation to one another according to their wealth, power, and prestige. In addition to achievement, marriage also could boost a lineage's status, especially when the father's clan was of high status and the marriage perpetuated an ancestral pedigree. The status of the father's clan also could be important in determining individual status and rank, and paternal ties provided knowledge of and access to places controlled by his matrilineal kin.

5. *House.* As Tlingit society expanded demographically and geographically, clan lineages were aggregated (into the above-mentioned super matrilineages or moieties) and subdivided into localized matrilineages known as houses (*hít*) or house groups. The Tlingit term *hít*

refers to the residential houses themselves, which were named for and sheltered members of a matrilineage or sib and their conjugal families. Where clans were small, residing in a single multifamily structure, the clan and house group were effectively the same entity. But a growing population and other pressures naturally led to the formation of new houses and sublineages over time. House leaders carried the title *hit s'áati*.

The Yanyeidí clan's history illustrates how a house group becomes named and eventually forms a clan. According to Elizabeth Nyman (Nyman and Leer 1993:9–35), a Yanyeidí elder from Atlin, British Columbia, the Yanyeidí took their name from a hemlock tree, which they were cutting down to make a house when their adze broke. At that time, the Taku River was bisected by a glacier, with people living on both sides. Mourning the loss of their adze, the people on the upriver side of the glacier were heard by those on the downriver side, and eventually the two peoples were united when the downriver group crossed the glacier to meet those on the other side. The downriver people also brought with them adzes, and thus the upriver people were able to finish building their hemlock house. "So that we will have a name to be called by, this is Hemlock House" (19), Xuts, the leader of the upriver group, proclaimed. As the lineage expanded, other houses were built, and they became known collectively as the Yanyeidí, or "Hemlock House People," a clan.

House groups had both a physical and a sociopolitical reality. Physically, houses, like clans, were always intimately linked to their birthplace, even if the original house itself was destroyed or relocated. Sociopolitically, a Tlingit was always a part of his or her mother's house, regardless of where he or she resided; the only exception to this was when a sublineage formally established a new house in the context of a potlatch (Mauss 1967; Kan 1989; Emmons 1991). The house group was also the core unit in the domestic mode of economic production. While the multifamily clan houses have been replaced as physical structures by nuclear family dwellings, the sociopolitical house is still recognized, and matrilineal ties are still reckoned through it. House groups maintain their integrity not only through the framework of kinship and ancestry (*shagóon*) but also through leadership (*hít s'áati*), property (*at.óow*), and coordinated social, ceremonial, and economic activities (*ḵusteeyí*).

6. *Person.* Finally, at the level of personhood, all Tlingits were

bestowed with birth names that were considered *at.óow* of the house or clan and inherited matrilineally. As components of personhood, names distinguished not only clan/house identity but also hereditary social rank, as the names themselves had different values (Emmons 1991:261). The lowest-ranking members of coastal Tlingit society, slaves (*gux*), were not always given proper Tlingit names because of their status as property rather than persons within the political system. In contrast, the high-ranking members of free society, the *aanyádi* (children of the village), were given the more valuable names at birth. As a consequence, birth names ultimately placed significant constraints on their carriers' future political status. Below the *aanyádi* stood the commoners, the largest strata of the social structure, whose names were typically selected by the oldest women or by the clan mother of the mother's group and ritually bestowed through a potlatch.

Angoon Deisheetaan elder Lydia George identified naming as the single most important aspect of cultural training among the Tlingit. "Your name tells you your history . . . who you are and how you are related to people." At the metaphysical level the Tlingit term for name (*saa* or *ya saa*) corresponds with breath (Langdon 2000:149). Names, especially high-status names and titles, were recycled and reanimated through ritual, in which participants were paid by hosts to endow and breathe life into the name by repeating it aloud at least three times as it was invested in the initiate. Without a Tlingit name, social identity is drastically weakened—short of breath—and the individual may be considered adrift, lost, without a spirit, and without a place (*l'aan gooshu*, "without country"). De Laguna (1972, 2:790) observes, "It is through his name, and the meaning of his name, that a Tlingit knows himself. His name or names identifies the spirit or spirits, formerly animating a long line of forebears, that have come to live again in him, shaping his body or lending character to his personality."[6] The fact that many personal names are directly tied to places of historical significance further strengthens their embrace. A recent birth announcement exemplifies how this connectivity is realized: "On January 18, 2000, Shawaan Jackson-Gamble was formally given the name Chaak'ti, which translates to 'Caretaker or Keeper of Hamilton Bay.' Hamilton Bay is an historically important bay to the Tsagweidí families and is still used today by Kake people for subsistence activities" (in Langdon 2000:154). The embracing connectivity of Tlingit names so impressed one observer, he was led to assert: "It would be difficult to exaggerate the importance of naming among the Tlingit. In a culture where everything is related to everything else and nothing was spiritually meaningless, names not only classified, they defined social roles, conferred mythic significance, and they were often lovely" (Carpenter 1977:288).[7]

Traditionally, a person's clan, moiety, and individual status could be reckoned from his or her name. European naming practices have confused matters. As Deisheetaan Ida Calmagane (Thornton 2004b:39) explains, "The white man came and they just give anybody any name, any kind of name." In contrast to singular matrilineally inherited Native names, in the nineteenth century Europeans began giving Natives anglicized first and last names, with the surnames being patrilineally inherited, in direct conflict with the aboriginal way. Perhaps in response, some new naming patterns emerged, including the practice of tying a person's first name (which was not patrilineally inherited) to his or her land. Examples of such naming include Berners Bay Jim, Lituya Bay George, Hot Springs Charlie, Sheep Creek Mary, Situk Harry, and Taku Jim. This pattern of naming provided better resonance of individuals' ancestral and practical ties to place than the Euro-American way of "giving any kind of name."

Personal status, however, was not solely the product of one's name, birthright, or ascription. The highest-ranking names of a particular lineage were reserved as titles and were given only to highborn members (or, rarely, to exceptional commoners) who merited chiefly status through their own achievements. These were almost exclusively men whose achievements were measured by their success in organizing economic production, taking care of lands and resources, and expanding the redistribution of goods and sociopolitical alliances through trade, marriages, ritual potlatching, and other means. As elites, these title-holders also controlled clan *at.óow*, including the distribution of non-material possessions, such as clan histories, songs, stories, names, and other specialized knowledge.[8]

From the standpoint of Tlingit ethnopsychology, personal wealth, prestige, status, and character were all deeply rooted in place. Accordingly, sacred places constituted a special type of *at.óow*. In discussing the sacredness of particular legends of the trickster/demiurge Raven that are localized in his clan's Chilkoot territory around modern-day Haines, the Lukaax.ádi leader Austin Hammond (*Daanaawáak*; see Kawaky 1981) emphasizes how these *at.óow* connect place to individual and social being in a life-sustaining nexus:

> It was at Chilkoot that they [my grandfathers] taught me things about our Tlingit ways. My grandfathers said, "The time will come when these things we're going to tell will need to be heard again."
>
> I tell you for years and years we found in the river our livelihood and our food, the strength of our families. . . . And all along these shores were special places where the salmon come. And each place has its own name.
>
> It was Raven who showed us how to get our food. Raven knew what was good for us, and taught the Tlingit how to live. Raven exists in our legends and in our lives. Sometimes Raven is powerful and wise, and at other times Raven seems foolish. But always the stories of Raven hold special meaning for us. It was Raven who hung by his beak suspended from the clouds at the time of the Great Flood. It was Raven who taught our people to catch salmon.
>
> These are the stories my grandfathers passed on to me. These are the things I'm trying to teach my grandchildren. It is these stories which help guide our people as we live with the land. . . .
>
> For Raven taught us, if we live with the land, not against it, the land will take care of us. The land, the river, they hear us!

As *at.óow*, sacred places and the stories they hold are important for the earthly wisdom they embody and the character that they draw forth. As psychologist James Hillman (1999:11) notes, the Greek word *mythos* is perhaps best translated not as legend but rather as "plot." "The plots that entangle our souls and draw forth our characters are the great myths," he observes. "Myths show the imaginative structures inside our messes, and our human characters can locate themselves against the background of the characters of myth." Places, the settings of myth, give resonance to these plots and make them tangible to the future generations who follow their ancestors' footsteps, or *shuká*. Therefore, it is not only that the land and the river "hear" Tlingits but also that Tlingits, through *at.óow* and other frames, "hear" the lands and waters speak their wisdom and use this guidance to construct personal behavioral models and meanings (Cruikshank 1990b, 1998), thereby helping them to realize their *shuká* as both heritage and destiny. How individuals construct these models becomes fundamental to their character. As Hillman also observes, character is more than a set of traits to be identified or instilled: it is a process of self-realization embodying a unique constellation of characteristics or traits that become more clearly inscribed (to use a term etymologically linked to character) on the individual, and thus perceptible as lasting and defining images, only with age and experience. Thus character requires "additional years" and the important physiological and psychological changes that come with aging, in order to be fulfilled.[9]

At.óow represent this organic relationship between person and place in other ways as well, including mapping the landscape of the world and of history onto the landscape of the body as constitutive elements of personhood. This is done most poignantly through naming and the donning of regalia that clothe the body in clan crests and ornaments, which, in turn, clearly emplace the wearer geographically and socially. According to de Laguna (1972, 2:758), Tlingit personhood may be conceptualized as possessing three aspects: "the body, a virtually sexless, immortal spirit or soul which is reincarnated in a series of bodies . . . and the name or names which indicate and also establish personal identity." Like clan or house-group identity, names and titles are passed on from generation to generation and may be of geographic origin (see de Laguna 1972, 2:789; Thornton 1997b, 1997c, 2000) or allude to particular landscapes. Such names fuse place and personhood in clear and inextricable ways. Similarly, as *at.óow* and *shagóon*, names evoke elements of character.

I would argue that bodily *at.óow*, such as ceremonial headgear, Chilkat blankets, and other regalia, as well as ornamentation such as tattooing, face painting, and the like, effectively constitute a fourth dimension of Tlingit personhood. Through the embodiment of *at.óow* designs, these adornments literally extend and project the person as a social being. They also reveal social rank. According to Sergei Kan (1989:77–102), the ideal person in Tlingit society is the leader (*hít s'áatí*, "master of the house") or "aristocrat" (*aankáawu*, "person of the village," or *aanyádi*, "child of the village"), who is symbolized as being heavy, stationary, and dry like a rock, as opposed to wispy, fleeting, and wet like a leaf. Accordingly, the ideal person is conceptualized as situated and emplaced, like a feature of the land itself, but also as "heavy" in adornments and possessions, or *at.óow*.

In fact, the Chilkat and button-style blankets and other regalia that adorn Tlingit leaders are literally heavy, but more important they represent "weighty" and anchoring components of the collective being, including stellar features of the landscape, such as rivers and mountains, which figure prominently in the clan's *shuká*. These places are sacred sites for the clan that displays them and are considered possessions (*at.óow*) through a transaction or "purchase" event (Dauenhauer and Dauenhauer 1994:15), often in which a clan member was "exchanged" (typically involuntarily) for the land. In the film, *Haa Shagóon* (Kawaky 1981), Lukaax.ádi leader Austin Hammond wears the precious Sockeye Point Robe (*X̱'aakw X'aayí Naaxein*; see fig. 2.1) and explains the event it symbolizes and the purpose of its display:

> Woven into the blanket that I wear is an important legend. Two young boys were racing in their canoe when it capsized. As one boy pulled himself out of the water, up from the lake's depth appeared a giant sockeye salmon taking hold of the remaining boy, to disappear beneath the waters. And after several days people from both clans gathered there to mourn his loss. It was decided to call the place Sockeye Point [*X̱'aakw X'aayí*]—the name repeated four times to carry the weight of the law and the emblem woven into a blanket. And to those who come asking, "Where is your history?" I answer, "We wear our history." Traditionally, we have not been writers of books. We did not have surveys or titles. But we wove into our blankets our brother the sockeye. On our clothing is the ownership and history of our land.

By this and other means, *at.óow* serves to merge place and identity in ways that reinforce social group and geographic affiliations as well as Tlingit notions of personhood, social rank, and resource tenure. As Austin Hammond's example demonstrates, *at.óow* also inscribe character and serve as touchstones for character building. In the case of Sockeye Point, the place is the carrier of an important life-sustaining lesson about the dependence of the collective upon the salmon. The sacrifice of one of the clan's members to the sockeye allows his descendants to continue to harvest salmon in a delicate moral and ecological balance suggestive of mutual respect between equals.

FIG. 2.1. Austin Hammond displays the Sockeye Point Robe (X̱'aakw X'aayí Naaxein), a sacred object (at.óow) of his clan, at a 1981 ceremony near Chilkoot Lake in Haines, Alaska. Among other things, the robe encapsulates important clan history and signifies title to the lands and waters around Chilkoot Lake, where freshwater (spawned-out) sockeye salmon (x̱'aakw) are harvested. Photo by R. Dauenhauer

THE SOCIAL ORGANIZATION
OF GEOGRAPHIC KNOWLEDGE

Having shown how the basic units of Tlingit social structure relate to one another and to place, I now examine the organization of Tlingit geographic knowledge at the level of the individual in more detail. To do this I return to my ethnogeographic interviews with Herman Kitka Sr., whose place in the social structure is outlined in table 2.4. He is a four-named elder of the Box House of the Kaagwaantaan clan of Eagle moiety, from Sheet'ká Ḵwáan (i.e., dwelling in Sitka, the anglicized name for Sheet'ká, meaning "Oceanside of Shee [Baranof Island]"). He is a child of the L'uknax̱.ádi clan.

But the birth of the Kaagwaantaan as a clan begins not at Sitka but in Hoonah territory, in the shadow of the present-day Glacier Bay National Park and Preserve (see map 2.1). According to a story told to

TABLE 2.4. Tlingit Social Organization, with a Profile of Herman Kitka Sr.

Level	Social Unit	Herman Kitka Sr.
1	Nation	Tlingit
2	Moiety	Eagle/Wolf
3	Ḵwáan	Sheetk'á Ḵwáan
4	Clan	Kaagwaantaan (L'uknax̱.ádi Yádi)
5	House	Ḵook Hít
6	Person (Names[s])	Kusataan, S'áaxw Shan, Naawul'aada, Kindaa

John Swanton (1909:326–46) by Herman Kitka's great uncle, Deikeen-aak'w, it is from a place near *Xákwnoowú* (Sandbar Fort) in Dundas Bay (*Listee*) that the proto-Kaagwaantaan hero, Ḵaakeix'wtí (also known as "the man who killed his sleep"), a *Xakwnukweidí* (person of the people from Sandbar Fort), struck out on an epic quest to the interior after killing his sleep, which appeared to him in the form of a bird. Looking for seals, he canoed into Cross Sound, moving west toward a place called *Naguḵhéen* (Rolling Creek, a small sockeye system at Cape Spencer). After rounding Cape Spencer (*Naguḵyada*), he headed inland on foot to Mount Fairweather (*Tsalx̱aan*, "Land of the Ground Squirrels") and then returned to the coast, emerging near Lituya Bay at a place called *Yakwdeiyí* (Canoe Road) near *Laḵásgi X'aayí* (Seaweed Point). He continued his journey north to Dry Bay (G̲unaax̱oo, "Among the Athabascans") and then navigated up the Alsek (*Aalseix̱'*, "[Resting Place?]") and Copper (*Eeḵhéeni*, "Copper River") rivers to the interior, where he lived among the Athabascans for two years, teaching them how to trap and prepare certain fish and animals efficiently and in quantity. After two years, Ḵaakeix'wtí packed his belongings and returned with the Athabascans to Glacier Bay. Reentering Tlingit country, they reached the coast at *Chookanhéeni* (Straw Grass Creek), home of the Chookaneidí (People of *Chookanhéeni*) clan; but the Chookaneidí shunned the visitors, telling them instead to head across the bay to *L'ei-wshashakee Áan* (Glacial Sand Hill Town) at Bartlett Cove. Here they encountered the group that would become the Kaagwaantaan. After the advance of the glaciers in Glacier Bay (another story; see Dauenhauer

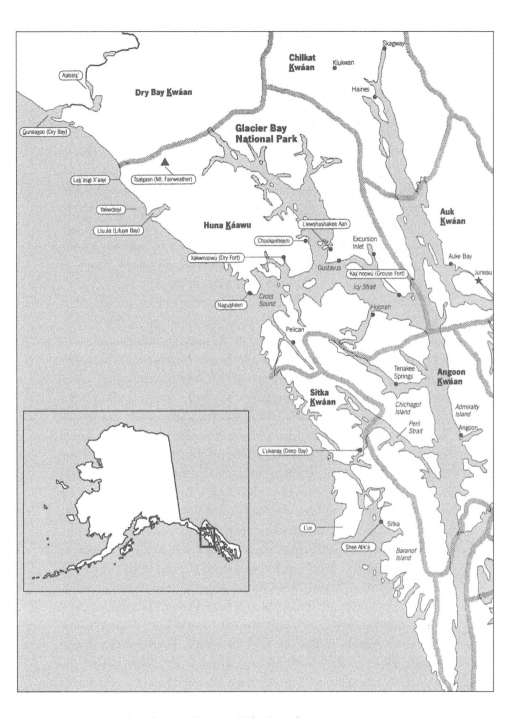

MAP 2.1. Selected sites in Herman Kitka Sr.'s place-name inventory
(Thornton 1997b)

and Dauenhauer 1987:245–92), K̲aakeix'wtí and his group moved with the Kaagwaantaan to *Lulxágu* (Fireweed Pebble Beach), where they built several large houses and a fort (*Ka̲x'noowú*, "Female Grouse Fort") and sponsored lavish potlatches with their newfound wealth from the interior trade. Timbers for one of these houses were damaged by fire, and, consequently, the dwelling earned the name *Kaawagaani Hít*, or "Charred House." It is for this house that the Kaagwaantaan are named. Afterward some of the Kaagwaantaan moved to Sitka. As Deikeenaak'w (Swanton's consultant [1909:346]) put it, emphasizing ancestral ties to the landscape: "Because we are their descendants we [the Sitka Kaagwaantaan] are here also. They continue to be here because we occupy their places." As Herman Kitka puts it, working backward, "Some of us came to Sitka, but we all stem from Glacier Bay."

The journey of K̲aakeix'wtí is Kaagwaantaan history. Because Herman Kitka draws his identity from these events, he knows this geography, even where he has not set foot in the territory. But the man who killed his sleep is also hero to the L'ukna̲x.ádi, Herman Kitka's father's people (see also Swanton 1909:154–65).[10] The Kaagwaantaan, it is said, were the wives of the L'ukna̲x.ádi (161) and vice versa. They lived together at Glacier Bay and later at Sitka. The L'ukna̲x.ádi, too, gained wealth through favorable trade with the Athabascans, including native copper through the Copper River trade corridor. According to oral tradition (160), in the spring after they hosted the Athabascans, the L'ukna̲x.ádi traveled to the mouth of the Copper River (*Eek̲héeni*), where they established a village, *Kus'eix̲ka*. Swanton's other consultant, Kadashan, notes: "All along where they went they gave names. A certain creek was called [*Naguk̲héen* (Rolling Water, at Cape Spencer)], and they came to a lake which they named [*Ltu.áa* (Inside the Point Lake, Lituya Bay)]" (160). Also named were the two tallest mountains of northern Southeast Alaska: Mount Fairweather (*Tsalx̲aan*, "Land of the Ground Squirrels") and Mount Saint Elias (*Waa'eit'ashaa*, "Mountain Inland of *Waas'ei Yík*" [known in English as Icy Bay]). Because Herman Kitka's father was L'ukna̲x.ádi, with ties to the famous Dry Bay village of *Gus'eix̲*, where the first Sleep House was built in honor of these events, he also knows these places from the stories told by his paternal relatives.

Although *Kaawagaani Hít* and *Ka̲x'noowú* have long been abandoned, they remain sacred. As sacred places, they are remembered, honored, and frequently utilized as potent symbols to achieve important social objectives. In potlatches and other ceremonies in northern Tlingit country, Kaagwaantaan orators still use the phrase *Ch'a Tleix' Kax̱'nuwḵweidí* (We who are still one People of Grouse Fort) to achieve at least three ends: (1) to promote solidarity and *communitas* among the now dispersed *Kax̱'noowú* clans; (2) to reiterate their inextricable ties to this historic, collective dwelling place; and (3) to metaphorically transport the listeners to this sacred landscape so that they may be reunited with their ancestors, who likewise may be summoned forth by name.[11] In short, *Kax̱'noowú* serves not only as a chronotope, a place where time and space merge and cannot be understood without reference to each other, but also as a place that is "brought forth to reconfirm" (*gágiwdul.aat*; cf. Nyman and Leer 1993) *shagóon*, Tlingit being in the world.

The Coho clans possess their own phrase of sociogeographic solidarity: *Ch'a Tleix' L'uknax̱*.ádi (We who are still one People of *L'ukanax̱*). The original *L'ukanax̱* (literally Coho Community) may have been at Deep Bay in Peril Strait north of Sitka, where Herman Kitka maintains his father's subsistence camp to this day (cf. de Laguna 1972, 1:226). Mr. Kitka can trace his family's presence there back at least eight generations. In oratory, the phrase *Tleix' L'uknax̱.ádi* is also used to refer to Dundas Bay, Lituya Bay, and Dry Bay on the west coast of Glacier Bay National Park. Dry Bay and Lituya Bay are famous as birthplaces of new Coho clans. As one L'uknax̱.ádi, the late Paul Henry, remarked, "From Lituya Bay we migrated away from each other." He added jokingly, "Maybe we kicked each other out of there" (Dauenhauer and Dauenhauer 1981:52a), an acknowledgment of the main motivation for clan fission among the Tlingit: conflict. Lituya Bay is especially rich with place-names and cultural associations and is homeland to the T'aḵdeintaan branch of the Coho clan, which stems from the L'uknax̱.ádi.

Similarly, Herman Kitka noted in our interviews that "Dundas Bay has a lot of history." Among other things, it is celebrated as the site of the original two-story clan house (Eagles Nest House), what he jokingly terms "the first Tlingit condominium." Occasionally, the phrase *Ch'a Tleix' Xakwnukeidí* (We who are still one People of *Xakwnoowú*) is also used in oratory to the same effect as the Kaagwaantaan phrase. Like *Kax̱'noowú*, *Xakwnoowú* is a very old site; material recently excavated at the fort site suggests occupation dating as far back as sixty-five hundred years.[12]

It is primarily through these interwoven social histories and the wellsprings of *at.óow* and *shagóon* that Herman Kitka has come to know the sacred geography of his clan and that of his father's people. Place intelligence comprises both traditional ecological knowledge (TEK) and traditional social knowledge (TSK), and both are necessary for success in Tlingit country. TEK provides the individual with a foundation to comprehend and adapt to local ecological conditions. TSK provides the individual with a foundation to comprehend how people have evolved in relation to the land and to one another.

CONCLUSION

There are two important geographies in Tlingit: the physical and the social. The basis of claims to ownership and use of territory and resources was founded in knowledge of both geographies and their interrelationship. Tlingit place-names were an important link between the two landscapes and formed an important basis for social identity and the maintenance and transcendence of sociogeographic boundaries. Strategically deployed in rituals and other communicative interactions, placenames and their cultural associations function not only to distinguish groups but also to unite them. Toponyms embody both ecological and sociological knowledge, and Tlingits learn to think with the landscape to achieve a variety of material and social goals. Unfortunately, those who do not speak Tlingit—that is, nearly all those under age seventy—have a much more difficult time achieving these goals because the implicit connections between personhood and geography are absent or obscured in English. Similarly, many non-Native observers have missed these connections and oversimplified Tlingit geography as neatly bounded clan or ḵwáan territories, when the reality was much more dynamic and complex.

Tlingits who do understand the connections between person, social structure, and place through traditional ecological and sociological knowledge have a powerful technology at their disposal. It is something akin to a modern geographic positioning system, except that it is more adaptive because it is coordinates one's position along the physical, ecological, *and* sociological terrains. With this knowledge one can reckon not only one's place on the map but also one's place and ties in the multidimensional social structure that defines and governs that landscape, even if it is not the domain of one's own clan or <u>k</u>wáan. With this technology one can find an answer not only to the question, Where am I? but also to the equally critical question in Tlingit, How do I belong to this place?

This is why on a recent berry-picking trip to Glacier Bay National Park, Herman Kitka began thinking about place-names and about his relatives, maternal and paternal, who lived and subsisted in this part of Huna Tlingit country. At a memorial plaque in Dundas Bay honoring his dad's nephew, he and members of the Chookaneidí and T'a<u>k</u>deintaan (the Coho clan, once a house group of the L'ukna<u>x</u>.ádi) clans stopped to pay their respects and to recall their many relatives and ancestors who had dwelled in this sacred place. Turning to the younger leader of the T'a<u>k</u>deintaan clan, the recognized owners of Dundas Bay, Herman Kitka invoked the words of one of the man's maternal uncles, who had said to him, upon meeting the Kitka's boat anchored at Dundas Bay more than a half century ago, "You belong here 100 percent." "He knew I had Coho on both my father's and my mother's [mother's father's] side of the family," Mr. Kitka remarked with a smile, remembering the warm feeling of being "placed" and embraced by the web of Tlingit social relations. "That's right," his T'a<u>k</u>deintaan host replied, renewing the embrace with a link of his own: "You're my dad's people" (i.e., Kaagwaantaan). And with that all commenced picking *neigóon* berries, united again in the shadow of *Xakwnoowú*.

3 WHAT'S IN A NAME?

Place and Cognition

Ever since I was a boy I have heard the names of different points,
bays, islands, mountains, places where [we] get herring, [hunt]
and make camps, that is why I think this country belongs to us.
—KADASHAN, TLINGIT LEADER

"Dzántik'i Héeni is hard to spell. . . . It's impossible to pronounce . . .
sounds like Santa's Bikini! . . . And who wants to be a flounder!" These
were some of the protests heard in 1994 in response to a proposal to
name a new middle school in Alaska's capital, Juneau, after the Tlingit name for the city's downtown water source: *Dzántik'i Héeni* (Flounder at the Base of the Creek), known as Gold Creek in English. Many
citizens favored other contending names for the new school, most of
which were biographical names, honorifics to immortalize worthy individuals, among them a Tlingit civil rights leader, Elizabeth Peratrovich.
But influential members of the Native community pressed the issue as a
means of affirming not only the increasingly threatened Tlingit language
and geographic identity (despite a growing non-Native population, Juneau
is still a Tlingit community) but also Tlingit ways of place naming, which
are richly descriptive and seldom biographical. Despite its phonologi-
cal, orthographic, and semantic problems for English speakers, *Dzántik'i Héeni* prevailed as the name for the new middle school and paved
the way for a renaissance of Tlingit place naming.

It is tempting to dismiss the charges against *Dzántik'i Héeni* as mere
cultural insensitivity. After all, a number of the Russian and Spanish
names that dot Southeast Alaska are also difficult for English speakers
to pronounce. But there is more to it than this. Because it is a descriptive place-name, *Dzántik'i Héeni,* as a symbol, presents certain prob-

lems when translated into English and applied to a new locale. The new middle school is not at the mouth of Gold Creek (indeed, some local Natives preferred the Tlingit name for the school's actual locale, *Shaanáx̱ Tlein*, or "Big Valley"), and in transferring the name one cannot avoid also transferring its other symbolic links. Thus, "gathering flounder" may come to be associated with children gathering on the grounds of the new school. Interestingly, flounder, a perfectly respectable creature and subsistence resource in Tlingit culture, suffers from a sullied image in English. Few students want to be thought of as "floundering." Consequently, the gathering of flounder, a cause for celebration in Tlingit culture, becomes a dubious metaphor for contemporary English-speaking middle school children in the mostly non-Native city of Juneau. Such is the power of names as symbols and ways of knowing places in diverse cultures.

This chapter analyzes Tlingit place-names both as a universal domain of human knowledge and as a particular cultural system of meanings.[1] Unlike Dzántik'i Héeni Middle School, most indigenous place-names have arisen out of organic processes of experience rather than bureaucratic processes involving nominations, committee meetings, and votes. I begin by mapping a cognitive terrain defined by a set of Tlingit place-names arising through organic experiences described in the well-known Tlingit "Salmon Boy" myth. I show how this myth defines, connects, and frames certain named sites in time and space, and coordinates with the knowledge and experience of contemporary Sitka elders who still inhabit this storied landscape. Then I move on to address four key cognitive questions using a linguistically informed anthropology of experience: (1) How are Tlingit place-names constructed syntactically, and how does syntax relate to Tlingit environmental perception? (2) What is named, and how does the distribution of indigenous place-names reflect patterns of movement, settlement, and subsistence? (3) What are the major semantic components of Tlingit toponyms, and how do they compare to the English toponomy in defining places? (4) Pragmatically, how are place-names deployed and interpreted within the broader context of Tlingit cultural genres and systems of meaning? Overall, my objective is to go beyond a mere descriptive listing and translating of toponyms, as is so often the custom with place-name studies, and to analyze them in a framework that allows for cross-cultural comparisons and insights into how Tlingits in particular, and humans in general, conceptualize their relationship to the lands they inhabit.

The Tlingit language has certain structural and relational capacities that enable a speaker to communicate an enormous amount of information about the qualities of a place within a single toponym—information that would be burdensome if not impossible to express in an English place-name. By contrasting the structure of Tlingit place-names with English toponyms in a single area, Glacier Bay National Park, one sees that there are important similarities and differences in place-naming patterns across cultures. I argue that similarities in place-naming patterns may be linked to certain cognitive universals, such as the use of the body and kinship as metaphors, whereas differences in naming are illustrative of key differences in perceptions of and attitudes toward the environment. After fleshing out these differences and similarities, in the final section of the chapter I relate these findings to Tlingit cultural ideals of place naming and relational ecology as expressed by the Tlingit cultural hero and place maker par excellence: Yéil (Raven)

THE MAP IS NOT THE TERRITORY
BUT A COGNITIVE TERRAIN

Mapping names on a two-dimensional grid consisting of longitude and latitude is itself a cultural act of representation, and it should be emphasized that, as the linguist Alfred Korzybski said, "the map is not the territory" (see Bateson 1979:32; Hunn 1996:6). Indeed, all maps are representations and distortions, if not "lies" (cf. Monmonier 1991). As has been shown, Tlingits had their own ways of mapping territory, especially through sacred property (at.óow), such as ceremonial regalia, which too might be "mapped" onto the body as an element of personhood. In my research I found that, while many Tlingits were comfortable working with official paper maps, especially fisherman and hunters, who often scrutinize topographical maps and nautical charts, others preferred being there, or, when that was not possible, orienting themselves and the audience on an imaginary journey and pointing to named features of the invisible landscape in the air as we "approached" them.

Beyond awareness of cultural differences in mapping, it is important to recognize that there has been a history of intercultural mapping between Tlingits and Euro-Americans. Perhaps the earliest and most unique mapping experiment involving Tlingit place-names was that of George Davidson (1901), who set out in 1869 to map the lands above the Chilkat River extending to the Yukon River, which had previously been terra incognita to Euro-American cartographers. He enlisted the help of the G̲aana̲xteidí leader Kohklux (also known as Chatrich'), whom he reportedly had to bail out of jail to employ in this endeavor. In an inspiring exercise in cross-cultural communication, Davidson engaged the Chilkat leader to work with paper and pencil for several days creating a map of this area. As Davidson tells it, the endeavor "cost him [Kohklux] and his two wives two or three days' labor with pencil and no rubber. . . . It began at Point Seduction, in Lynn Canal, with islands, streams and lakes; and with mountains in profile" (76). To this Kohklux added information about distance (in terms of days' travel by foot), camping places, and geographic names. Needless to say, Davidson was quite impressed. For his part, Kohklux was equally impressed with Davidson's ability to transcribe Tlingit sounds on paper such that the geographer could read Native place-names back to him in his own Tlingit tongue. Fortunately, this exemplary piece of collaborative research was recorded and can be used by Chilkat and Chilkoot Tlingits and interior groups as a source of aboriginal place-names, historic trails, trade routes, and other valuable information.[2]

Another explorer who was sensitive to indigenous names on the land was Edward J. Glave, who accompanied the Frank Leslie Exploring Expedition to the Yukon interior in 1890. Reporting on the local geography, he wrote:

Throughout my letter I have retained the native names of geographical points wherever I could learn them. In my opinion, this should always be studied. The Indian names of the mountains, lakes and rivers are natural land marks for the traveler [sic], whoever he may be; to destroy these by substituting words of a foreign tongue is to destroy the natural guides. You ask for some point and mention its native name; your Indian guide will take you there. Ask for the same place in your substituted English and you will not be understood. Travelling in Alaska [sic] has already sufficient difficulties, and they should not be increased by changing all the picturesque Indian names. Another very good reason why these names should be preserved is that some tradition of tribal importance is always connected with them. These people have no written language, but the retention of their native names is an excellent medium through which to learn their history. (In Cruikshank 1991:113)

Glave (1890:86) was especially impressed with another Chilkat Tlingit leader, Indiank' (Indayaneik), who was "proud of his geographical knowledge and takes great delight in imparting to us items of information. . . . His map [rendered in the sand], when complete, generally covers a space five or six yards square."

Unfortunately, other explorers were anxious to ignore or remove the Native names in favor of their own monikers of discovery. The explorer and travel writer Eliza R. Scidmore early on condemned this form of cultural erasure, chastising the unfortunate tendency of Euro-Americans to ignore the indigenous geographic nomenclature in favor of giving landmarks "the name of some inconsequent and now forgotten statesman whom it seemed officially desirable to flatter at the time" (1896:143).

As a result, only a fraction of the total inventory of Tlingit place-names survives today. Even without problems of cultural erasure, language loss, and colonial renaming, aboriginal place-names are fragile linguistic artifacts. Unlike other domains of knowledge, such as terms for plants and animals or body parts, place-names are not necessarily widely shared. Though key landmarks may be known region-wide, names for other geographic landmarks may be restricted to those who have material or social ties to them, as emphasized in the previous chapter. Even the most knowledgeable of elders knows only a subset (as discussed below, usually no more than about five hundred) of the total inventory of Tlingit place-names.

Unfortunately, for many Tlingit clans and house groups, the last surviving elders with traditional geographic knowledge of particular lands have passed away. As much as 50 percent of Tlingit toponymic knowledge may be lost already, and this loss could accelerate as Tlingit becomes increasingly endangered as a spoken language. At present, fewer than five hundred Tlingits, mainly the eldest generation, speak their native tongue fluently, and, even for them, it is typically not their dominant mode of discourse (see Dauenhauer and Dauenhauer 1998). Place is increasingly crystallized through the English language and the Euro-American place-names that dominate the landscape. The implications of this linguistic shift (and loss) are profound. As the last Tlingit-speaking elders from particular landowning groups die, so too do many of the names, metaphors, narratives, and other knowledge related to specific places within these areas. Even when language revitalization is successful, ethnotoponymic knowledge may not be recovered. As one elder lamented: "I used to know the Tlingit names of these places, but now I don't remember them all. . . . [And] there's no one left to ask." Such realizations have spurred efforts to conserve the Tlingit place-names, following Linnaeus's dictum that, "if you don't know the names, your knowledge of things perishes." Adapting Linnaeus to a Tlingit proverb, T'akteintaan elder Ken Grant states, "Lyee sakoowoo saawx' ch'a tleix ee jeedax goox la haash ee koosteeyi" (If you don't know the names, your [Tlingit] way of life will drift away forever) (see HIA 2006).

Many Tlingit-speaking elders have taken this proverb to heart. Indeed, given the selective forces working against them, it is amazing how many Native place-names elders do remember. Often they remain sedimented in the mind, below the surface of conscious recall, only to be stirred up into memory in certain experiential and cultural contexts that connect to them. A number of times during fieldwork I was fortunate to be able to re-elicit an aboriginal name from an old map, chart, or report. "Oh yeah, I remember that one—that's a good one!" elders would often exclaim upon hearing the name again: "—[a relative] used to talk about that place." Inevitably this would lead to further reminiscences on the social history of named places, as elders began to connect geographic names to one another and to people in *storylines* of individual and collective experience. Such storylines ultimately weave together into maps of experience and configurations of *shagóon*, which, in resonance and interanimation with the canonical myths and sacred clan histories and geographies (and other *at.óow*), help Tlingits make sense of the world and their place in it. This is why, having heard the names and knowing their webs of significance, Kadashan can assert with confidence that "this country belongs to us."[3]

To illustrate the process of how place-names and personal and canonical storylines intermesh and interanimate one another, I map a version of the Tlingit "Salmon Boy" myth in relation to modern Tlingit experiences. Widely distributed among peoples of the Pacific Northwest Coast, the myth concerns a boy's capture and yearlong odyssey among the salmon people before returning to his people and becoming a powerful shaman. The oldest written version of the story, recorded by John Swanton (1909:301–10) from Deikeenaak'w in Sitka in 1904, is also the richest in toponyms. In April 2000 I had the opportunity to map this story with Sitka elders Herman Kitka and Ethel Makinen, Roby Littlefield, and Sitka Tribe staff, as part of an effort to retranscribe and retranslate the story part for a place-based school curriculum (see Littlefield et al. 2003). We went over the story line by line in both English and Tlingit, with a special eye toward identifying and "getting the story behind" named sites in the text. The results highlight not only the resonance between place-names, memory, and experience but also how an ethnogeographical reading of myth can enrich the understanding of indigenous peoples' sense of place and the links between language, land, and identity.

The story map (map 3.1) charts eleven place-names in the order of their appearance in Deikeenaak'w's version of the story. Deikeenaak'w was a Kaagwaantaan granduncle of Herman Kitka and a child of the Kiks.ádi, the matrilineal clan most closely tied to the story. Though Deikeenaak'w died when Herman Kitka was young, Mr. Kitka heard the story from elders numerous times. Moreover, as a lifelong commercial and subsistence fisherman in the Sitka area, he was intimately familiar with its geographical and ecological context. Deikeenaak'w assumed that his audience possessed this background knowledge and could actively apply it in interpreting the story, including the specific geographic locales he names or alludes to in passing. This is precisely what Herman Kitka and Ethel Makinen did, adding at least six additional important geographic sites (nos. 12–17) that are indirectly referenced in Deikeenaak'w's narrative.

Our discussion of the story began with the title. Swanton chose to call the story "Moldy-End," after the unflattering name given to the boy protagonist by the salmon people, whom he insulted by disparaging and casting aside a moldy piece of dryfish offered him by his mother. The proper Tlingit title for the story, the elders agreed, should be Aak'wtaatseen (Alive in the Eddy), the honorific that was bestowed on the boy after he returned from his year with the salmon tribe and

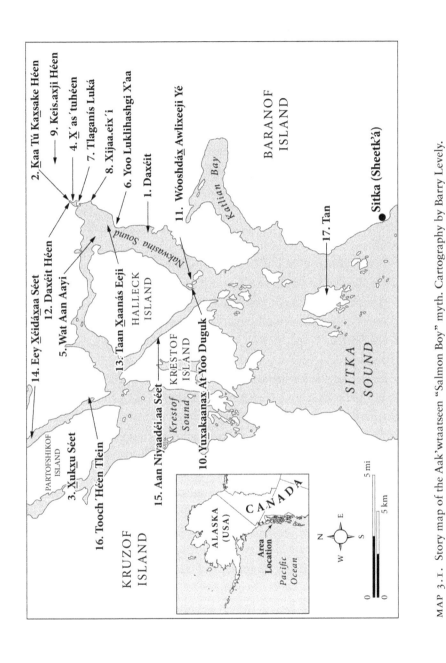

MAP 3.1. Story map of the Aak'wtaatseen "Salmon Boy" myth. Cartography by Barry Levely.

became a shaman. Significantly, Aak'wtaatseen also embodies a geographic reference, for when the boy returned to his people after having been transformed into a salmon, he chose to seek out his mother in an estuary, or eddy, at the mouth of the stream, where he attracted her attention by behaving in an especially "lively" manner. Hence, the name ties person to place directly.

The first place-name mentioned in the story, *Daxéit* (Fallen Stunned, no. 1), is an important bay, Nakwasina Sound, where the Kiks.ádi maintained a large seasonal salmon fishing camp. According to Herman Kitka, this name comes from another piece of oral history, alluded to by Deikeenaak'w, in which a group of Kiks.ádi explorers came down the Nakwasina River (*Daxéit Héen*, no. 12) on a raft (*Taan X̱aanás,* "Sea Lion Raft") and were submerged in the rapids at *Keis.ax̱ji Héen* (Noisy Waterfall, no. 9), save for one man who grabbed a tree branch and pulled himself to safety. The survivor reported back to his relatives that the others had perished, but in fact they had simply "fallen stunned" (i.e., had the wind knocked out of them) and been washed downstream. From this event the name *Daxéit* emerged. The raft too washed downstream and into Nakwasina Sound, where it became the reef known as *Taan X̱aanás Eejí* (Sea Lion Raft Reef, no. 13), an important navigational landmark today.

The second place-name refers to the creek where Aak'wtaatseen was taken by the salmon people after he insulted them. *X̱aa Tú Kax̱sake Héen* (Peaceful River, no. 2; translated by Swanton as "Amusement Creek") is a name that did not appear in our original place-names survey, perhaps because it is used exclusively by the salmon people in what appears to their boy captive as "the far out land." Interestingly, however, it appears that *X̱aa Tú Kax̱sake Héen* is actually part of the *Daxéit* watershed. Herman Kitka identified the creek as a small narrow tributary of *Daxéit Héen*, where "it is fun" to catch fish (in summer) because the river runs narrow and clear and "it is easy to pick the fish you want" to harvest. Thus, Tlingits commonly refer to it as *X̱aa Toowuk Sigoowu Héen* (Amusement Creek). By comparison, from the perspective of the boy who is captured by anadromous salmon in summer and reborn as a young, downstream-bound salmon the following spring, ready to embark on his journey to "the far out land" of the ocean, the creek does become peaceful. Looking downstream toward *Daxéit* in springtime, the busy Tlingit fishing community lies dormant, the people having left their smokehouses for the winter village, and the salmon boy sees only birdlife, especially sandhill cranes and brants.

After they migrate to sea and spend one or more winters feeding in the ocean, the salmon people return to their natal stream to spawn (at varying times according to species, with coho salmon the last because, as the story relates, they have "holes in their canoes"). The third place-name in the story is a passing reference to a shallow saltwater strait (*séet*), through which the salmon must pass on their return to *Daxéit*. Here the salmon are buffeted by strong, shifting tides and sometimes scrape against the rocks and become scarred. Herman Kitka identifies this site as X̱ukx̱u *Séet* (Going Dry Strait, no. 3), a long channel that often goes dry at low tide and in which he has seen salmon struggle, scrape, and sometimes become scarred or trapped. This also occurs in other salmon passes, including Neva Strait (*Eey X̱éidáx̱aa Séet*, "Tide Rips Strait," no. 14) and Olga Strait (*Aan Niyaadéi.aa Séet*, "Closer Strait," no. 15).

Next the salmon go ashore at a place where "it appeared like they would throw hot rocks on each other" and where "the skin of some of them moved like fish skins being roasted on hot rocks" (Littlefield et al. 2003). According to Herman Kitka, this is a reference to the *Tooch' Héen Tlein* (Big Fish Roasting Creek, no. 16), another Tlingit fishing camp on a creek in Neva Strait, where salmon collected were caught and roasted over a fire on special flat roasting sticks.

Farther along their journey back to *Daxéit*, the salmon people encounter the herring people, who also return en masse to spawn in Sitka Sound each spring. Natural rivals (salmon eat herring), the two species engage each other and trade insults. The salmon tribe taunts, "If only your cheek meat [which herring lack] satisfied people's hunger." The herring tribe responds, "We fed them before you" (herring spawn earlier than salmon spawn). "Our eggs are our cheek meat" (Tlingits prize herring eggs). "Maybe now your backbone will get dirty" (a reference to the fact that while herring spawn and live to see another day, salmon spawn and immediately begin to decompose, beginning along the backbone) (Littlefield et al. 2003). In addition to clarifying the ecological context of these insults, Herman Kitka notes that the site of this encounter was likely by *Tan* (Jumping [Fish], no. 17), an island in Sitka Sound where herring collect in great numbers and may appear to the incoming salmon like "a cloud far down the horizon," as the story relates.

As they approach *Daxéit* from Sitka Sound, the salmon people divide and choose their destinations. The pink (humpback) salmon say they will be going to *X̱'as'tuhéen* (Saliva Creek, no. 4). "That's what the humpy [humpback salmon] people call it," Herman Kitka observes. Elaborating, he explains that the choicest parts of the spawning rivers are taken by other salmon species, so the "humpies" chose to spawn in the lower reaches of the streams, where the tidal action and foam give the water a saliva-like appearance. The name poses a metaphoric analogy between the mouth of the river and a being's mouth.

Aak'wtaatseen, a dog (chum) salmon, is destined for the upper reaches of *Daxéit Héen*. He follows a path the salmon tribe calls *Wat Aan Aayí* (Right to Town, no. 5), referring to the Tlingit settlement at the mouth of the Nakwasina River. Just before reaching the village, they encounter *Yoo Luklihashgi X'aa* (Floating Point, no. 6), from whence they can see the Tlingit smokehouses, which at first appear to them like forts. Optical illusion is also significant in Tlingit perceptions of this point. Herman Kitka relates that if the point appears to be floating when you approach it on a sunny day, it is a sign rain will come the next day. Tlingits used *Yoo Luklihashgi X'aa* as a means of forecasting weather.

The next named place on their journey is *Tlaganís Luká* (Sapling Point, no. 7), where the people gathered and sharpened the green saplings "so the fish would jump on them." This is another name that may belong exclusively to the salmon people. The point lies at the mouth of the Nakwasina River. Once inside this point the boy sees his father, and the salmon encourage him to "stand up," meaning to jump for him. This Aak'wtaatseen does, impressing his mother especially. Later, after the other harvested salmon are half-dried, he eagerly presents himself to her in the eddy (the event from which Aak'wtaatseen's name, Alive in the Eddy, is derived), where she is cleaning fish. The salmon boy is then gaffed and clubbed by his father and given to his mother for cleaning. She is unable to make the first cut to clean him, however, because the salmon boy's neck is protected by the same copper choker he wore as a child. Examining the fish closely, Aak'wtaatseen's parents discover the copper necklace and realize their son has returned. They proceed to put him in a finely woven basket (*léet'*), cover him with bird down, and place him on the roof of the smokehouse and perform a ceremony to restore the salmon boy to human form.

The remainder of the Aak'wtaatseen story is a shamanic sequence, detailing the transformation of the salmon boy back into human form, after which he becomes a powerful shaman and leader among the Kiks.ádi people. Aak'wtaatseen's shamanic activities produce their own unique landscape and a set of toponyms chronicling his exploits. The small pond near *Daxéit*, where Aak'wtaatseen bathes and drums for power, becomes *Xijaa.eix'i* (Beating Time Slough, no. 8); the place where he spears the powerful land otter becomes *Yuxakaanáx At Yoo Duguk* (Point It [the Spear] was Thrown Across, no. 10); and the place where the shaman cuts out the otter's tongue and fasts for eight days takes the name *Wóoshdáx Awlixeeji Yé* (the Place Divided, no. 11). So powerful was Aak'wtaatseen that "he lived for more than 100 years. Even as he was dying, his spirits were so strong, that he sat and they moved him in a circle in a trance" (Swanton 1909:310; Littlefield et al. 2003).

Aak'wtaatseen is still remembered for the lessons he teaches about Tlingits' moral and ecological relationships with the salmon people, for the way he followed the salmon and learned to see the world from their point of view, and for the powerful shaman he became upon his return from the oceans. Up until the late nineteenth century, when missionaries and the state undertook to actively suppress it, shamanism was a powerful institution throughout the Northwest Coast. Shamans distinguished themselves through their extraordinary abilities to sense places and communicate with and control the sentient constituents of the landscape, sometimes even transforming into nonhuman beings, like salmon, to experience the world from their sensory perspective. Hence shamanism was a powerful technology for understanding and negotiating (and even transcending) local landscapes. So, too, is fishing experience a powerful technology, as evidenced by the deep ecological reading Herman Kitka is able to give to the salmon boy story. Having engaged the salmon in the same places, his experience resonates with events in the story. To become a good fisherman, he says, not unlike Aak'wtaatseen, "you have to make a study" of the salmon. This involves not only observing salmon but also learning to think and sense like a salmon—to develop an appreciation of their worldview.

The story of Aak'wtaatseen can be read in many ways. In this brief ethnogeographic mapping of one old version of the story, I have emphasized the abundance of traditional ecological and toponymic knowledge that is embedded in the myth and how an understanding of the plot and setting is enlivened and enriched by contemporary elders who still possess such knowledge. Only those with such expertise can comprehend the ethnogeographical and ethnoecological "grammar" that underlies the salmon boy's adventures and gives order and meaning to the particular constellation of named places that constitute the story's dynamic and sentient setting.

HOW ARE NAMES PUT TOGETHER?
THE SYNTACTIC STRUCTURE OF TLINGIT TOPONYMS

How naming systems develop is a function of language, culture, and environment. Cognitive anthropological and linguistic research has shown convincingly that, while language and culture are not so arbitrary as to actually constitute the environment, as the extreme form of the Sapir-Whorf, or linguistic relativity, hypothesis suggests, they do play a powerful role in shaping perceptions of the landscape (cf. Lakoff 1987). Thus, cultures inhabiting the same terrain may conceive of and act on the environment in very different ways.

Tlingit is classified as an isolate in the Na-Dene language family first proposed by Edward Sapir (1915) and consists of four mutually intelligible dialects or speech areas: the Gulf Coast, Inland, Northern, and Southern (de Laguna 1972, 1:15–16). Like Athabascan languages, Tlingit is characterized by its grammatical emphasis on the verb and its complex prefixing and classificatory structures that allow whole phrases to be built out of a single verb stem. Typically the verb stem appears toward the end of a word, with as many as twelve prefixes and three suffixes modifying it. Important prefixes for place naming include relational nouns or theme prefixes (Naish and Story 1973), directionals, classifiers, and possessives. Commenting on the possessive suffix in place naming, Ken Grant instructed me that it reflects the Tlingit notion that places, like human beings, can "possess things," even people. Indeed, Tlingits respect lands, as they do people, for what they possess.

In a verb-centered language like Tlingit, place-names may incorporate complex verb phrases that have the capacity to define the environment in terms of its actions, motion, and processes. This linguistic emphasis on action is mirrored in Tlingit metaphysics in that actions are attributed not only to what English speakers would define as "animate" objects or beings but also to inanimate ones, such as rocks and trees, and indeed the earth itself (de Laguna 1972, 1:21). In addition to this "enlivening" influence of the Tlingit verb, the Tlingit system of incorporating relational nouns and other specifiers into the verb enables the speaker to describe complex actions with a precision and economy that is hard to match in English.

To understand how this works, one can take as an example the English and Tlingit names for Glacier Bay, which, although similar in their geographic referents, convey different meanings. The English name, Glacier Bay, is a classic binomial compound, consisting of a generic physical feature of the landscape (bay) with a specifier, in this case a noun (glacier), preceding it. Many English place names conform to this pattern. The Tlingit toponym *Sít' Eeti G̲eeyi* (Bay Taking the Place of the Glacier) also is typical in its construction. Like the English, the Tlingit includes the generic (*geeyí*, or "bay"), but the specifier is not an adjective or a noun, as is commonplace in English; rather it is a relational verbal noun (*eeti*) implying action in time ("taking the place of") and relative location. This place-name illustrates well the capacity of the Tlingit toponyms to concisely communicate a complex phenomenon.

Even more intriguing than its grammatical construction, however, is the idea that the Tlingit toponym conveys. It is fundamentally *ecological* in that it relates the way the bay and the glacier interact. While the English name implies only the *presence* of glaciers, the Tlingit name denotes a geographic *process* of glacial recession and the consequent formation of a bay in its place. Unlike the English name, the Tlingit toponym clues into important geological and hydrographic events that have occurred in this place. Furthermore, the Tlingit name is both phenomenal and historical in revealing how Tlingits have experienced the changing landscape over time. The indigenous names for Johns Hopkins Inlet, *Tsalx̲aan T'éidí Wool'éex'i Yé* (Inlet That Moves toward behind Mount Fairweather), and Hugh Miller Inlet, *Anax̲kuyaawal'ix'i Yé* (Where the Glacier Ice Broke Through), are other examples of this kind of action-oriented naming, describing a process that has occurred, or is occurring, over time. The first name requires a seven-word English phrase to translate it.

The key to ecological, action-oriented naming is the Tlingit verb. Analyzing the last two Tlingit place-names one finds that they are specific forms of the verb stems "to move" and "to break." In Tlingit there are more than twenty ways to say "move" or "break" in a complex verb.[4] Examples from Constance Naish and Gillian Story (1973:134-38, 34-35) include the following:

- move along (a number of objects all together and not having their own power of motion): *ka-ya-soos*
- move along: *ya-gaas'*
- move along, be moved along: *li-gaas'*
- move through the air (especially in a downward curve, like an arrow or shooting star): *ya-li-gaas'*
- move, often imperceptibly; move (of event): *ka-di-yaa*
- move forward with considerable momentum, keep moving from momentum: *k'a-ya-ya-daax̱*
- move (of textile [or skinlike object]), move around: *ya-wooḵ*
- move heavy object a little at a time (first one end and then the other): *ya-li-t'aaḵ*

Similarly for the verb "to break" one finds a wide variety of specific forms, including the following examples:

- break across (especially long objects), often by bending: *li-l'eex'*
- break in pieces, crumble: *ka-ya-x'eil*
- break, snap (especially ropelike objects): (1) *ya-k'oots*; (2) *li-k'oots*
- break off pieces (of food) with hand: *ya-waal'*

Why are such subtle distinctions worth making? Again, the answer lies in the ecology of Tlingit language. Distinctions within the verb tend to highlight phenomenal "differences that make a difference." For example, the verb *ya-waal'* (to break off pieces with hand) is inherently relational; it speaks of how something breaks in relation to the human hand. The verb denotes an action that can be done only by human hands, without special tools or superhuman force. Especially for hunter-gatherers, who were consistently engaged in harvesting, processing, transporting, and otherwise handling materials with their hands, such distinctions are worth noting. Other verb-centered names encapsulate salient messages about perception of the land, such as *Yoo Luklihashgi X'aa* (Floating Point); or travel, as in the cautionary name *Tleilkee Ya* (Place You Can't Go Through); or subsistence, as in the name *Xaataadugich Yé* (Pitching the Fish Place). As these examples illustrate, when incorporated into place-names, verbs provide the interpreter with valuable qualitative information about the nature of landscapes. The relational capacity of Tlingit makes it especially well suited to describing the world in ecological terms.

Another key to the descriptive power of Tlingit toponyms lies in the fact that multiple relational nouns and directionals can be incorporated or "stacked" into place-name syntax to describe position and location with phenomenal precision. The place-name *Geesh K'ishuwanyee* (Just on the Edge of the Base of the Kelp) exemplifies this polysynthetic or "stacking" quality of Tlingit by accommodating no fewer than four relational nouns to indicate a specific place in the sea where halibut can be located and caught. Literally translated the name can be deconstructed as follows: *Geesh* (kelp) *K'i* (base) -*shu* (end) -*wan* (edge) -*yee* (place below). Relational nouns commonly incorporated into place-names are well suited to describing conditions on both land and sea (see table 3.1). English place-names typically lack such expressive power because relational terms cannot easily be incorporated into their syntax.

Like English, Tlingit makes frequent use of binomial compounds in which a descriptive modifier is combined with a geographical generic. Some commonly incorporated generic terms for geographic features are listed in table 3.2. Eugene Hunn (1996) reports an aversion to binomial compounds in Sahaptin place naming, which he cautiously attributes to the "agglutinative nature" of Sahaptin and a general bias against binomials in hunter-gatherer semantic domains (C. Brown 1985; Hunn and French 1984; but see Berlin 1992:275–90). Tlingit, Dena'ina Athabascan (see Kari 1989), and other Na-Dene languages do not share this aversion to binomial compounds or generics. In fact in Tlingit place-names that lack generics there are typically major landmarks, such as prominent mountains like Mount Fairweather (*Tsalxaan*) or major mainland rivers such as the Alsek (*Aalséix*), Chilkat (*Jilkaat*), Taku (*T'aaku*), and Nass (*Naas*), though not Stikine (*Shtax'héen*). A similar pattern is apparent

TABLE 3.1. Common Relational Nouns Found in Tlingit Place-Names

Relational Noun	Translation	Example	Translation
a daa	around or about it	Taas' Daa	Double-Headed Tide Around It (Lemesurier Island)
a t'áak	back inland from it	Saaxw T'áak	Back Inland from the Cockles
a k'í	at the base or foot of it	Dzántik'i Héeni	Flounder at the Base of the Creek
a t'éik	behind it	Tayx'ayí T'eikgeeyí	Bay behind Tayx'ayi
a seiyi	below it	Neixinté Seiyí	Below the Green Rock
a t'aak̲	beside/inside it	Yat'ak̲héen	Creek beside / inside the Face of It
a x̲'áak	between them	Tsaa Tak̲di X'áak	Between Seal Harpooners
a wán	edge of it	Wanachích	Edge of a Porpoise (an island)
a yá	front of it	G̲il' Yaká	In Front of the Cliff
a shá	at its head	Taan Shaayí	At the Head of the Sea Lion
a x̲oo	amid, among	X'áat'x'i X̲oo	Among the Islands
a x̲'é	its mouth	Yéil X̲'ek'	Raven's Little Mouth
a ká (shakée)	on top of it (on top of the hill or mountain)	L'eiw Shaa Shakee.aan	Town on top of the Sand Hill
a t'iká	out toward the open sea from it	Sheey At'iká (Sheet'ká)	Oceanside of Shee (Baranof Island)
a eetí	place where it was (or taking the place of)	Sít' Eeti G̲eeyí	Bay in Place of the Glacier

in northern Athabascan languages, suggesting a possible refinement of the binomial aversion theory in these areas.[5]

Among the most important theme prefixes in Tlingit place-names are body referents. As noted earlier, the body is an important metaphor and man's most basic environment. Thus, like many languages, Tlingit makes use of classifiers that describe environmental phenomena in relation to human anatomy. In his *Grammatical Notes on the Language of the Tlingit Indians*, Franz Boas (1917:68–70) observed that body referents constituted the majority of modal prefixes that occupy first, second, or third positions of the verb complex. When incorporated into nouns, he notes, the meaning of these body prefixes can be instrumental, directive, or locative (68), as in the place-name *Ltu.áa* (Inside the Nostril Lake). When body parts are incorporated into verbs, they may represent qualities of

TABLE 3.2. Common Geographical Generics in Tlingit Place-Names

Feature	Tlingit generic	Example	Translation
bay	*geey*	*Xóots Geeyí*	Brown Bear Bay
cliff	*gíl'*	*Kuts'een Gil'x'i*	Rat Cliff
fortified place	*noow*	*Deikee Noow*	Far Out Fort
glacial silt, sand	*l'eiw*	*L'eiw Shaayí*	Glacier Silt Mountains (cutbanks)
glacier	*sít'*	*Sít'k'i T'ooch'*	Little Black Glacier
hill	*gooch*	*X'aan Goojí*	Fire Hill
hole	*tuwool*	*Yéilchuwatuli Yé*	Raven Bored a Hole There
hole (below freshwater)	*ísh*	*Ishkahít*	House on Top of the Fishhole
hole (below saltwater)	*eet*	*Chaatl Eedi*	Halibut Hole
island	*x'áat'*	*Kóoshdaakaa X'áat'i*	Land-Otter Man Island
isthmus, portage	*góon*	*Aangóon*	Isthmus Town

TABLE 3.2. *(continued)*

Feature	Tlingit generic	Example	Translation
lake	*áa*	*Áak'w*	Little Lake
mountain	*shaa*	*Nuskw Shaayí*	Wolverine Mountain
point	*x'aa*	*Teey X'aayí*	Yellow Cedar Point
rapids	*eey*	*Eey Tlein*	Big Rapids
reef	*eech*	*Yées' Eejí*	Large-Mussel Reef
river, creek	*héen*	*Tilhéeni*	Dog Salmon Creek
rock	*té*	*Teyeiyí*	Rocks Alongside
rockslide	*ḵaadí*	*Ḵáa Tlénx'i Ḵaadí*	Slide of the Big Men
sandbar	*xákw*	*Xakwnoowú*	Sandbar Fort
spring (freshwater)	*goon*	*Tinaa Gooní*	Copper Shield Spring
strait, channel	*séedi*	*Taan Té Séet*	Sea Lion Rock Strait
trail, road	*dei*	*Deishú*	End of the Trail
valley	*shaanáx̱*	*S'eek Shaanáx̱*	Black Bear Valley
village, settlement, land	*aan*	*Kasa.aan*	Beautiful Town (Kasaan, AK)

appearance or character "in the sense that these qualities are permanent" (112). This pattern is illustrated by the name *Yoo Luklihashgi X'aa* (Floating Point [Point that Moved Up and Down in a Perching/Squatting Posture]), which refers to a point of land that appears to move up and down like a person alternating perching and squatting. Many place-names use common anatomical prefixes, including the mouth (*x̱'é*), face (*yá*), head (*shá*), nose (*lu*), or nostril (*lutú*). Data on the frequency of anatomical referents in place-names are given in table 3.3. Similar patterns are evident in other Native American languages (cf. Boas 1934:14–18), as well as in English (e.g., Hilton Head), suggesting that anatomical image

TABLE 3.3. Semantic Referents in Place-Names

Semantic Category	% Tlingit Toponyms in Glacier Bay (n = 130)	% English Toponyms in Glacier Bay (n = 205)	% Native Toponyms in Southeast Alaska (n = 2186)
Biological	43	9	30
Animal	29	6	23
Plant	12	1	8
Topographical	59	25	41
Hydrographic	42	11	32
Terrestrial	16	13	9
Biographical	1	50	1
Habitation Sites	12	0	14
Historical	13	9	7
Metaphor	7	1	6
Anatomical	7	1	4
Other	NA	NA	2
Navigational	NA	NA	1
Subsistence Activity	NA	NA	2
Relationals	NA	NA	13

schemata are a cross-cultural phenomenon in place naming.[6] As the primary landscape that humans inhabit, the body provides the most natural "technology" by which to measure and conceptualize the broader landscape. In short, we all have embodied minds (Varela, Thompson, and Rosch 1991).

WHAT IS NAMED: SEMANTICS AND TOPONYMIC DENSITY

Like material artifacts, place-names lie in particular contexts and assemblages, and their distribution and patterning are important to understand. Examining what features of the environment are distinguished and labeled by place-names enables one to assess basic issues of environmental perception and classification as well as environmental change and land use over time.

As might be expected, many similar geographic features tend to be named across cultures, although not with the same frequency. In oral cultures, a "mental economy" (Hunn 1996) seems to exist, whereby not every landscape feature is named, but rather only those worth remembering. To label all features, regardless of cultural interest, would be both superfluous and taxing on memory. In contrast, in literate societies blank spaces on the map seem to stimulate the naming impulse and the map itself is an aid to memory. Nevertheless, it is clear that certain environmental forms invite names across cultures. These include large persistent geographic features such as large rivers, islands, mountains, and valleys.

In an earlier study (Thornton 1995), I charted the correspondence between named features in English and Tlingit for the same landscape, Glacier Bay National Park and Preserve (see table 3.4). The survey showed that, although most types of geographic features were named in both nomenclatures, each culture favored certain categories. For example, English favored the naming of mountains (25 percent of the sample, compared to 5 percent in the Tlingit name set) and glaciers (18 percent vs. 5 percent) while Tlingit emphasized the naming of islands (13 percent vs. 9 percent in the English sample), bays (20 percent in both), streams (19 percent vs. 8 percent), and habitation sites (12 percent vs. none). By comparison, points (8 percent), rocks (3 percent), and valleys (1 percent) comprised roughly the same proportion of each name set. Like English, Tlingit has generic terms for these features.

This comparison suggests that perceptual salience by itself does not guarantee that a place will be named. In theory, the number of perceptually salient features is infinite. Thus a selection process is called into play as a basis for making meaningful distinctions in the environment. Tlingits tend to name only specific features of interest to them—for example, refuges, key navigational landmarks, and productive hunting, fishing, and gathering locales—while the places in between remain a "relatively undifferentiated landscape" (de Laguna 1960:20). Especially among societies without written records, where names and

TABLE 3.4. What Is Named

Geographical Feature	% Tlingit Toponyms in Glacier Bay (n = 130)	% English Toponyms in Glacier Bay (n = 205)	% Native Toponyms in Southeast Alaska (n = 2,186)
Streams	19	8	24
Habitation sites	12	0	14
Points	8	8	14
Bays	20	20	12
Islands	13	9	8
Lakes / lagoons	2	4	7
Rocks	3	3	5
Passages / straits	3	1	4
Sand / beach	NA	NA	4
Cliffs	2	0	3
Glaciers	5	18	3
Mountains	5	25	3
Valleys	1	1	2
Tide / current	NA	NA	2
Caves	0	0	1
Slides	2	0	1
Holes	NA	NA	1

other knowledge were passed down through oral tradition, cultural interests influenced not only the selection of sites to be named but also
whether or not the names were to be retained in the collective memory.
Cultural interests in place naming play a similar kind of practical or
"utilitarian" role to those shaping ethnobiological classification systems
(Hunn 1982).

Cultural interests may differ, however, even among cultures inhabiting the same or similar environments. Glacier Bay, being a wilderness

park in the American consciousness rather than a place of human dwelling, does not inspire habitation names. It does for Huna Tlingits, however, who refer to Glacier Bay as "our homeland" and "our icebox" (Thornton 1999b; Hunn et al. 2003).

As befits a maritime culture, hydrographic and shoreline features figure more prominently than inland landmarks in the Tlingit toponymy, while mountains are relatively neglected (see table 3.3). Bays, streams, and islands are the geographic features most frequently named. Although most of these features also have English names, collectively they constitute a smaller percentage of the English name set. For Tlingits, bays and streams had cultural value not only as outstanding geographical landmarks but also as subsistence resource areas and habitation sites.

As elsewhere, in Glacier Bay localized Tlingit clans laid exclusive claim to wealthy, defensible pockets of natural resources, especially salmon fishing streams. Berg Creek, or *Chookanhéeni* (Straw Grass Creek), is a case in point. A productive sockeye and coho fishery and sheltered habitation site, this area was claimed by the Chookaneidí clan. The Chookaneidí not only occupied and possessed this bay but also took their name from it. The name Kuyeik.ádi, belonging to a now extinct segment of the Lukaax.ádi, can be translated as "People of Excursion Inlet."[7] A group called the T'ikanaa (People of the Pacific Side) at one time may have occupied Taylor Bay (*T'ikaa*) and parts of the outer coast. And finally, the T'akdeintaan, a clan still well represented in Hoonah, apparently took their name from a small island in Lituya Bay upon which they used to camp. In addition to clans, individuals too were named for places. In this way place-names were inextricably linked to identity, property, and other important aspects of social life. These links were sanctified and reinforced in ritual. Only members of the possessing clan were free to interpret the geography and history—including the toponymy—of a territory, which they did through oratory, songs, dances, and regalia and other visual art, as well as through the very act of place naming.

What is and is not named may also be a function of the evolution of the landscape itself. For example, in Glacier Bay patterns of glacial advance and retreat have had a profound impact on the distribution of names. Mapping named sites shows a significantly higher density of names near the mouth of the bay than at the present head of the bay, which was inaccessible one hundred years ago. Tlingit oral history and the western scientific literature both highlight the significant glacial recession that has occurred in the bay over the past several centuries. The Tlingit traditional narratives also note the rapid advance of a single, large glacier to the mouth of the bay prior to the modern glacial retreat, an advance that destroyed their main settlement at Bartlett Cove, *L'eiwshaa Shakee Aan* (Town on Top of the [Glacial] Sand Dune). Prior to this encroachment, Glacier Bay possessed a different name, *S'e Shuyee*, or "Drainage at the End of the Glacial Mud." Tlingit history traces this earlier reference to a time when the bay was "a great valley" with a single, muddy river flowing through it (Hall 1962:41). Thus *S'e Shuyee* and *L'eiwshaa Shakee Aan*, despite perceptual obsolescence, are retained in the assemblage of geographic names at Glacier Bay. What is more, by unpacking the sequence of names an important insight is gained into the natural history and cultural evolution of the region.

Beyond Glacier Bay, throughout the Southeast Alaska region, similar patterns are found, as summarized in table 3.4. Again waterways dominate the name set. Perhaps the most striking difference between the regional name set and the Glacier Bay inventory is the higher ratio of stream names to bay names. This is likely a function of there being many more streams than bays. It is probably true that every major bay and inlet in Southeast Alaska had a Native name, for even those bays that did not possess resources of value to Tlingits held significance as navigational landmarks. This is not the case with streams, however, as there are simply too many to mark with names; nor do all streams possess the navigational salience of bays.

In addition to looking at what is and is not named, the density of names in a particular area can also be measured. As with material artifacts, a high density of names on the land implies a strong cultural interest in the landscape and, potentially, a dense population. Toponymic density is a measure of the number of named places per square mile within the range of a speech community. It is derived from the broader concept of lexical density, which Hunn (1994:81) defines as "the ratio of the number of named elements within a semantic domain or subdomain to the size of the referential space spanned by the terminological set." In the case of place-names, such a measure is designed to facilitate cross-cultural comparisons in naming patterns relative to physical space. But, theoretically, lexical density can be applied to terms in any referential space, including color space (e.g., Berlin and Kay 1969; Kay and McDaniel 1978), genealogical space (Atkins 1973), and other semantic spaces.

After plotting toponymic densities for Sahaptin-speaking peoples of the Columbia River region, Hunn compared these figures to toponymic and population densities of ten other hunter-gatherer groups, including the Tlingit (based on the author's data), and one horticulturalist society. He found striking correlations between population densities and lexical densities, which he attributes to the "Magic Number 500." It appears that few individuals remember more than about five hundred names in any lexical domain. Similarly, the Magic Number 500 also seems to define the upper limits of personal relationships that individuals can maintain in foraging societies, as first suggested by Joseph Birdsell (1953) in his concept of the "dialectical tribe." Thus, "the strong positive correlation . . . between population density and toponymic density may be understood as the consequence of a domain size-limitation imposed by the constraints of individual human memory" (Hunn 1994:85).

A basic analysis of Tlingit ḵwáan toponymic densities can be calculated by dividing the total number of toponyms in a ḵwáan by the ḵwáan's population density (population divided by ḵwáan area).[8] These calculations show that toponymic densities generally decrease as one moves from south to north, with the southernmost Sanyaa Ḵwáan and Taant'a Ḵwáan having the highest place-name densities and the northernmost Yakutat the lowest. Although the earliest and most comprehensive place-name surveys were completed in the southern ḵwáans, I suspect that the higher densities are also a function of historic population densities and migration trends. The earliest Tlingit population centers were in the southern mainland ḵwáans, and it is from these areas that many of the northern groups migrated. Thus, the highest toponymic densities would be expected in southern Tlingit country.

The Tlingit data also support the Magic Number 500 as a limitation on individual memory. Thomas Waterman's (n.d.) richly dense toponymic survey of over 850 Tlingit place-names in Sanyaa and Tongass ḵwáans was carried out primarily with two consultants, although exactly how many names came from each is not known. Similarly, Sitka interviews with elders Charlie Joseph Sr. and Herman Kitka Sr. produced between four hundred and five hundred place-names from each. This is not to suggest that the informants did not know or would not recognize more Native names (and most of the English name set that overlays them), but rather that they these four hundred to five hundred names were the ones they could recall from memory and had some knowledge about in their cognitive "files."

WHAT'S IN A NAME? SEMANTIC REFERENTS

Analysis of the linguistic structure and topographical distribution of place-names provides a partial view of how cultures perceive their environment. A semantic analysis helps to complete the picture by tracing out other references contained in toponyms besides generic topographical features. Semantic patterns are especially important in evaluating place-names as sources of TEK, or traditional ecological knowledge, for they communicate much about *why* people are interested in particular environmental features. Like the syntactic construction of names, a semantic analysis highlights the descriptive force of Tlingit names in constructing mental images and cognitive maps of a particular geographic region and the inhabitants who have dwelled there.

The typology in table 3.3, based on those developed by Waterman (1922) and Hunn (1996), provides a basis for comparing semantic referents in Tlingit and English place-names in Glacier Bay National Park. As in the case of geographic referents, the Tlingit semantics can be compared to the analysis of the regional place-name data for Tlingit.

The first category, biological references, includes animals, plants, and anatomical and mythological allusions. In Glacier Bay, animals are evident in 29 percent of Tlingit place-names, referring to twelve different species of fish and wildlife. In English, animals are evoked in 6 percent of names, referring to ten different species of wildlife but no fish. The majority of these associations in both languages are *metonymic*, meaning that these places are characterized by the presence of a particular resource (ordinarily plant or animal), usually in abundance. For example, Goose Cove was a name suggested by the scientist W. S. Cooper, who observed there "a number of young wild geese, who still unable to fly, were flapping over the water" (Orth 1971:379). References to human populations are also included in this category. The English name Tlingit Point is a metonymic association referring to Hoonah seal hunters who camped there. Similarly, the Tlingit called Tidal Inlet *Gus'k'iyee Kwáan Geeyí* (White Man's [People Dwelling at the Base of the Clouds] Bay) because of the presence of whites at that place. The Tlingit names for Bartlett River, *Gaat Héeni* (Sockeye Creek), and for Beartrack River, *Gaat Héeni Tlein* (Big Sockeye Creek), reflect not only the concentration of this species at these locations but also the Tlingit cultural interest in these fish. Indeed, sockeye salmon (*Oncorhynchus nerka*) were among the most coveted of resources because of their attributes as a food source (taste, high oil content, and extended harvestability in freshwater) and their narrow distribution compared to other salmon (cf. Langdon 1989:306; Thornton, Schroeder, and Bosworth 1990). Consequently, sockeye streams were highly valued, carefully guarded, and often named for this key resource. In comparison, the lack of references to fish in the English name set is indicative of a bias toward upland resources, especially those that are easily viewed.

In the regional name set, there is a negative correlation between the frequency of fish streams containing various salmon and their semantic frequency in place-names (see table 3.5). Pink salmon streams, the most frequent type, are least commonly referred to in toponyms, while sockeye streams, the least common (along with king salmon and steelhead streams), are the most recognized. As the most common and least desirable of the major Pacific salmon, it seems that pinks were recognized in names only if there was something otherwise exceptional about their run, such as size, timing, quality, or exclusivity. King salmon, the most desirable of the species along with sockeye, are also commonly referred to in names. With respect to the other two species, dog salmon and coho salmon, it appears that a key factor in their being semantically incorporated into names was their temporal existence vis-à-vis other salmon. In streams where they coexist with other salmon, dogs or cohos are often the last species to return in the summer or fall. Late salmon runs were of great value because they supplied a concentrated source of fresh fish when other summer resources were becoming increasing scarce. The primacy of other key foods, such as harbor seals, is similarly reflected in a high frequency of semantic references in place-names.

TABLE 3.5. Semantic Frequency of Selected Subsistence Resources in Toponyms

Animal	Percent Toponyms	
Salmon	3	% Salmon Names
Red	1	43
Coho	1	21
King	0	13
Dog	0	14
Pink	0	14
Other	0	7
Halibut	1	
		% Marine
Marine Mammals	5	Mammals Names
Harbor seals	2	56
Sea lions	1	28
Sea otters	1	16
Whales	1	38
Land Mammals	1	
Deer	0	
Bears	1	
Birds	4	
Raven	3	
Seagull	1	
Duck	0	

Metonymy also characterizes plant references in both languages. In the English toponymy for Glacier Bay, Strawberry Island is an example of a metonymic plant association based on abundance. *Chookanhéeni* (Straw Grass Creek), *Keishish.aní* (Alder Country), and *Wudzidugu Geeyí* (Bay Wooded with Cottonwoods) are examples of this pattern in Tlingit. Interestingly, one Tlingit name for Strawberry Island was *L'eiw X'áat'i,* or Sand Island, indicative of the island's habitat at an earlier stage of succession, prior to the presence of significant patches of strawberries. The relative dearth of plant names in both toponymies may be a reflection of glacial scouring and the lack of culturally significant plants (despite a superabundance of berries; see Thornton 1999b) in Glacier Bay as compared to other habitats. Although 12 percent of the Tlingit place-names reference plants, many of these are redundant (table 3.3).

Analysis of the regional Tlingit place-name data shows reference to a much wider array of plants than in Glacier Bay, although the frequency of plant place-names is roughly the same (8 percent). Common plants cited include various berries, roots, seaweeds, yellow cedar bark, and other edible plants, as well as those that are employed in technologies, such as yew wood (used for bows and other tools, and found only in parts of southern Tlingit land), saplings, spruce roots, and red and yellow cedar. Here are a few place-names: *Kaltl'àak'wach' Shis'k* (Having Fresh Wild Rhubarb), *Laxx'áat'ak'u* (Red Cedar Islet), *Kalsaksk'i* (Little One That Has Yews), *Kóox X'áat'i* (Wild Rice Island), *Yaana.eit Xágu* (Wild Celery Sandbar), *Taganis* (Sapling [Poles]), and *Xaat Áa Duls'el' Yé* (Place Where They Dig Spruce Roots). Animal references are more common than plants but also comprise a smaller portion of the regional name set (23 percent) than in Glacier Bay.

Humans subsist not only on plants and animals but also on minerals and water. The last two categories also manifest themselves in names. One inlet, for example, is simply known as "Grindstone" for the value of the materials gathered there in manufacturing and sharpening tools. Despite the plethora of creeks and rivers, especially good sources of drinking water are referenced often in names, such as *Gunhéeni* (Clear Springwater) and *Tinaa Gooní,* (Copper Shield Springwater). In another case it appears that the absence of freshwater is highlighted in a place-name that is freely translated as "Where the Saltwater Comes Up and

People Moan for Freshwater." Thus toponyms are named not only for their manifest characteristics but also for their latent or anomalous qualities, or those that they fail to manifest.

Another important set of references found in place-names concerns the body. As suggested above, anatomical references are common in place naming as in other referencing systems because of the primacy of the body as man's most basic landscape and instrument of measure. Place-names such as *Yáay Sháak'ú* (Whale's Little Head [Point Carolus]) display a *metaphoric* association, positing an analogy between a geographic feature and an anatomical feature based on visual resemblance. Even generic topographical references may be couched in terms of the body. In Tlingit a word often used to describe a point of land is *lutú,* which means nose or nostril, as in *Ltu.áa* (Inside the Nostril Lake), or Lituya Bay in English. Body references characterize 7 percent of the Tlingit place-names in Glacier Bay. Anatomical metaphors are also invoked in the English toponymy (e.g., Dicks Arm), but less frequently.

At the regional level, roughly 4 percent of place-names utilize anatomical references, or what George Lakoff (1987:271) calls "kinesthetic image schemas." In examining this category of associations, certain patterns of naming emerge that are consistent with larger cultural themes concerning the body noted by other researchers (cf. de Laguna 1972; Kan 1989). These include a marked preference for naming places after external bodily features, as opposed to internal ones; a particular emphasis on the head, face, or specific facial features; and a general avoidance of the mention of bodily effluvia.[9]

Among the external features of the body, the head, face, and specific facial features are stressed. This pattern is quite consistent with the Tlingit emphasis in other spheres, such as visual art. According to de Laguna (1972, 2:761): "The head or face was the most important motif in art. This not only represented the actual head of a person or animal, but when repeated on other parts of the animal's body signified the indwelling anthropomorphic soul (qwani [ḵwáani]). Faces or heads were also used to symbolize the spirits of mountains, rivers, glaciers, rocks, raindrops or hailstones and other entities which we conceive as wholly inanimate objects or natural forces." It is not surprising that references are found, for example, to Human Head Island (*Ḵasha X'áat'*) and to the heads of other beings, such as *Shála Ẋeishk'w* (Head like [That of a] Steller's Jay), referring to a mountain with a crestlike ridge. Similarly, other topographical features are linked to specific parts of the head, including the face, nose, mouth, and jaw.

De Laguna (1954) also emphasizes the potency associated with bodily effluvia. Perhaps because of this potency, few direct references to bodily effluvia are found in place-names. Yet external orifices of the body, such as the mouth (*Taay X'é,* "Hot Springs Mouth"), nostrils (*Ichlugè* "Inside the Nose Reef"), and rectum (*Xalnù Tukyee,* "Below the Anus of *Xalnú*"), through which these substances pass, are commonly referred to in place-names. As in the body (see Walens 1981), landscape "orifices" often link one domain with another, such as the "mouth" connecting a bay to a strait or an underground spring to a surface pool.

In addition to the above naming patterns involving parts of bodies, there are also metaphoric references in toponyms to whole forms, human (*Tsaagwáa Shaanák'u,* "[Hood Bay] Old Woman"—a mountain; or *Nás'ginấx Kaa,* "Three Men"—islands) and nonhuman (*Yáay,* "Whale"—an island). As a schema, anatomy provides a tool for organizing disparate geographic elements into meaningful wholes.

The importance of metaphorical and metonymic association in naming and of image schemata like the body in classifying the environment helps explain redundancy in naming. Northwest Coast ethnogeographer Thomas Waterman (1922) correctly observed that indigenous naming principles bred certain patterns of replication, wherein similar sites in different areas would inspire the same name. Even so, the logic of repetition involves more than unreflectively applying old names to new sites that resemble the originals. Like naming offspring after ancestors, naming places after similar predecessors involves a certain contemplation and comprehension of their character. Perhaps for the same reason, the geographies of mythic stories are often relocalized when groups move to a new setting. There is an important mitigating factor, too: distance. In general, features with the same name cannot be too close together. Thus not found are two creeks named *Gaat Héeni* (Sockeye Creek) in the same area. The logic of this rule would seem to be one of avoiding confusion in identifying key sites in practical navigation and in memory. Significantly, this pattern applies to the social world as well, where it is important that persons possessing the same name (especially honorific names and titles) not be too close together in social space (e.g., within the same localized house group) and time (e.g., the same generation), lest there be confusion.

There is another process that I term *ensemblage*, which also has been reductively characterized as mere redundancy by early ethnographers. A geographic ensemblage is a grouping and relating of various landscape features into a meaningful whole through naming. Ensemblage creates regions out of otherwise disparate points. Typically one key landmark serves as the central organizing feature for a whole constellation of named sites within a circumscribed area. For example, there is a small island called *Kéin* at the entrance to the narrows above the village of Kake in central Southeast Alaska. *Kéin* (an unanalyzable term) is the central organizing feature for a geographic ensemblage that also includes *Kéin Séet* (Kéin Strait/Pass, east of Kéin) and *Kéin Yatx'i* (Children of Kéin, a set of islands southwest of Kéin). Although small and seemingly insignificant in itself, *Kéin* is a very important landmark for orienting travelers approaching and leaving Kake to the northeast. Its significance as a signpost is cross-cultural, as underscored by the fact that the island, known as Turnabout Island in English, now houses a federal navigational marker for boats. But in the English toponymy there is no ensemblage—the subsidiary features of the island are not even named. Larger toponymic ensemblages in Tlingit may contain as many as ten or twelve names related to a central feature.

The *Kéin* grouping is one of two ensemblages at the entrance to Keku Strait. The other one—the *Teik* ensemblage—orients the traveler approaching or leaving Kake to the northwest. Like *Kéin*, *Teik* is a small island, but in this case its derivative names refer to features on the island itself and are anatomical in nature, *Teik Lunáak* referring to the "nose" or point of the island, and *Teik Tukyee* to its "rear end" or outlet.

The metaphor of kinship offers another schema for relating places. Especially common is the "child of" metaphor, which defines a small feature proximal to its larger "parent"; *Kéin Yatx'i* (Children of Kéin) is an example of this paradigm. Such ensemblages and schemata both reveal and shape Tlingit sensuous perceptions of the landscape, rendering the character of their country in human terms. Not far from *Kéin* is a place called *Kéex' Luwoolk'i*, or "Hole at the Base of the Nose [Rock] of Kake" (i.e., "Little Nostrils of Kake") (see fig. 3.1). Kake Tlingit dancers used to adorn themselves with large nose rings to emulate the shape of

FIG. 3.1. _Ḵéex̱' Luwoolk'í_ ("Little Nostrils of Kake") is a descriptive name using anatomical metaphor to characterize this historic village site first settled by the ancestors of Kake people before the Flood, according to the late Johnny C. Jackson. So picturesque was the descriptive name that those returning long after the Flood, who had never seen the place, could recognize it from the name. Photo by N. Matsumoto

this rock, which had been a landmark to them during their migration north and still serves as a marker today.[10] This too constitutes a form of ensemblage. As with the Lukaax.ádi sockeye blanket discussed in the previous chapter, this kind of bodily adornment maps the character of the land onto the body as an element of personhood. But the central feature of the geographic ensemblage is not a place but persons, who place elements of the geography on their bodies in order to mutually inscribe their character on the land and the land on their character. Through ensemblage, not only does space become "a society of named places," as Lévi-Strauss (1966) observed, but members of society also become landscapes of named places.

Having highlighted some semantic patterns in names on the land, it is important that I stress that place naming is not merely a mechanistic or rationalistic process in which places are identified and grouped for their metaphoric relations to the body or kin, or metonymic associations to key resources. Toponyms are carriers of mythopoetic traditions as well, invoking shared historical experiences and legends and grounding them in a material reality of the continuous present. The semantics of Tlingit toponyms also reveal a concept of place that incorporates dimensions other than the physical here and now, that implicitly accepts the unseen as part of that which is seen, and that nests what once was in the realm of what clearly is now. Many Tlingit place-names are evocative of the mythical and historic past, insofar as they serve to cement the traditional relationship between a particular group or clan and the territory that continues to sustain them.

In Glacier Bay and elsewhere associations are found that hearken back to mythological and historical events. For example, *Kuts'een Gíl'x'i,* or "Rat Cliff," refers not to an abundance of ordinary rats at the cliff below Spokane Cove but rather to a single extraordinary rodent of epic proportions that once, long ago, kidnapped a young Tlingit maiden and took her to his cliff lair to be his wife. The villainous varmint eventually was subdued by the young woman's brothers in a nasty battle at the site.[11] Such toponymic references serve as historical citations on the text of the land, bringing events of the past into the present for new generations to learn. Mythological animal and plant references comprise 4 percent of the Tlingit toponymy in Glacier Bay; they are all but absent in the Euro-American toponymy.

A special set of mythological references in Tlingit place-names are those that refer to the trickster-demiurge Raven. Though blessed with supernatural powers and a clever mind, Raven nevertheless had to labor to survive in the world. As the legends recount, he had to steal the various elements that comprise the world, and, after helping to transform the world, he embarked on a quest to gather together those items necessary to sustain (human) life: freshwater, firewood, and various food resources. His Tlingit relatives are still engaged in the quest and follow the trail he has left. People hunt, fish, and gather in the vicinity of *X'as'tuhéen* ([Raven's] Driblet Creek), created by the drops that spilled from Raven's mouth as he flew away from Petrel after stealing the latter's springwater; collect intertidal resources at *Yéil Kawóot* (Raven's Beads), amid limestone fossils that Raven once used to fashion a necklace for his wife; land their boats at *Yéil Kiji Yakwdeiyí* (Raven's Wings Boat Road), where he calmed the sea and created a smooth trail amid the rocks so he could land his canoe; and fish in the vicinity of *Yéil Geiwú* (Raven's Web or Fishnet), now petrified in stone above the tide line, the "webbing" still visible. Other aspects of Raven are similarly enshrined in the landscape.

Beyond biological referents to mythological or mundane plants, animals, and humans, a second major category of semantic references consists of topographical associations. These may be divided into two basic categories: (1) hydrographic, or those alluding to aquatic or shoreline features, and (2) terrestrial, or those referring to upland features of the landscape (see table 3.3). Topographical references other than generics make up 41 percent of the regional name set, with an overwhelming emphasis on hydrographic names (32 percent). Topographical references other than generics make up 59 percent of the Tlingit name set and 25 percent of the English. Significantly, 42 percent of all Tlingit place-names contain hydrographic references, another reflection of the culture's maritime orientation. The majority of nongeneric Euro-American topographical referents, in contrast, are associated with upland features.

What is more, Tlingit topographical referents in place-names are synesthetic. Tlingit names reflect not only the visual sense (what things look like) but also the auditory (*Dàalagàaw,* "Hollow Sound"), olfactory (*Téey Chan G̲éeyak'w,* "Little Bay Smelling of Yellow Cedar"), and even gustatory senses (*X̲'alinukdzi X'áa,* "Sweet Tasting Point"). Even the play of light and shadow is commented on. This contrasts with the English toponymy in the region, which tends to favor the static and the visual, and the terrestrial over the hydrographic. The English name set is also topographically impoverished in comparison to the Tlingit because of its overwhelming emphasis on biographical naming—places named for people—a phenomenon that is very uncommon in Tlingit, where people are named for places rather than vice versa.

The Euro-American preoccupation with biographical names is especially evident in Glacier Bay, where only about one-third of the English toponyms contain biological or topographical referents beyond generics. Instead the English toponymy honors a vast array of individuals, from explorers (e.g., La Perouse Glacier, Dixon Entrance, Muir Inlet) to scientists (e.g., Geikie Inlet, Reid Glacier, Adams Inlet); missionaries (e.g., Young Island, Brady Glacier); entrepreneurs (e.g., Bartlett Cove, Willoughby Island, Ibach Point); inventors (e.g., Wilbur [of the Wright brothers] Mountain); surveyors (e.g., Riggs Glacier, Lars Island, Netland Island); treasurers of the British Navy (Dundas Bay), and a host of other characters, many of whom never came within a thousand miles of Glacier Bay. Even Tlingits were enshrined in the landscape by whites. Sitka Charley (Charley Glacier) and Tyeen (Tyeen Glacier), members of John Muir's expedition, were memorialized in glaciers, as were the Hoonah leader Kasohto (Kahsoto Glacier) and the Chilkat leader Kohklux (Kloh-Kutz Glacier).[12]

Ironically, such naming would be deemed odd, if not inappropriate, in Tlingit. Indeed, biographical naming is virtually absent from the Tlingit toponymy. As shown, rather than name places after people, the Tlingit custom was more commonly to name people after places. This aversion to biographical naming is a common feature among Native Americans and perhaps indigenous peoples in general. Moreover, the few exceptional places that are named for Tlingit individuals are derived from the salient presence and activities of the person at the named site and generally do not constitute a claim on the land in the individual's honor.

This difference in naming practices is undoubtedly linked to differing attitudes toward and interactions with the landscape. In the Euro-American perspective the individual was the basic social unit, the discoverer and possessor of the landscape. In the process of colonizing America it was natural for European explorers to honor their patrons, cohorts, and countrymen with place-names as a means both of paying tribute and of marking the land as their own. Many places were named prior to any significant interaction with the landscape and thus probably could not have included biological and topographical referents worthy of distinction. Similarly, the tradition of naming objects for prominent intellectual forebears is very strong in Western science. In Tlingit, by comparison, clans and house groups were the key social units, and property, political power, and even identity were concentrated at those levels. Tlingit scientific discoveries concerning the environment tended to be memorialized in toponyms with biological and topographical references whither the people derived their living. In these and other ways, cultural differences have contributed to different patterns in place naming.[13] And, as the conflict over the naming of the Dzántik'i Héeni Middle School in Juneau attests, these differences persist to the present day.

Finally, another divergence in Tlingit and Euro-American naming patterns concerns habitation sites. Six percent of the Tlingit names refer directly to dwelling sites, including villages and forts, while no such references are found in English. The lack of references in English is not surprising considering that Euro-American habitation sites are often biographically named (e.g., Bartlett Cove, Gustavus, Juneau) and that permanent settlements came late to Glacier Bay and were outlawed in the course of its development as a monument, park, and preserve. In Tlingit the affix *aan* denotes a village, and *noow* denotes a fort or refuge. Forts were strategically important in the context of intra- and interethnic warfare dating back at least to the protohistoric period (Moss and Erlandson 1992). Place-names denoting habitation sites help keep ancestral dwelling grounds in memory. Similarly, as linguistic artifacts, they provide archeologists with important keys to understanding settlement patterns in Tlingit country.

PRAGMATIC DIMENSIONS OF PLACE-NAMES

Keith Basso (1996) and others (see Thornton 1997a, 2004a) have demonstrated the power of place-names in achieving pragmatic cultural ends when deployed in discourse, such as the promotion of morality, healing, identity, character, wisdom, historical consciousness, and other prerogatives. When a place's cultural associations are shared by the speaker and the audience, these cultural ends can often be achieved merely by speaking the place-name because the story and lessons behind it are already well known. In other cases, the story behind the name must be unpacked and contextualized to be understood. Given the wide variety of contexts in which place and place-names are evoked, their pragmatic functions are not easily classified. Broadly speaking, however, three important cognitive orientations that are embedded in place can be identified: social identity, time-space, and normative orientations.

As shown, the intimate links between personal identity, social identity, and place are reflected in the fact that people, collectively and even individually, are often named for places. Clan and house-group histories form an important genre of Tlingit oral literature and pedagogy. Through these narratives a Tlingit person can trace the contours of his or her individual identity in relation to the evolution of the social group within *Lingít Aaní*. To the extent that social groups with distinct identities have a shared history, place-names and narratives may transcend social group boundaries to emphasize unity in historical time, as evidenced in the statement *Ch'a Tleix' Xakwnuwkeidí*, or "We who are still one People of Sandbar Fort," used to reference and rekindle solidarity among several Tlingit clans who descend from a settlement at *Xakwnoowú* (Sandbar Fort) in Glacier Bay National Park. The semiotic convergence between identity, place, and property is particularly emphasized in clan histories. Thus, when Robert Zuboff, a member of the Angoon Ḵak'weidí (People of *Ḵak'w* [Basket Bay]) clan, recounted the history of Basket Bay, or *Ḵak'w* (Little Basket), he remarked: "This is how the history is told, / about / Basket Bay, from the time it's been ours . . . ages. / It was long ago, / it's been long, / since the histories have been told of us; / we are named for it, / Ḵak'weidí" (in Dauenhauer and Dauenhauer 1987:67; translated from the Tlingit).

Such narratives continue to be deployed to defend territory, mainly against non-Natives who disrespect Tlingit sovereignty and cultural patrimony. An illustrative example of this occurred in Glacier Bay National Park in the early 1990s. Park management had for years refused to recognize Tlingit claims to land and resources in its jurisdiction and had gradually frozen them out of their homeland (in what some Tlingits derisively termed "a second ice age") through various prohibitive regulations and enforcement acts. On Memorial Day weekend in the spring of 1992, the major Tlingit clans from nearby Hoonah gathered in Glacier Bay National Park to mourn their deceased relatives and to protest the National Park Service's denial of their customary and traditional rights. The bulk of the ceremony was concerned with recounting—through narrative, song, and dance—the ancestral ties that each clan maintained to places within the boundaries of the park and preserve. The recounting of ancestral names caused an emotional outpouring, especially among the older participants, who recalled their presence in Glacier Bay. Later, a written resolution was presented to the park superintendent and read aloud in Tlingit. Outlining the basis for the Huna Tlingits' rights in Glacier Bay, the resolution included the assertion that the history of Glacier Bay was "recorded in the regalia, songs, stories, and *names* of the descendants of Glacier Bay" (see HIA 1994; emphasis added). Similarly, in proposed legislation for the U.S. Congress concerning Huna Tlingits' rights in Glacier Bay, the Hoonah Indian Association (HIA, the tribal government) chose to deploy the oldest of three Tlingit names for the bay, *S'e Shuyee* (Drainage at the End of the Glacial Mud), to emphasize the Hunas' antiquity and aboriginal rights in the area "identified by the federal government as 'Glacier Bay National Park.'" Like Robert Zuboff and Kadashan (quoted at the head of this chapter), Huna clan leaders submitted their knowledge of names as a fundamental part of their claim to the territory.

Beyond social group identities and boundaries embedded in clan histories, spatial and temporal orientations are constructed in other ways through stories and names on the land. I have already touched on the mythic time events involving Raven and other extraordinary beings who literally shaped the landscape through their activities and whose deeds are immortalized as chronotopes (places in a community's geography where time and space are fused) in Tlingit *shagóon*. Like the Australian aboriginal concept of the Dreaming, *shagóon* posits a dynamic fusion of time and space in the landscape. The land constitutes the ground of being, a potent congelation of historical activities, and, to the extent that it embodies the wisdom of the ages and powerful ancestral spirits, a compelling force in contemporary life. Correlatively, it is through the landscape and one's knowledge of its historical and sacred places that the underlying order of the cosmos—and by extension one's *shagóon* or place within it—is revealed. As with T. G. H. Strehlow's (1947:31) Northern Aranda, the country is for the Tlingit individual a "living, age-old family tree" that continues to grow and resonate through his or her own being and dwelling on the land. It must be this way; as the Lukaax̱.ádi song declares: "Lest my ancestors' land lie desolate, you will always hear my voice there." Thus, according to his Dreaming—his *shagóon*—Lukaax̱.ádi elder Austin Hammond aspires to continue to fish for sockeye in the same locale where his ancestral relative was taken by the giant red salmon at Chilkoot Lake and to dwell in the same landscape that his ancestor, Raven, helped create through various deeds that are commemorated in toponyms like *Yéil Áx'sh Wulgeigi Yé* (Place Where Raven Swung, a cut between two peaks) and *Yéil Daa.ax̱u* (Raven's Luggage, a constellation of rocks in Chilkoot River) (SENSC 1995–2002). His own being on the land will maintain and extend his *shagóon* as well as that of his clan.

It may be that this kind of place consciousness, common to hunter-gatherers of Australia and North America and elsewhere, is part of our deep, collective human heritage. Significantly, the Dreaming and, less commonly, *shagóon* are sometimes translated as "the law." This is indicative of the powerful role of place not only in defining time in space but also in maintaining normative orientations. Just as Basso's Western Apache use stories embedded in place-names as moral touchstones, so too do Tlingits use stories to convey important lessons about morality and normative behavior. Glacier Bay again serves as a richly illustrative example.

Glacier Bay has been shaped by the advance and retreat of the mammoth tidewater glaciers that now sit at the head of the bay. The most recent advances of the glacier correspond to changes wrought by the Little Ice Age commencing about seven hundred years ago. Tlingit oral history documents their presence in the bay prior to the Little Ice Age (and archeological evidence suggests human habitation in the area dating back almost ten thousand years), and Chookaneidí clan history links the glacier's most recent and tragic advance to the violation of a taboo by a young Chookanshaa (female member of the clan) (see Dauenhauer and Dauenhauer 1987:244–91; Thornton 1995; Cruikshank 2005:158–60). The woman, Kaasteen, violates her prescribed seclusion at menarche by communicating with a glacier. A sentient being itself, the glacier (*Sít'k'i T'ooch'*, "Little Black Glacier") responds by advancing rapidly and destroying the tribe's settlement (*L'eiwshaa Shakee Aan*, "Town on Top of the [Glacial] Sand Dune"), claiming the life of a female member of the clan who remains behind and forcing the exodus of the Tlingit from Glacier Bay. Because the glacier claimed the life of a Chookanshaa, the clan in compensation now claims the landmark as a crest, or *at.óow*. This claim and the story behind it are referenced in many media, including a button blanket (fig. 3.2), which, like the sockeye blanket in the previous chapter, serves simultaneously as a cultural map, historical icon, moral text, and legal title to the landscape. In presenting the story of Kaasteen as *at.óow*, normative orientations of moral behavior, relations between human and nonhuman beings and spirits, and ties between people and places are reinforced in powerful ways.

Perhaps most powerful are the songs. Songs are an important genre of *at.óow* and place making that engender strong cognitive and emo-

FIG. 3.2. Chookaneidí Glacier Bay button blanket. This button-style blanket (*x'óow*) maps sacred sites and stories of the Chookaneidí clan in Glacier Bay, including *L'eiwshaa Shakee Aan* (Town on Top of the [Glacial] Sand Dune), where Kaasteen (bottom center), a young woman in menarche, called to the glacier *Sít'k'i T'ooch'* (Little Black Glacier; center), violating her taboo of seclusion, thus causing the glacier to advance and destroy the village and forcing her people to evacuate. The blanket also features other crests of the Chookaneidí, including the brown bear, and serves as a historical and legal record of Chookaneidí ties and rights to Glacier Bay. Photo by T. Thornton

tional ties to place and homeland. With their accompanying gestures, dances, and mimetic reflections of place, songs amplify and re-present the content and sentiments expressed in clan histories. Among the most poignant examples of this are two grieving songs composed by Chookaneidí during their exodus from Glacier Bay. Centuries after the fact, these songs still evoke and encapsulate the feelings of despondency that accompanied the Chookaneidí's loss of their relative and homeland. The first song, composed and sung as they departed *L'eiwshaa Shakee Aan* (at Bartlett Cove, site of the current park headquarters) just ahead of the advancing, earthshaking glacier, mourns: "Won't my house / be pitiful / won't my house / be pitiful / when I leave on foot /. . . . Won't my land / be pitiful / won't my land / be pitiful / when I leave by boat" (in Dauenhauer and Dauenhauer 1987:283). Later, a second song of mourning was composed just outside Glacier Bay at *Wanachích* (known today as Pleasant Island): "My land, / will I ever / see it again /. . . . My house, / will I ever / see it again?" (287–89).

Because of the profound feelings of sadness they evoke, these songs are typically only voiced on "heavy" occasions, such as a funeral or memorial potlatch. When they are sung, their geographic context is always emphasized, and afterward the Glacier Bay diaspora is traced with each clan initially going to a separate settlement—the Chookaneidí to Spaaski Bay (*Lakooxás' T'akhéen*), the Wooshkeetaan to Excursion Inlet (*Kuyeik'*), and the Kaagwaantaan to Ground Hog Bay (*Kax' noowú*)—before eventually reconsolidating at the modern village of Hoonah (*Xunaa*).[14] When Amy Marvin, clan mother (*Naa Tláa*) of the Chookaneidí, told this story to a gathering of scientists in Glacier Bay National Park in 1993 (see Culp et al. 1995:306), she confessed through a translator that "it was very difficult for my grandparents to tell this story—it always brought tears to their eyes. I experienced that difficulty when I was getting ready to come over here today. I have that same feeling." At the same time, she observed that the sorrowful songs are also a source of strength—a gift: "When we have problems, when we're thinking of our family that are deceased, and we're going to repay the kindness of the Raven tribe [the opposite moiety], that is when we use these songs." Similarly, when traditional Chookaneidí visit Glacier Bay today they may sing, pray, and leave gifts of tobacco or food to honor and feed the spirits of ancestors who dwelled and died on this land, so they don't "lie desolate." In this way, the ancestors' trails of inhabitation, suffering, and fortitude and the continuing presence of their spirits on the land serve to orient and inspire (literally to breathe spirit into) contemporary Tlingits.

CONCLUSION: NAMING, KNOWING, AND BELONGING

This chapter has examined the structure and content of Tlingit place-names in relation to universal cognitive schemata and particularistic cultural principles and interests. While certain cognitive universals apply to Tlingit place naming, such as the use of generics in identifying major geographical features, employment of the body as a metaphor for landscape, and the correlation of population and toponymic densities and the constraints of the Magic Number 500, ultimately the gestalt and resonance of naming (or non-naming) can be fully understood only in terms of Tlingit ideology and practice.

Places are conceptualized by individuals under specific ecological, social, and historical circumstances through cultural models of the way the world works. As a consequence, investigations of cultural and cross-cultural place-naming patterns should lead back to a theoretical understanding of the linguistic, cognitive, experiential, and other cultural models that motivate naming. Though the origin of most place-names is part of that "hoary antiquity" to which Waterman alludes (1922:175; see also Thornton 1997a), researchers are fortunate to have a cultural model of the Tlingit namer in Raven.

Through his adventures, misadventures, and quest to survive and make sense of the world, Raven apprehends and interacts with Tlingit country much as a Tlingit would. Similarly, his way of naming the land is emblematic of Tlingit processes of naming. In the course of his travels, Raven names both the corporeal beings he encounters and the places he discovers. Some of the toponyms he bestows commemorate events, such as the landmark that is named "after the name of a small canoe, because one of these was passing at the time" (Swanton 1909:21), or qualities of the place (i.e., "Noisy Beach"). Yet, for the most part, the place-names dispensed by Raven fall into the metaphoric/metonymic categories described above. For example, a hollow filled with trees that Raven perceives to resemble young men is named "Where There Is a Crowd of Boys" and a point on the coast subject to powerful undertow is called "Point Holding Things Back," and so on. Raven also was destined to "[show] all the Tlingit what to do for a living" (Swanton 1909:83); consequently, many of the toponyms he bestows serve this cultural interest, as when Raven informs Bear of "a good [halibut] fishing ground" in an area he named "Just on the Edge of the Base of the Kelp" (*Geesh K'ishuwanyee*, discussed above), indicating both a specific resource patch and a general principle for locating such places. Raven tales provide a model for naming and classifying places and suggestions for how to interact with them in appropriate ways.

Like Tlingits, Raven speaks to places, too, and makes sense of them in relation to each other, and to existing prototypes. Thus, when he arrived at the place he later was to name *Skanáx̱* (Noisy Beach; known as Saginaw Bay in English),

> Raven talked to it in order to make it into Nass [River] . . . but, when the tide was out great numbers of clams on the flats made so much noise shooting up at him that his voice was drowned, and he could not succeed. He tried to put all kinds of berries there but in vain. After many attempts, he gave it up and went away saying, "I tried to make you into Nass, but you would not let me." So you can be called [*Skanáx̱*]. (In Swanton 1909:15)

Though it resembles his beloved and prototypical Nass River, the affordances of *Skanáx̱* are not the same as those at Nass. Berries are perhaps not as abundant as at Nass, whereas clams are more bountiful, indeed so plentiful that their cacophonous "shooting up at him" overwhelms his senses, literally preventing him from redundantly creating another Nass purely out of want, longing, or nostalgia. In this episode Raven shows that place naming is an organic process involving a dialogue between the human senses, cultural models of experience, and key characteristics and affordances of the environment. Raven cannot simply impose a prototypical cultural model onto *Skanáx̱*. At a fundamental level the place must speak for itself, and the namer should listen.

Insofar as names of actual places are woven throughout Tlingit creation myths, these toponyms suggest a relationship to the landscape that differs from the dominant Euro-American paradigm on an ontological level. Toponyms that appear in creation myths by definition denote sacred spaces, which "[make] possible the 'founding of the world'; where the sacred manifests itself in space, the real unveils itself, the world comes into existence . . . and makes possible ontological passage from one mode of being to another" (Eliade 1959:63). The hierophanic concept of place makes mythopoetic Being continuous with mundane being, and subsistence, which may be translated as "real being" (Thornton 1999a), itself becomes a sacred act.

Clearly, the act of naming is a powerful one. Through naming, one may not only capture vital information about a location but also implicitly lay claim to a particular place by virtue of articulating one's special relationship to it. With naming comes knowledge, and with knowledge, power: the power not only to use, control, and possess but also, just as important, to define. As the Tlingit creation myth recounts:

> When his son was born, Kit-ka'ositiyiqa [Raven's father, Keetk'a Usitiyik Ḵá, "The Man Up There That Is"] tried to instruct him and train him in every way and, after he grew up, told him he would give him strength to make a world. After trying all sorts of ways Raven finally succeeded (Swanton 1909:3).

That which is created is not fully real until it has been named; this is not the least of the lessons of Raven in his quest to make a world.

Following Raven, Tlingits keep going back to places in their own quest to make a world. So writes the Kake Tlingit poet Robert Davis (1989) in his poem "Saginaw Bay: I Keep Going Back":

> He dazzles you right out of water
> Right out of the moon, the sun and fire.
> Cocksure smoothtalker, good looker,
> Raven makes a name for himself
> Up and down the coast from Nass River,
> Stirs things up.
> . . . .
>
> He moves north, Kuiu Island, Saginaw
> Bay—
> Wind country, rain country,
> Its voices try to rise through fog, the long tongue of the sea
> sliding beneath the bay.
> . . . .
>
> The Tsaagweidi clan settled there first,
> it was right. Beaches sloped beneath
> canoes
> greased with seal fat,

they carried the Seal clan to these creeks
Shaking with humpies and dog salmon.
. . . .

Sometimes it felt like the center of the
world,
mountains circling within reach.

At its mouth on a knoll
A fortress guarded against intruders.
They came anyway, from the south,
a swift slave raid.
They destroyed the village.
The people fled every direction.
. . . .

After the massacre, the battered clan
collected themselves and moved north
to Kupreanof island. That became the
village of Kake. Those became Kake-
kwaan.

And every once in awhile
One sees in his mind
Raven tracks hardened in
Rock at Saginaw
where Raven dug his feet in
and tugged the mudflats clear into the
woods.
He made a small Nass because he grew
homesick there,
and in those moments, they feel like
going back too
. . . .

When I was young everyone used Tlingit
And English words at once

Tlingit fit better.
. . . .

I know there's a Tlingit name for that bay
It means something like "Everything
Shifted,"
I don't remember the name
of the Halleck Harbor shaman
except he was most powerful
and I feel somehow tied to him.
Was he the one wrapped in cedar mat
sunk in the channel
only to reappear
at Pt. White ascending
the beach
to his own grieving ceremony?
I don't know. I get mixed up.
But I know my own name,
it's connected to some battle.
. . . .

Listen, I'm trying to say something—
always our stories stayed alive through
paintings,
always our stories stayed alive in retelling.

You wonder why sometimes you can't
reach me?
I keep going back.
I keep trying to see my life
against all this history,
Raven in the beginning
hopping about like he just couldn't do
enough.

Through this reflection can be seen the importance of names—place
names, clan names, personal names, and even names for *at.óow*—and

of Linnaeus's dictum that, "if you don't know the names, your knowledge of things perishes." Yet even when Tlingit names are forgotten, as in the case of Mr. Davis, he remains somehow possessed by them, and other cognitive frames—stories, songs, paintings, and, most especially, sensuous perceptions of the landscape itself—aid his memory in seeing his life "against all this history" (*shagóon*). Such is the nature of place intelligence in Tlingit cognition. It is not only, as Kadashan states, that knowing the names of places is why "this country belongs to us" but also that knowledge of place and seeing of one's life in the land "against all this history" makes Tlingits feel, inalienably, that they *belong to this country*. Despite the fact that "everything shifted," this impetus continues to inspire Tlingits to name new places, like Dzántik'i Héeni Middle School, and persons, like Chaak'ti (Caretaker of Hamilton Bay), with belonging in mind.

4 PRODUCTION AND PLACE

"It was easy for me to put up fish there."

As individuals express their life, so they are. What they are, therefore, coincides with their production, both with what they produce and with how they produce it. —KARL MARX, *The German Ideology*

Pausing in the middle of his 1946 statement on his people's use and claims to lands and waters around Kake, elder Fred Friday offered this vision of his Tlingit landscape: "The Native people know all the points and rocks and every little area by name. If I told you all the names of all the places that I know it would fill many pages. These areas were used so much that we were familiar with every little place" (Goldschmidt and Haas 1998:177). Previous chapters of this book underscore the first part of Fred Friday's claim: the vast majority of major terrestrial and hydrographic features of Southeast Alaska were named by the Tlingits and other indigenous inhabitants of the region. This chapter explores the second part of his vision, that of an indigenous landscape enlivened by the resonance of a rich geographic nomenclature and individual and collective experiences of using areas "so much that we were familiar with every little place."

What Fred Friday glosses as "use" is conventionally termed "subsistence uses," a form of economic production that has come to be defined in public policy terms as "the customary and traditional uses by rural Alaska residents of wild, renewable resources for direct personal or family consumption." In contrast to Friday's place-based vision of subsistence, this government definition, enshrined in the federal Alaska National Interest Lands Conservation Act of 1980 (ANILCA, P.L. 96-487, sec. 803), says nothing about the particular geographic settings of subsistence activities. This is not unintentional, for ANILCA is a sequel to an earlier piece of legislation known as the Alaska Native Claims Settlement Act of 1971, which formally extinguished aboriginal territorial, hunting, and fishing rights in favor of a business corporation model of land and resource title and development. ANILCA partially restored noncommercial subsistence use rights (for Alaska's rural residents as opposed to Natives), but in a limited context. ANILCA entitles rural community dwellers (in Tlingit country this means everyone but residents of Juneau and Ketchikan) to preferential use of defined fish, wildlife, and plant resources, but only if managers (typically state biologists) determine that these resources are scarce enough that they must be allocated according to the subsistence use priority (over sport and commercial users) and rural preference. In practice, this policy might translate into residents of a rural community obtaining a preference in time (e.g., an earlier opening for hunting or fishing); space (e.g., "subsistence only" fishing in a certain stream); or quantity (e.g., higher bag or possession limits). However, to date, the granting of such subsistence preferences have been the exception rather than the norm.

More important, there is no recognition of Native individual, house, clan, ḵwáan, or tribal ties to specific resource areas—to particular places—despite the fact that ANILCA maintains that subsistence "is essential to Native physical, economic, traditional, and cultural existence." In practice, the government has viewed subsistence not as a set of relationships to particular places but merely as a form of noncommercial economic use of wild "resources," whose practitioners receive preferential treatment only if commercial economic uses of resources (or other environmental factors) severely threaten "reasonable opportunities" (cf. Caldwell 1998) for subsistence uses in broad (and often culturally meaningless) regions defined by the modern state bureaucracy and its resource managers. In short, while subsistence has a place in Alaskan public policy, that policy typically is not sensitive to the fundamental role of place in Native subsistence economies.

Alaska Natives tend to take a different view. Tlingits, in particular, regard subsistence as an intricate and profound set of relationships with particular geographic settings where their social groups have dwelled historically. For them subsistence is *haa ḵusteeyí*, "our way of living," "real being," an "enriching existence," and not "the minimum (food, etc.) necessary to support life," as dictionaries and non-Natives often define it (see Thornton 1998, 1999a). Indeed, a recent reissue of a booklet originally titled *The Subsistence Lifeway of the Tlingit People* (Newton and Moss 1983) was retitled *Haa Atxaayí Haa Kusteeyíx Sitee, Our Food Is Our Tlingit Way of Life* (Newton and Moss 2005) to emphasize this very point. Tlingit, like all Alaska Native languages, emphasizes the broad, holistic, and fundamental meanings of subsistence. As the foundation for existence, Tlingits defined themselves by the pathways and projects they adhered to in obtaining, processing, and distributing what have come to be known as "subsistence resources." Collectively, these activities formed a seasonal cycle not only for material production but also for social, political, educational, and spiritual activities. Today, subsistence production remains foundational to Tlingits' identity, experience, and culture, but pathways and projects have changed in many cases, often in profound ways.

This chapter analyzes the relationship between place and material production in detail. Specifically, I argue that in pre- and early postcolonial Tlingit society, place and being were intimately linked to projects of production that were conceived of as existing on relative experiential cycles of time (season) and space (path). Changes in these cycles, functions mainly of technological innovation and increased competition and regulation of Tlingit production by non-Tlingits, have undermined this productive sense of place in various ways, depending on the degree of disruption or transformation.

Notwithstanding these changes, however, the role of places in nourishing and sustaining human life—even afterlife—continues to be of paramount concern in Tlingit culture, especially in communities and households where significant production of wild foods is still carried out.

THE NATURE OF TLINGIT PRODUCTION

"Production is the interaction of man and nature," says Karl Polanyi (1944:130). It includes not only hunting, fishing, and gathering of foods but also the manufacture of such things as technologies and art. As emphasized in previous chapters, productive interactions with nature also involve emotions (Milton 2002) and intuition and "poetic involvement" (Ingold

2000:25, 57) through the place-names, narratives, *at.óow*, and other means of engaging the field of relations that constitute the Tlingit life-world as *shagóon*. To neglect the role of the nonmaterial in production, or "procurement," to use Nurit Bird-David's (1992) relational term, would be to subjugate the important principles of Tlingit ecology, including its sentience, relational epistemology (Bird-David 1999), and relational sustainability (Langdon 2002). For hunter-gatherers like the Tlingit do not "approach their environment as an external world of nature that has to be 'grasped' conceptually and appropriated symbolically within the terms of an imposed cultural design, as a precondition for effective action . . . indeed, the separation of mind and nature has no place in their thought and practice." (Ingold 2000:42). As a consequence, "the differences between the [economic] activities of hunter-gatherers on the one hand, and singing, story-telling and narration of myth on the other, cannot be accommodated within the terms of a dichotomy between the material and the mental, between the ecological interaction *in* nature and the cultural constructions *of* nature. On the contrary, both sets of activities are, in the first place, ways of dwelling" (57).

Here I focus on the place-context of production through dwelling, particularly the harvest, processing, and meaning of food. In the abo-riginal Tlingit economy, food production was the dominant project in terms of not only time allocation but also ideology. Sitka elder Herman Kitka put it simply: "If we didn't put up our foods, we wouldn't have a culture." As food is a paramount element of culture, it is also a para-mount element of place. For to procure food—to subsist—is quintes-sentially to dwell, to gain sustenance and "real being" from places. And places, like all environments, "are constituted in life, not just in thought, and it is only because we live in an environment that we can think" (Ingold 2000:60).

Today, as in the past, specific foods are harvested and processed at specific times of the year depending on abundance, distribution, acces-sibility, and need. Typical Tlingit seasonal rounds have been described by various observers (e.g., Niblack [1890] 1970; Oberg 1973; de Laguna 1972; Thornton 2004b). However, it is important to note that every village's seasonal round—indeed that of every house group—varied to a degree as a result of micro-ecological differences affecting the factors listed above, though the primary periods for similar activities in different villages were often the same. Thus, in composing a generalized portrait of the Tlingit seasonal round, one way to account for variation is to distinguish between primary and secondary harvest periods by species. The appendix constructs such a portrait on the basis of conventional Western seasonality.

For Tlingits time was a function of hunting, fishing, and gathering seasonality, as opposed to the agricultural seasonality that underlies terms like spring, summer, and fall. Tlingit calendars were reckoned according to "moons" (twelve or thirteen months) marking key climatic conditions, ecological phenomena, and cultural projects that defined a community's dwelling at various times of the year. Table 4.1 shows sample calendars from northern Southeast Alaska. As can be seen, the names of the moons—*Héen Táanáx Kayaaní Dísi* (Plants Grow Underwater Moon) or *K'úxw dísi* (Marten [Trapping] Moon), rather than March, for example—highlight key processes and relationships in Tlingit living space, such as the maturation, reproduction, and harvest cycles of key plants (e.g., seaweeds in March), fish (e.g., salmon in June and July), and animals (e.g., marten in March, and many others in May and June).

Beyond seasonality, another way to analyze the subsistence round is in terms of time allocation to various activities. The only ethnographer to construct a rigorous time-activity portrait (but not a time-space portrait à la Hägerstrand) of the Tlingit is Kalervo Oberg (1973), who worked in Klukwan in 1931–32. His calculations are reproduced in figure 4.1. As with the generalizations about seasonal activities, Oberg's generalizations about time budgeting for Klukwan are not strictly applicable to every community, as a result of local environmental and economic variations. Oberg's portrait also represents the temporal commitments of a postcontact, mixed economy, though the study was done in the depression era of self-reliance and in a community still regarded as isolated and "old-fashioned" and highly dependent on wild foods.

Together, these two sources of information provide a composite sketch of both the duration and intensity of particular activities over a given year. However, what are missing from these idealized portraits of the seasonal round are the settings of production, the places in which subsistence activities occur. Every production activity or project takes place in one or more specific locales that are intimately linked to that activity

TABLE 4.1. Island and Mainland Calendars (Moons) among the Northern Tlingit

Island (e.g., Sitka or Angoon) Calendar	Mainland (e.g., Chilkat/ Chilkoot) Calendar (Emmons 1991; see also Oberg 1973)*	Approximate Month
Xáat Dísi (Salmon [Harvesting] Moon) or Atka Taa dísi ("[Animals] Fattening Moon)	Asxukw Disi (Drying Moon) / Tlexa Aatxaan Dísi (Smoking Salmon Moon)	July
Shaa Xeiyí Dísi (Mountain Shadows Moon)	Shaa Xeiyí Dísi (New Snow on Mountains Moon) or Kuk'eet (Berry Picking)	August
Dís Yádi (Child Moon; referring to the weaning of young animals); also Kaxweix Dísi (Highbush Cranberry Moon)	S'aax Tlaa Dísi (Groundhog Mother Moon) / Kaxwéix Dísi	September
Dís Tlein (Big Moon)	Kusi.áat K'áchk'w (Little Cold)	October
Kukahaa Dís (Digging / Scratching Moon [bears dig winter dens])	Kukahaa dís or Dleit K'áchk'w (Little Snow)	November
Shaanáx Dís (Head through Moon; hair shows on a seal fetus's head)	Shaanáx Dís Kukaxeit (Digging / Scratching Moon)	December
T'aawák Dísi (Canada Goose Moon)	T'aawák Dísi (Goose Moon) or She warchel [?] (Leaves Falling)	January
S'eek Dísi (Black Bear Moon; when cubs are born)	Kutí Káchk'u Dísi (Small Weather)	February
Héen Táanáx Dísi (Underwater Leaves [Sprout] Moon)	K'óox Dísi (Marten [Trapping] Moon) or Héen Taanáx Kayaaní Dísi (Plants Grow Underwater Moon)	March
X'éigaa Kayaaní Dísi (True Budding Moon; land plants sprout)	Kahaakw.ish (Fish Egg [Eulachon, Herring] Spawn)	April
At Gadaxeet Yinaa Dísi (Ripening [of Animals] Moon)	Kayaaní Dísi (Plants Moon)	May
At Gadaxeet Dísi (Birthing [of animals] Moon)	Xáat Dísi (Salmon Moon)	June

NOTE: Compiled from Emmons 1991, Oberg 1973, McClellan 1975, Thornton 2004, and field notes.

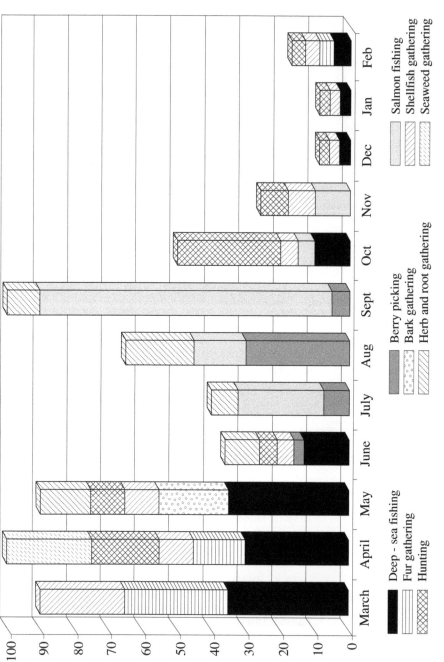

FIG. 4.1. Time spent (%) resource gathering, Klukwan, 1931 (reproduces the calculations of Oberg 1973).

in memory. Following Giddens, I have termed these activity centers "locales," emphasizing their position as hubs of socioeconomic activity.

Implicit in each locale are not only an activity and a physical setting but a social setting as well. In this sense, material production is not only what is produced but when, where, and how it is produced and with whom—what Marx termed the "relations of production." These implicit connections are made explicit when people talk about place.

To understand these connections, I use the following extended example. In April 1994, Herman Kitka, an eighty-year-old elder from Sitka, spoke to a session of the Alaska Anthropological Association on his knowledge of Native place-names in the Sitka area. He chose to speak on the constellation of places that were most important to his own being, and he stressed the spatiotemporal and social coordination of specific activities or "projects" in relation to two focal places: his winter village of Sitka and his family's seasonal settlement at Deep Bay. As with the conventional Tlingit calendar, his year begins in the late spring, when his family moves from the winter village to the fish camp.

My family was very lucky in selecting Deep Bay for their customary and traditional subsistence use. Deep Bay was called L'ukanax̱. My family moved to Deep Bay in May after the herring roe harvest in Sitka Sound.

Black seaweed and ribbon seaweed was picked from the beaches in Salisbury Sound, which was only about three or four miles from Deep Bay. The teaching was done by an uncle in each clan. The uncles taught the young people the names of the places, months, and what tide to pick the seaweed. The next lesson was how to go about drying the seaweed to preserve it for use year round.

The taking of our customary, traditional food supply was taught by uncles through all families of Southeast Alaska.

With seaweed all taken care of, the next undertaking was to fish for halibut for drying. Bait for the halibut hooks has to be gotten. Uncle took us to Rapids Island at low tide. We learned to look for octopus dens at low tide's edge. We learned from Uncle how to catch the octopus with a gaff hook.

Next, our uncle split the young group into two groups. One group was told to cut down alder wood for the smokehouses; the other group was shown how to bait the hooks. Uncle took us into the narrows outside of Deep Bay.

Uncle showed us the halibut fish hole, which he called *eet* in Tlingit. Next, we learned how to line-up the Halibut *eet* or fish holes by lining up two points on the beach. Today I still use this Halibut *eet* line-up to catch my subsistence halibut for drying at Deep Bay.

With enough halibut caught and drying in the smokehouses to satisfy all the families in Deep Bay, halibut fishing stopped. Uncle noticed how we enjoyed the fishing; he told us that to fish for the halibut for fun we would be wasting our food supply—to do so would offend the Holy Spirit [*Haa Shageinyaa*] and cause us to lose our blessing and go hungry.

Back to winter homes in Sitka to store our subsistence foods for next winter use.

In my lifetime a change in living took place—going to canneries for summer work and seine fishing. All our families moved to Ford Arm cannery, which was first called Cape Edwards Packing Company, later renamed Deep Sea Salmon Company.

All the older men went seine fishing for salmon for two months. The women all worked in the cannery.

After the fishing season closed, the families all moved back to Sitka again.

The families again got camping equipment and collected to go to fish camp at Deep Bay; also jars for canning berries were taken, along with fishing gear for catching late summer dog and coho salmon for drying.

Uncle again told his trainees, "We can only take enough salmon for all the needs of each family in Deep Bay." Smokehouses were loaded with the fires being attended by our elders.

Next, Uncle took all available persons berry picking. The berry picking places were out in the straits outside of Deep Bay among all the islands. Each island had a Tlingit name, so we can remember where to get the blueberries in the future when we get old enough to go on our own.

The next project was to go seal hunting. Only the older boys were taken. I was lucky to be one of the seal hunters. We were taught how to shoot. The seal hunting areas were outside Deep Bay on certain islands, reefs, and narrow passes between the islands. After a lot of misses by each hunter, we finally learned the proper way to shoot at the seals in the water.

Uncle showed us how to skin the seals, save the fat, meat, and skins.

We learned how to make stretchers using green, small alder poles. Sealskins were dried for winter projects in Sitka.

The fat and some meat were saved from young seals for smoking. Fat was rendered out and put in containers. Seal hunting stopped when all families in Deep Bay had enough for use through the year.

Next project—Uncle showed us how to make deer calls. A deer hunting party was selected, three persons to each party. Uncle took the hunting party up the mountain on the west side of Deep Bay—half way up in a basin on the mountain. Uncle told us to spread out and keep very quiet while he blew his deer call—one a little long call, the next very short. He called in three deer while he was showing us how to use the deer call.

The three deer were shot by the hunters selected to do the shooting.

We got all three deer. Then Uncle showed us how to clean and fix the deer for packing back to camp. Two hunters in each group of three were selected to each pack a deer apiece back to camp, one person in each group had to be a look-out for safety reasons in bear country, and to take turns in packing the deer back to camp. All the hunters were successful that day. Deer were all skinned and cut for smoking and hung up in the smokehouses. After three days of smoking, the deer meat was taken down and cut into small chunks for cooking in pots. After cooking, the deer meat was put on racks again up in the smokehouses and then dipped in seal oil and packed in containers and covered with seal oil. This type of preserving smoked deer meat kept without spoiling through the winter to be eaten as "cold cuts." All fish, meat, and berries preserved, the families again moved back to Sitka, our winter homes.

The next project—the older men prepared for the winter trapping season that would start in December and January.

My grand folks, my dad, and uncles went to Emmons Island at the entrance of Hoonah Sound, just ten miles north of Deep Bay. Each family from Sitka also had their own trapping areas.

Some of our subsistence foods were gotten from our winter homes at Sitka. Gathering of clams and fishing for bottom fish, rockfish, flounders, halibut, crabs and shrimp were done from our winter homes at Sitka.

Before the [commercial] herring sac roe fishery, the Sitka Tlingits used to engage in herring roe fishing from small rowboats. The herring caught in small rowboats was used for making herring oil. Herring roe was taken and dried in trees among the islands around Sitka. All the small islands have Tlingit names and were used together with all other families in the Sitka area.

This herring was done the last week in March and the first two weeks in April, mostly under Uncles' directions to each family group.

All this teaching was done where our customary, traditional subsistence food supply was gotten. This teaching was what made each Tlingit a good citizen in each community. The young people learned to respect the land they live on. They also learned to take only what each family needed to make it throughout the year. We need to keep on teaching our children our subsistence lifestyle and our culture and religion. Without this teaching our Tlingit cultures will be lost forever.[1]

This is a phenomenal portrait of subsistence, giving full weight to the spatiotemporal setting as well as to the richness of particular places through individual experience and communal pathways and projects on the land. In his narrative, Mr. Kitka naturally weds particular food production projects to particular places. Procurement of food is a year-round endeavor and, as such, constrains not only where he travels but when and with whom. In such a subsistence economy, the spatial, temporal, social, and project contexts become integral parts of one's conceptions of places—their boundaries, their links, their meanings—and the basis for place intelligence (Thornton 2004a). In this way, Deep Bay is a nexus not only for subsistence but also for learning and growing up, for family ties and social structure, for continuity and change, and, in the end, for Mr. Kitka's own being and Tlingit culture itself.

PATH AND PROJECT

For Herman Kitka, locales for subsistence projects are fundamentally linked in time and space by paths en route to activities. These paths are constrained by the spatiotemporal organization of natural resources in the environment as well as by the organization of society in relating to that environment. Thus, Mr. Kitka went to Deep Bay not because it was the best or nearest place to harvest salmon but because it is a good place to harvest salmon and his family *owns* it and he *knows* it well. While resource availability and territoriality influenced where one harvested foods, the seasons influenced when. The sequencing of food production projects, then, took place in a geographical and social time and space.

Path and project are the two fundamental building blocks of time-geography (Pred 1986:10):

According to the path concept, each of the actions and events consecutively making up the existence of an individual has both temporal and spatial attributes. Consequently, the biography of a person is ever on the move with him or her and can be conceptualized and diagrammed at daily or lengthier scales of observation as an unbroken, continuous path through time-space, subject to various types of constraint.

A project, moreover, may be defined in time-geographic language as "the entire series of simple or complex tasks necessary to complete any intentional-inspired or goal-oriented behavior. Each of the sequential tasks in a short- or long-term project is synonymous with the coupling together in time and space of the uninterrupted paths of two or more people or of one or more persons and one or more tangible inputs or resources" (10). The conjunction of particular individual paths with particular cultural (or institutional) projects at specific temporal and spatial settings is what makes place "a historically contingent process," in Allan Pred's terms, and *shagóon* (heritage and destiny) and *haa ḵusteeyí* ("our way of living") in Tlingit terms. Mr. Kitka's Deep Bay narrative exemplifies this experience of subsistence.

TRADITIONAL SEASONAL PATHS

Since food production was until the mid-twentieth century the dominant and sustaining project in social life, it remains intimately bound up with notions of path and place. Consequently, when they were asked to testify about their possessory rights (Goldschmidt and Haas 1998) to specific locales and what these places were used for, Tlingit respondents invariably made reference not only to their social connections to the landscape but to the productive projects that took place at particular sites. This testimony was, as often as not, organized according to where the place lies on the traditional seasonal path (Thornton 1998).

A typical theme was for a witness to describe a locale, the path to get there, and the activities that took place there. For example, "There was also a hooligan [eulachon] camp around Haines for smoking hooligans in the spring after the first run. This camp was at Taiyasanka [*Deyeisaank'i*] Harbor. Toward the end of May or the beginning of June the people camped and put up hooligans at the Four-mile and Ten-mile camps. There was a village and camp at Berners Bay where fish was smoked. We hunted and fished there and gathered berries during the summer" (James H. Lee, no. 7, in Goldschmidt and Haas 1998:101–2). The emphasis here is especially on habitation sites, the seasonal camps where people dwelled during subsistence production. In the witness's memory, the seasonal path moves smoothly from spring into summer. Yet, in following the temporal path of production, Mr. Lee must make a spatial jump from the hooligan production camp at Taiyasanka Harbor to the salmon smoking camp at Berners Bay, more than forty miles to the south. This is revealing not only of the paths of production but of the environment itself, which can be conceptualized as a patchwork of very productive locales separated by pathways of travel.

This productive emphasis is reflected more generally in Tlingit conceptions of space. As de Laguna (1960:20) has observed, unlike Westerners, who feel their geographic knowledge to be incomplete "so long as there remain blank spaces on the map," Tlingits refer not to areas or measures of space but rather "to specific spots: fishing streams, coves, berry patches, or house sites, etc., and the terrain or waters between these places are simply the relatively undifferentiated landscape through which one travels in going from one to the other." In other words, subsistence paths and projects, along with social structural links, were the relational axes of Tlingit navigation rather than some absolute or uniform scheme of reckoning such as the cardinal directions or the calendar (Thornton 1997b).[2]

Similarly, relationships and possessory rights over lands were articulated and modified on the basis of path and project. Thus, in reflecting on the ownership of Taiya Inlet, another Goldschmidt and Haas witness, Haines elder Paddy Goenette, qualifies his group's (the Chilkoot Kaagwaantaan clan's) initial claim to the whole territory on a detailed consideration of the specific locales for production and the paths and projects of other clans (especially the Lukaax.ádi, which he is a child of) throughout this area:

I was born at the village of Chilkoot, and am a member of the Kaagwaantaan clan. . . .

Dyea and Skagway are claimed by my people. There are three streams at Dyea, and there are three smokehouses there. The people did not live there the year around, but used the place a great deal. All three of these smokehouses were owned by Lukaax̱.ádi people. They controlled a large area of land. This place was used for berries as well as for smoking fish. The Indian people also hunted there and smoked meat. They generally went up there in the fall of the year. Some of the people would go up to pick berries and then rush back to Chilkoot to put them up. During the hunting season, however, they stayed up there a long time. We used to get seals at Skagway when I was a boy. I remember one man who lived there the year around, because things were easy to get. This man was related to my father. We would hunt seals in the fall. He hunted up the Skagway River. There was a big smokehouse on an island up the Skagway River where a stream comes in from the southeast. This place was called X'wat'héeni [Trout Stream]. This was a good place to get mountain goats. The Skagway area belongs to the Kaagwaantaan clan. (Goldschmidt and Haas 1998:108)

Again the narrative follows the seasonal flow of activity, moving in this case from summer to fall. Also evident is a distinction between harvest and processing locales for some resources during this era (i.e., the first half of the twentieth century). Thus, rather than bring jarring supplies to the seasonal camp, people instead "rush back to Chilkoot to put them up." During hunting season, however, this is not a practical means for processing meat, and so they dry it out on the hunting grounds and, consequently, stay out "a long time." One also finds that some people prefer certain harvest locales because resources are "easy to get," a phrase that is often heard even today and reflects not merely resource abundance but also accessibility, harvestability, local knowledge, and the psychological comfort and security that comes with harvesting in places one knows and to which one belongs through social and historical ties. At the same time, other locales, such as those for seal hunting, have changed since Mr. Goenette's childhood; though easy to get at one time, seals are no longer taken in quantity at Skagway, perhaps because it is too far to go (i.e., not worth the cost in time and resources), too developed, or other foods like mountain goat can no longer be taken easily there along with seal.

The above statement is remarkably similar to another one made by a witness in Saxman, Charles T. Johnson, who also classifies ownership according to productive locales—again three fish streams.

> Burroughs Bay belongs to the Joonax̱ (Unuk) Teiḵweidí. There are three streams up there, the Joonax̱ (Unuk), Shaax̱ Tá [Grant Creek], and Sháa Héeni. [Klehini River]. The Unuk is the biggest one. We had two houses up there where we got hooligans [eulachon] and dried them and made hooligan oil. Henry Denny also had a house there, and so did Frank Howard. My father's brother had a smokehouse at the mouth of the Shaax̱ Tá River. Now whites are taking up homesteads in that area. We also gather crabapples up there and just recently a homesteader has taken over the place where we got crabapples. In the fall, we used to dry bear and goat meat, smoke fish, pick cranberries (highbush) and crabapples. We go to this area about March 28 every spring to get hooligans. I went there year before last but this year I didn't feel well enough. Joe Williams went up there.
>
> Denny had a smokehouse on Grant Creek [Shaax̱ Tá]. Whites kept him out. One of the men had a rifle and was standing in the doorway when Denny came there. His wife got scared and they left and never returned.
>
> Fitzgibbon Cove (Shaaya G̱eeyí) was a place where we used to get hemlock bark in the spring. Joe Johnson's father had a cabin there and he would go there before fish were available in the spring. There is a small creek on the north shore of Behm Narrows, just where Behm Canal comes in where the people could get early dog salmon and kings. This also belonged to Joe Johnson's father. He was a Teiḵweidí. (165)

Here again, the witness follows the seasonal flow of productive resources, duly noting the interruptions in the cycle caused by competition from whites. Harvest sites for the first fish of the season, whether herring in Mr. Kitka's case or hooligan or early dog and king salmon in Mr. Johnson's case, hold a special significance in Tlingit environmental consciousness and sense of place.

Similarly, late salmon runs also were highlighted in the geography of production because they extended the harvesting activity with the highest material payoff well into the fall. Especially important were fall dog salmon. Mr. Kitka regularly obtained these at Deep Bay through October, in a fishery that he and his father created in the mid-twentieth century by transplanting and fertilizing fall dog salmon eggs from a stream at Excursion Inlet (see Thornton 1997b), an ingenious act of indigenous aquaculture. Other fall salmon locales were similarly celebrated, such as a small creek north of Lemon Creek in Juneau, called *Eix'gulhéen*, known as "a very good stream, especially for a late run of dog salmon, but also for cohos" (Goldschmidt and Haas 1998:113). Security Bay (*Ḵúchx'w*), near Kake, is also famous as a place where "they get dog salmon late in the fall" (176). While dog and coho salmon were valued fall resources, sockeye, the most durable of the Pacific salmon upon reaching freshwater, could in some cases be harvested into the winter. Chilkat elder Susie Nasook (102) remarked on one particularly long-producing stream, the Tsekhini [*Tsikhéeni*], as "a place where fish were easy to get, and we have fished there from old times to the present day for sockeyes and cohos. We can get fish there until New Year."

In the ethnographic literature of the Northwest Coast, the winter months are often characterized as sedentary because the weather is poor and resources are scarce. Winter is highlighted as a time for ceremonies, storytelling, and household chores rather than wayfaring subsistence production. As the above examples illustrate, however, this is not strictly the case, either traditionally or in the postcontact era. While travel is often more limited in winter, food production does not cease. As Mr. Kitka's narrative indicates, though the salmon may be gone, fishing for bottom fish such as halibut, flounder, and rockfish continued, as did localized shellfish (especially crab, clam, and cockle) gathering. Oberg (1973:67) also notes that shellfish were gathered, preserved, and stored from October through June. Recently, Madonna Moss (1993) has suggested, based on archeological and ethnographic evidence, that shellfish, while not highly prized, were an important dietary staple, especially among certain segments of society, such as women and those of low rank.

Winter village life became decidedly less sedentary with the advent of fur trapping in the postcontact era. The winter months were when furbearers were considered prime, and trapping thus became an intensive winter project. To obtain furs, trappers, mainly young to middle-aged males, created new paths—traplines—which they followed throughout the winter months. As Oberg points out, the intensification of the fur trade encouraged Tlingits to pursue terrestrial furbearers and to stake out individual trapping territories. In terms of individual paths and projects, this change in the relations of production meant that a "group formerly collective in its principal economic enterprises [became] individualistic in productions accompanied by the parceling out of original undivided territory" (Oberg 1973:60–61), though it was often a territory to which the Native could claim some aboriginal right through kinship. This transformation came at the expense of the house group, which previously had been the central unit of production.

The intensification of trapping also meant that men were on the move throughout the winter, reversing the tide of sedentism and consolidation associated with modernization. In some cases new habitation sites were constructed to facilitate the production of furs. A family from Klukwan, for example, might move fifty miles south to Endicott River to trap for "mink, lynx and other animals" (Goldschmidt and Haas 1998:110), building a cabin there as a base. Walter Goldschmidt observed that, "where trapping does not require the establishment of permanent camps, the older ownership pattern is often overlooked" but that "Natives never trap an area specifically claimed by a living descendant of the original clan owning an area. There is considerable resentment among the Natives of the fact that white trappers do not respect such ownership rights" (24).

In addition to trapping, tending gardens, especially potato crops, rapidly became a part of the seasonal flow of the postcontact economy. Tlingit cultivation of plants was not new; berry patches and perhaps other plant resources had been actively managed prior to contact (Thornton 1999b). Nor did Natives give up fishing for farming, as "civilizing" agents might have hoped. Instead, gardens, whether located near fish camps or elsewhere, simply became another station on the path of production. Billy Jones's testimony regarding his relationship with Kelp Bay reflects this integration: "In the old days we went to Kelp Bay in March and would stay there all summer and smoke fish and gather food for winter use. About fall we would come back to Angoon and harvest our potatoes" (Goldschmidt and Haas 1998:71).

Seasonal paths of production were instrumental not only to making a living but to the very definition of what constituted places and their reckoning in time, space, and memory. In discussing objective claims to the lands and waters of Southeast Alaska in 1946, Tlingits consistently situated places within the spatiotemporal context of material production. Thus, people did not just own places or use them; rather, they lived in them and off them and through them in particular ensemblages of paths and projects that, collectively, defined the seasonal round and, to a large extent, the places themselves.

THE SOCIAL ORGANIZATION OF PRODUCTION

Along with the seasonal distribution and availability of resources, social organization has played a vital role in shaping how Tlingits make their living. Traditionally, various productive tasks took place in particular social organizational contexts that were flexibly suited to carrying them out. As Wayne Suttles (1968, 1974) and, more recently, Allan Richardson (1982) have pointed out, the considerable variations in social organization of production on the Northwest Coast are at least partly attributable to environmental variations. Generally, as one moves north along the coast there are fewer types of resources, and more seasonal and local variation, but perhaps less year-to-year fluctuation among them. In Southeast Alaska, the northern fringe of the culture area, resources tend to be much more concentrated in time and space than in northern California, the southern fringe. These conditions posed special problems for the organization of labor in the north. When salmon runs are concentrated in dispersed streams over periods of weeks rather than months as in the south, it is important to be able to command a significant labor force to harvest and process that resource while it is available. The northern matrilineal system of labor organization and land tenure, including exclusive control of productive patches of resources—among the Tlingit, Haida, and Tsimshian—can be viewed as a response to this spatiotemporal concentration of resources. For Tlingits, localized segments of the matrilineages, clans and house groups, provided the corporate means, along with slavery (see Donald 1997), to harvest enough resources to support large populations relative to other hunter-gatherers. Thus Richardson (1982:105) found, "The most noteworthy aspects of resource control on the Northwest Coast are the general gradient of increasing resource control from south to north (with a peak in the extreme north [i.e., Tlingit country]), and the gradient, also from south to north, of increasing emphasis on descent-based kin groups."

Kinship, then, was central to production. In Tlingit country, almost all production took place in the context of lands and sites that were owned, defended, and inherited through these clans and house groups. As shown, this social geography was intimately bound up not only with concepts of place but also with individual and social group identity. Kinship, and particularly clan organization, shaped the core and peripheral contours of an individual's geographic knowledge. Similarly, kinship provided a specific framework for the teaching of geography, through material and symbolic production, and therefore a resonant context for the remembrance of place. For this reason Tlingit discussions of place are nearly inseparable from discussions of family. Hence, Herman Kitka consistently references his uncles when referring to his knowledge of Deep Bay and other productive sites around Sitka.

Kinship structured not only how one came to know places but how one talked about them as well. Proper ancestral links were a prerequisite for speaking authoritatively on place. These ties symbolized a social group's continuity on a particular landscape as well as the group's relationship to the land. In Tlingit law, the basis for ownership of specific territories was always deeply rooted in history. History, embodied in stories and other expressive cultural forms, recorded how people came to own places. Tlingits considered representations of place history, such as blankets, hats, and regalia, as *at.óow* (sacred possessions), forming a kind of deed of trust or title to the sites they referenced. This is why, in his testimony on possessory rights of his clan, Angoon elder Billy Jones felt compelled to state, "I could tell long stories about each of these places and about how our people came to own them, but that would take very much time, so I am just telling who owns them now" (Goldschmidt and Haas 1998:150). Jones clearly did not prefer the shorthand approach, for it was tantamount to reading the signatures on the deed (the names of those who now own the property) without bothering to conduct a "title search" or examine the historical record itself (the story of how the owners came to possess the property). Moreover, for Tlingits at least, the invocation of ancestral names served to summon forth that record of ownership and title and make it tangible, personal, and continuous—in short, legitimate. By that same logic, Jones challenged the legitimacy of the U.S. government's claims to the land, asking rhetorically, "Can any government official name his grandfather or grandfathers that have occupied any of our land, like we can? This land is our[s] and we shall fight for it!" (1948 affidavit in Curry and Weissbrodt n.d.) Similarly, Herman Kitka's father, Frank, challenged the U.S. government's rights to possess his beloved Deep Bay, asking a Forest Service official, "Which one of your grandfathers put a claim on this land?" For these men, white claims to property were not legitimate without a bona fide ancestral history, a kinship link, *shagóon*.

Reciting clan histories and invoking the names of deceased relatives were two important ways that ancestral knowledge was invoked in support of claims to productive sites and other valued places. It is still common today for an authoritative statement about the history of a place to be bolstered by the phrase "I know this because I heard it from my uncle" or "my grandfather" or "my auntie" or, simply, "by those now dead who came before us." If the relative or ancestors are respected, such invocations carry great weight in the court of public opinion and are analogous to producing sworn testimony, if not incontrovertible material evidence, in support of a case in a modern American court. The words of Billy Jones are again illustrative, though in this case he (a Deisheetaan) is testifying on behalf of another clan (the Dak̲l'aweidí).

> Eliza Harbor is called *Gúnx̲* and belongs to the Dak̲l'awedí clan. When they left Stikine River they first went to Eliza Harbor and established a village at Loon Point. Later they found this place unsatisfactory and moved to Angoon. *I heard all this from the old people* and have seen the remains of houses. I also have seen one smokehouse on Liesno Island, which the native people call *Teey X'áat'i*. A man named Tłese'ic from Angoon, who now lives at Tyee, claims that place. He belongs to the Dak̲l'awedí i clan. He goes there to hunt and trap and he lets other Native people trap there. (Goldschmidt and Haas 1998:150; emphasis added)

Even though, in the context of the land claim investigation, he does not feel he has time to "tell the stories," Jones still manages to encapsulate the entire migratory history of the clan in a few short sentences. Moreover, he combines this ancestral knowledge with firsthand experience and personal knowledge of current conditions of production, ownership, and access as if it was a natural fulfillment of heritage and destiny, or *shagóon*.

RESPECT, RECIPROCITY, AND THE ACT OF PERMISSION

Although Tlingits exercised a high degree of territorial control over key production sites, access, even to non-matrikin, was typically extended *if permission was sought*. The great Tlingit attorney William Paul (n.d.) stressed, "In . . . olden days, the boundary lines demarking the areas claimed by adjoining tribes [or clans] were by consensus and were protected by respect." Yet, the boundaries were permeable. "According to the unwritten Tlingit law it was incumbent upon everyone belonging to a phratry [e.g., Raven or Eagle/Wolf] to house and feed any other members who should visit him, no matter from how great a distance he might come" (Swanton 1908:427). But non-matrikin were expected to show respect by seeking formal permission from the host group before penetrating their territory. As with title to property, permission of access was sought and granted through the idiom of kinship. This procedure, in effect, validated the host's claim to the site by recognizing his ancestral ties to the place. To ask permission was to explicitly recognize and respect the host's natural rights to the land. Thus, the communicative act of obtaining permission served as a symbolic reinforcement and maintenance of social boundaries while at the same time allowing for permeation of those boundaries to meet material needs and engender reciprocal ties.

Anthropologist Ronald L. Olson (1967:vi), who was adopted by the Chilkat Gaanaxteidí of the Raven moiety, explains how this principle might be put into practice upon entering an "alien" village.

> In 1934 I was in the village of Klawak when the coastwise maritime strike stopped all communications with the outside world. Food supplies ran short and we had to depend almost wholly on salmon. Since the local area, including the salmon stream, was property of the Ganaxadi [Gaanax.adi] (the equivalent of the Chilkat Ganaxtedih [Gaanaxteidí]) I had the necessary right to harpoon salmon there. I was also able to borrow a harpoon from a Tlowahaddih [Lkuweidí?] man who was, of course, my "brother-in-law." If he refused it would have shown how little he respected my wife who was automatically

a Kagwantan [Kaagwaantaan] Wolf and his "sister." Seeing his lack of respect for her, I might have divorced her, causing her clan to lose face. This is the Tlingit attitude. He *could not* refuse the loan so long as he had the harpoon which he was not using at the time. Had I been counted as a Wolf I could then have gone to a "brother-in-law" Ganaxadi and asked *his* permission to spear salmon in his stream. For a like reason he could not have refused. All in all, the rivalry between the moieties is largely ceremonial in nature. The reciprocal rights and obligations are and were operative to a far greater degree.

By asking permission and emphasizing proper kinship ties, an individual could under most circumstances obtain temporary use rights to virtually any territory in Tlingit land. In fact, one's extensive network of rights was perhaps limited only by one's own creativity, knowledge of the social structure (what I have termed TSK, or traditional social knowledge), and ability to navigate the social space between host and visitor. Perhaps the only exception was during times of resource stress or vulnerability, when conservation became paramount, but even then guests might still be accommodated through other means of sharing. Unfortunately, as Olson suggests, this dynamic aspect of land use and territoriality has often been overlooked in discussions of property and resource tenure, especially among groups that rely on hunting, fishing, and gathering (cf. Myers 1982; Williams and Hunn 1982; Carrier 1987; Berkes 1998; Thornton 1999b).

Failure to seek permission could bring censure, or the trespasser might be "educated" in a more polite way. For instance, "If a man was camped at a creek claimed by his clan and household and a man of the opposite moiety came there, the visitor was not openly told of the ownership, he was invited in, feasted, and told how the host's ancestors always came there to fish. A small gift was made to the visitor. This was, in effect, telling him the creek was claimed" (Olson 1967:12). The problem of "freeloaders" was similarly handled by a culturally sanctioned means of censure, or even violence. Those who abused their privileges by staying too long, or taking too much, or violating some local ordinance, were "called by a special term of contempt, *(n)icka-qa'wu* [*nichkaḵáawu*]" (Swanton 1908:427), or "person of the beach." This term stands in opposition to the Tlingit cultural ideal of the *aanḵáawu*, or "person of the village," a term reserved for the aristocracy. By contrast, the *nichkakáawu* was an outcast—marginal and uncivilized, without home, property, country, or legitimate social relations (cf. Olson 1967:vi; Kan 1989), in short, *displaced.*

This moral framework was extended to interactions with nonhuman relatives, such as bears, whose permission might be sought to harvest salmon or berries in dense patches used by both groups. Such a request was made by the late Amy Marvin, clan mother of the Huna Chooka-neidí, upon landing on the shores of Dundas Bay to pick nagoonber-ries in August of 1996. Because the brown bear is a totemic ancestor of her clan, she addresses the bears as "my mother's grandfathers," a particularly respectful approbation.

> Have pity on us
> my mother's grandfathers.
> We are moving about here
> searching for our food.
> Our numbers are growing small.
>
> Have pity on us
> and allow us through.
>
> Have pity on us.
> Let it be as though you have
> poured good luck into our path.
>
> Wherever we should go
> Move away from our path.
> Have pity on us [literally, We are in a pitiful state].
> Please hear our voices.
> My mother's grandfathers
> Have pity on all of us.
> (*A Time of Gathering* 1999; translated from the Tlingit by John Marks)

On this occasion the bears abided and left the group alone. If not, they may have risked becoming outcasts themselves. Like *nichkakáawu*, bears could be ostracized by their own kind for violating prescribed, respect-ful norms of interaction with humans (Thornton n.d.).

The practice of asking permission continued to be exercised regularly throughout the early twentieth century and in some places continues to be observed to this day. According to Sitka Native George Lewis, whose family had possessory rights of Goddard Hot Springs near Sitka, this courtesy also was regularly followed by the Russians, who, he said, "never used these hot springs without first getting permission from the owner and bringing gifts of food, blankets, or clothing" (Goldschmidt and Haas 1998:64–65). Despite a long tenure under American common property law, in 1946 Tlingits were still respecting clan boundaries by seeking permission from the local *hít s'áati* (house-group leader) or clan leader to use foreign hunting and trapping areas. With approval, a member of a Wrangell clan recalled, "Last winter some of the Tlingit people came up from Saxman and were good enough to ask our people permission to trap there and to find out if any of us were going down before they went to use the area" (76). It seems that this sanction was operable for subsistence activities, particularly hunting and trapping, though not for commercial fishing, which came to be viewed in a different light. Among more traditional Tlingits, this courtesy is still extended as a sign of respect to the recognized steward of a place when hunting, fishing, or overnighting there. As Herman Kitka, a Kaagwaantaan leader and child of the L'uknax̱.ádi clan centered at Deep Bay, told me: "A lot of the people still ask my permission to use Deep Bay when they're going up there to get their subsistence foods; I never say no. 'I don't own it,' I tell them, 'I'm just taking care of it.'" This typifies the Tlingit attitude toward conservation: it is a matter not so much of "resource management" as of "taking care" of places.

LOCAL KNOWLEDGE (TEK), CONSERVATION, AND TAKING CARE OF PLACES

Conserving or taking care of places requires intimate local knowledge of their natural and social history. Local knowledge, also called traditional ecological knowledge (TEK) or indigenous (environmental) knowledge (IK) (cf. Hunn 1993; Berkes 1998; Ellen, Parkes, and Bicker 2000; Bicker, Sillitoe, and Pottier 2004), of place is a primary, though not always sufficient, impetus for conservation (Krech 1999; Hunn et al.

2003). However, without intimate local knowledge of an ecosystem, and a desire to "take care of it," conservation might be impossible, even if there is effective control over access and demand of natural resources.

In this light, the restriction and permitting of access and use to selected resource sites should be seen not simply as a matter of territoriality but also as an opportunity to seek local knowledge on *how* to properly interact with particular places from those who have dwelled there sustainably for generations. Even prior to contact, it is clear that Tlingits had the technologies and wherewithal to drastically alter the distribution and abundance of resources in localized areas. The prescription to seek local permission provided a means for local resource managers to counsel visitors on the best places and ways to harvest without compromising the resource. For example, in Yakutat Ḵwáan, Icy Bay and Yakutat Bay were two important marine hunting areas because of the high density and predictability of seals. But as de Laguna (1972, 1:374) discovered, access to these areas was strictly controlled not only because of these factors but because these bays were sensitive breeding places. As one expert told her: "If there are young seals, then the mothers will stay with them, and there is not as much chance of scaring the whole herd away. . . . The chief [*hít s'áatí*, or house leader] would also say that the men had to get seals with spears. He didn't want people to shoot [with guns] because they would scare the seals. If anybody went sealing before the seal had pups, they would scare the whole herd away." Tlingits realized the need to prevent seals from dispersing and possibly relocating prior to pupping and placed social and technological controls on hunters to prevent the seals from being disturbed. In another case at Wrangell, hunting was allowed on a certain island but camping was prohibited, "so as not to chase off the game" (Goldschmidt and Haas 1998:76). Local knowledge and behavioral sanctions also applied to dealings with the supernatural elements of particular sites. Local owners developed such prescriptions and proscriptions (*ligaas'*, or taboos; literally "against nature") on the basis of collective experience and the desire to ensure a sustainable supply of resources. If guests ignored them or otherwise threatened the resource, they were subject to punishment, as was the case preceding a nineteenth-century massacre of Aleuts by local Tlingits at Kayak Island in northern Tlingit country; having been extended the privilege of harvesting seals in the strait east of the island, the Aleuts were said to have taken too many, thereby provoking reprisals from the Tlingit.

Generations' following the same seasonal paths and projects led to a wealth of accumulated knowledge and an intimacy with place through the communion of food production. This communion was manifest not only in one's adaptation to the contingencies of a particular environment but also in the profound sense of familiarity, comfort, integration, and security that came with knowing how to live off the land. This meant understanding the rhythm and flow of a place, along with its resources. In this context, production, which might ordinarily be thought of as work, came to be viewed as natural, enjoyable, and even easy. Seagull Creek near Hoonah was "an easy place to get fish" (Goldschmidt and Haas 1998:59), and nearby Neka Bay a place where "it was easy to get high bush cranberries, blueberries, salmon berries and loganberries" (59).

Such statements illustrate how a high degree of local environmental knowledge facilitates production so as to reduce anxiety and create positive feelings of comfort, satisfaction, and integration with the environment—a strong and sustaining sense of being-in-place. Indeed, among the Tlingit it is common for topophilia to be expressed in the idiom of production, which, in turn, was always linked to kinship and ancestry. Reflecting on her relationship with Sitkoh Bay, the late Deisheetaan elder Mary Willis (fig. 4.2) put it this way:

Oh, I used to like it there.
Always fish there, summertime.
Gaat Héeni they call it—
Sitkoh Creek, by the cannery.
Lots of sockeyes there.
Oh I used to like it . . .

It was *easy* for me to put up fish there.
There's a fish hole—
Ísh they call it.
We used to set the hooks there.
Sometimes get two or three at once . . .
Oh, I used to like that place . . .
I used to like to stay over there.

FIG. 4.2. The late Mary Willis holds the Deisheetaan button blanket proclaiming her clan's organic ties to Sitkoh Bay in central Southeast Alaska and referencing key landmarks, including *Yéil Katóogu* (Raven's Cave), *Gaat Héeni* (Sockeye Creek), and Tinaa Gooni (Copper Shield Springwater). Photo by T. Thornton

> It was easy for me to put up food there.
> I fix the sockeye.
> We get halibut near the point.
> I fix it too . . .
> Every year we used to go there . . .
> My [maternal] uncle owned that place . . .
> All our foods were there for us.
> Oh, I used to like that place.

Perhaps this is why on her last trip to Sitkoh Bay in 1990, Mrs. Willis, then in her eighties, wanted first to see the sockeye in *Gaat Héeni* and, upon seeing them, exclaimed to our boat captain, "Where's the net?" For Mary Willis, food production comprised the ebb and flow of life at Sitkoh Bay, and she vaulted from the skiff ready to fish. Other "good places" (cf. L. Johnson 2000) were similarly defined by their productive habitats and the foods they provided. Returning from our trip she remembered *Atahéen* (Creek at the Head) at the head of Sitkoh Bay, which we had not had time to visit. She told me its Tlingit name and added, "[We] used to get the [wild] rice from there—*kóox*—and *tl'aak'wách'* [Indian rhubarb—it's] like a spinach, the leaves; we used to get it from there, the long leaves. Some day I'll show you. . . . *Kóox* is good with blueberries too." The land continued to speak to her all the way back to Angoon. And much of the remainder of her life was devoted to trying to conserve Sitkoh Bay as a Deisheetaan landscape and a good place to put up food.

TECHNOLOGY AND THE EXPERIENCE OF PLACE

Production and, by extension, Tlingits' relationships to places were mediated by the technologies employed in making a living. Extensive local knowledge of the environment through tradition and practice was one such technology (Ridington 1990). The body itself was another. As outlined earlier, the body constrains our experience and communion with place by its very capacities and limitations. Our bodies can be engaged in only one place at a time, so we encounter places serially with some near and others far. "When we say that an object is huge or tiny, nearby or far away, it is often without any comparison, even implicit with any other object, or even with the size and objective position [i.e., the simple location] of our own body, but merely in relation to a certain 'scope' of our gestures, a certain 'hold' of the phenomenal body on its surroundings" (Merleau-Ponty 1962:266). The phenomenology of perception vis-à-vis the body-subject is emphasized in Tlingit travel narratives, such as the following story about a Kwáashk'i Kwáan (Yakutat Raven) group traveling along the Gulf Coast from Copper River toward Yakutat (note too the phenomenology of production):

> Then the people thought they saw a wolverine. They used it for a compass and walked towards it. When they came to it they saw it was a little mountain, an island with trees on it, just a little hill. . . . That night a wolverine came to the fire. The hungry people killed him and ate him. They cut him up in little pieces to feed all the people. Then they walked on again.
>
> Pretty soon they saw a rabbit sitting on the snow, far away. They walked

FIG. 4.3. Mount Saint Elias (*Waas'eit'ashaa* [Mountain Inland of Icy Bay]) is celebrated as a sentient being and crest in this Yakutat Kwáashk'i Ḵwáan tunic with blanket. A beacon for travelers, the mountain appeared in various guises to clan members during their migration to Yakutat from Copper River; its form was often determined by factors such as weather, the travelers' orientation and distance, and other circumstances. Tlingit perceptions of the mountain's indwelling spirit are reflected in the lower portion of the design. Sheldon Jackson Museum SJ-I-A-329

towards the rabbit. After two days walking they saw it was the top of a mountain, but they kept on walking anyway. Finally they came to Mount Saint Elias. It was a compass for the people. (De Laguna 1972, 1:32)

In another story the peak of the same mountain is perceived by ocean-voyaging Tlingit mariners as a "seagull" above the clouds—"Every day it was getting higher"—before finally revealing itself as Mount Saint Elias (see fig. 4.3) when the distance between observers and object narrows. These perceptual phenomena are worth noting in oral tradition, for they remind the listener that things are not always what they seem, or, phrased in Tlingit metaphysics, landscape features, as beings, may take more than one form.[3] Thus, in Tlingit cosmology, the morphological changes of Mount Saint Elias are more than just optical illusions: they are navigational cues, portents of the future, transformations of sentient beings, signs to be read. Reading the mountain as a series of animal encounters emphasizes the phenomenal experience of travel, perception, subsistence, and interspecies encounters along the rugged Gulf Coast of Tlingit country. Like the human body, nonhuman forms are truly metaphors to live by.

Tlingit language is also attentive to this phenomenon of perceptual change according to relational distance. For instance, there are the following terms: *hé*, indicating an object that is very near and always present; *yaat*, denoting an object that is a bit farther off but still in one's "scope," to use Maurice Merleau-Ponty's term; *yut*, indicating something so remote that it can be used as an impersonal article; *wé*, suggesting an object so far away that it is almost invisible or barely in one's perceptual "hold"; and, finally, *wuyík*, relating to something that is beyond all perceptual recognition.[4] The relational efficacy of such fine-grained distinctions for a maritime hunting-gathering people can hardly be overestimated. Indeed, this may be true for all indigenous, oral cultures, for whom

places are never just passive settings. Remember that in oral cultures the human eyes and ears have not yet shifted their synaesthetic participation from the animate surroundings to the written word. Particular mountains, canyons, streams, boulder-strewn fields, or groves of trees have not yet lost the expressive potency and dynamism with which they spontaneously present themselves to the senses. A particular place in the land is never, for an oral culture, just a passive or inert setting for the human events that occur there. It is an active participant in those occurrences. Indeed, by virtue of its underlying and enveloping presence, the place may even be felt to be the source, the primary power that expresses itself through the various events that unfold there. (Abram 1996:162)

The technology of the body and its influence on phenomenal experience is particularly evident in descriptions of production. Place memories are often memories of the paths taken to various hunting, fishing, or gathering sites. Mary Williams's 1946 recollections of the Tsirku River (Goldschmidt and Haas 1998:30) are illustrative:

At the Takhin Glacier in the upper portion of the Tsirku River two days by canoe there was a berrying place called *Dakhéen Xuká*. This could also be reached by way of the Takhin River, and the Haines people sometimes came up this way. This place belonged to the Kaagwaantaan clan. We gathered mountain blueberries and other berries there. Helen Hotch went up there with her father when she was a girl of less than ten (about 40 years ago). Our people haven't gone up there recently because it is too hard to get to by canoe . . .

The next place down the Tsirku River is called *Qatxalqiya* [*Katgalgiyá*?], between the confluence of Summit Creek and of Nugget Creek with the Tsirku. Berries and gophers were obtained from both sides of the Tsirku here. The Kaagwaantaan were recognized as owners but others went there. I only went there one time about 30 years ago. Mr. and Mrs. Kudeinahaa went up there frequently before his death about 15 years ago. Don't know of anyone going up there recently. At a place on the Tsirku River where two cliffs come together is a place called *Gil' X'aak*, which was used as a camping place and where a berry called tínx (bearberry), soapberries and blueberries were obtained. This was also a good place for mountain goats. It belonged to the whole Klukwan people.

Despite a thirty-year absence from this place, Mrs. Williams still recalls the details of the landscape in vivid detail, as if she were actually traveling up that river (two days by canoe) with her audience, reading the navigational cues (e.g., "where two cliffs come together") in sequence, and stopping at camps or productive sites to obtain foods (mountain blueberries here or soapberries there). The geography is remembered from an embodied perspective as it was experienced in subsistence or other productive ventures launched from the downriver settlement at Klukwan.

Geographer David Seamon refers to such time-space routines as "body ballets" (a more aesthetically pleasing term than "routines"), which he defines as a "set of integrated behaviors which sustain a particular task or aim" (1980:157). Following Merleau-Ponty, Seamon argues that the body is more than a technology, that it can become a kind of "precognitive" subject that by its very limits and capacities shapes behavior in a "preconscious way" (155). It is not that the body supplants the mind as agent but rather that the body and mind exist in a dialectical relationship, each structuring and feeding back on the processes of the other, and, as the narratives above suggest, both contributing to the memory and definition of place. The discussion of the use of the body as a metaphor and cognitive tool for place naming in previous chapters illustrates another aspect of this dialectical relationship.

Other technologies also had profound effects on the limits of production and the conceptualization of time, space, and place. The canoe, for example, as a means of negotiating the land and seascape was integral to people's understanding of place. Already identified as a genre of place is the famous Yakutat *gudiyé*, the "secret" sealing canoes exquisitely designed for the tight maneuvering required to hunt the ice-choked waters of a particular place: Icy Bay. Canoes of various types were constructed to facilitate production, be it hunting, fishing, warfare, ocean or riverine travel, or trade. Mrs. Williams's two-day journey to the Tsirku by canoe would have been impossible without the benefit of such watercraft. But production was also limited by technology. Thus, Porcupine Creek off the Klehini River was remarkable not just as a subsistence site but because it was "the highest camp site to which the natives could get by canoe" (Goldschmidt and Haas 1998:31).

The other important aspect of the relationship between traditional technologies and place was that tools and other manufactures were rendered from the local environment. Just as a place might be recognized and celebrated as a salmon fishing site, so too might a certain stand of timber be esteemed for its value in the production of canoes, paddles, houses, forts, temporary bark shelters, pitch, rope, baskets, adze handles, ladles, dishes, drums, bows, arrows, spear shafts, halibut hooks, and so forth. Thus, Emma Henry, a Klawock elder, remembered Sandy Point, east of Karta Bay, as "a very important place when I was a small girl" because her family camped there and, lacking "regular houses," had to fashion shelters out of bark (Goldschmidt and Haas 1998:87). The act of constructing dwellings from local materials became a signature means of cultivating the landscape and making it part of their being. Like food production, technological production was a means of sustaining life through a communion with place. Moreover, signatures of inhabitation could be read in such places as "figures in the landscape" (Bierwert 1999:36) through the culturally modified trees and other subtle tracks of the ancestors. As Angoon elder Billy Jones reads Kelp Bay:

"It is still possible to see the places in that area where the Native people gathered the bark off the yellow cedar trees, which they used for shelter" (Goldschmidt and Haas 1998:149).

With some technologies, such as the traditional halibut hook, there was even more to it than this. Early explorers marveled at the efficiency of Tlingit-style halibut hooks and Tlingits also favored them for their selectivity: different sized hooks could be shaped (through carving) and influenced (through magic, or *héixwa*) to target appropriate-sized halibut (preferably not too small or too large). Originally fashioned from local materials, including spruce (or yellow cedar), alder (or yew in the south), spruce root, and bone (or later iron for the barb), the hooks themselves were considered sentient beings, possessing shaman-like powers (see Jonaitis 1981), and each hook was decorated and named:

> The decorations on the hook are to influence the fish and so face downward. They also give the hook a kind of life, as does the individual hook's personal name. The fisherman would warm his hands in the sunshine and put them on his rig, and address the buoy, the line, and especially the hooks, telling the latter, "Go down to halibut land and fight!" Or he would tell them to go for the halibut's wife so that the husband would become angry and bite the hook (using a ruse similar to that employed by Raven when he made the king salmon so angry at the greenstone that the fish jumped ashore). And the hook answers the fisherman. (De Laguna in Emmons 1991:117)

To produce such a technology was to give birth to a social creature. Houses, canoes, and other technologies were similarly conceived. Accordingly, the rendering of natural products into technologies was analogous to the process of human reproduction itself and, as such, was traditionally considered a natural part of the seasonal and life cycles, and of the experience of place.

CHANGES IN PRODUCTION: ENCROACHMENT AND MODERNIZATION

Changes in production have been marked, especially since the 1880s when commercialization of the fisheries began in earnest. The encroachment of non-Natives, conflicts between Tlingit and Euro-American kinship and property law, and the introduction of new technologies and regulations have combined to change the way people relate to places through the means of production. Although Tlingits resisted these changes actively and with some success, competition and the loss of access to traditional resources combined with the demands of making a living in a developing capitalist economy necessitated accommodation. Through perseverance and good fortune some Tlingit communities have been able to conserve portions of their traditional land and resource base and minimize the deleterious effects of industrial development. These communities, it seems, continue to enjoy the highest degree of communion with place through traditional and modern means of production.

The history of Alaska, like other colonial settings, has been a story of increasing encroachment upon indigenous lands and resources by non-Natives. Of course there was significant intra- and interethnic fighting over territory prior to contact, but the postcontact incursions were much more intensive. They came in waves.

The first wave was that of the fur traders. The most important competitive influence was that of the Russian-American Company, though the Hudson's Bay Company and independent American traders also competed for furs in Southeast Alaska. It is generally acknowledged that, despite their claim to Alaska by right of discovery and conquest, the Russians' penetration of *Lingít Aaní*, especially outside of their regional center at Sitka, was very limited. Though Russians dominated the mercantilist fur trade economy, their penetration into other sectors of the economy was minimal in part because of Tlingit resistance. Indeed, the Russians remained highly dependent on Tlingits for labor, foodstuffs, and other necessities throughout the colonial period. The employment of Aleuts and Kodiaks by the Russians and other Native groups by the British and Americans to harvest furs posed a direct threat to Tlingit sovereignty and to the supply of key animal resources, such as sea otters. Consequently, the fur trade was a source of many conflicts. Tlingits destroyed the Russian settlements at Sitka in 1802 and at Yakutat in 1805, sacked the British Hudson's Bay Company outpost at Fort Selkirk in 1851, and periodically attacked Aleut and Kodiak hunters who violated Tlingit territorial sovereignty (Emmons 1991; J. R. Gibson 1992). Although the Russians recaptured Sitka in 1804, they were always wary of travel beyond the stockaded settlement. Clearly, "Russian control of the region was purely mythical" (Drucker 1958:41; see also Hinckley 1996).

Sea otters and other furbearers notwithstanding, the Russians otherwise respected Native property rights, even in the vicinity of their stronghold at Sitka. I have already cited the example of Goddard Hot Springs near Sitka, where the Russians reportedly "never used these hot springs without first getting permission from the owner and bringing gifts." The same practice was reported at nearby Redoubt Bay, where Russians "recognized the native ownership of this bay by giving the owner food and clothing. He was treated and dressed like a prince of the Russians" (Goldschmidt and Haas 1998:64). According to Stephen Langdon (1989:314), "One can conceptualize these Russian payments as rental or lease fees, as they apparently did not transfer ownership rights, a practice which Oberg (1973) indicated was proscribed in Tlingit society." From the perspective of production and relationships with place, the salient feature of these "leasing" arrangements was that they preserved the integrity of Tlingit "communal property" and resource management for fish and species other than furbearers. This remained largely the case though the early part of the American era in Alaska, from 1867 to 1889, after which the federal government began active management of Southeast Alaska fisheries.

The second wave of economic incursion came with the commercialization of the fisheries, which began in the 1870s. The effects of this movement have been well documented by Jefferson Moser (1899), Stephen Langdon (1977, 1989), and Robert Price (1990) and for the fishery at Sitkoh Bay by Thomas Thornton, Robert Schroeder, and Robert Bosworth (1990). By 1900 commercial fishing and fish processing had become big business in Alaska, and there were more than twenty canneries in Southeast Alaska alone (Moser 1899; Alaska Fisheries Board and Alaska Department of Fisheries 1949; Price 1990). Even in the early years the effects of single fishing and cannery operation could be widespread and devastating. For example, the Redoubt Bay cannery near Sitka, established in 1889, was within a year intensively exploiting fisheries more than fifty miles away at Sitkoh Bay.

As Langdon (1989) has shown, the struggle during this period was between traditional communal property rights of Southeast Alaska Natives and the "common property" rights favored by the invading commercial enterprises to maximize access. The latter, of course, prevailed under American law and, with the help of the U.S. military, was enforced against the Tlingits despite fierce resistance in many instances.

The case of Sitkoh Bay (Thornton, Schroeder, and Bosworth 1990) illustrates how this transformation came about. When fishermen from the Redoubt cannery began penetrating Sitkoh Bay, local Tlingits expected them to ask for permission to fish. Failure to follow the traditional protocol led to a standoff with the Deisheetaan Tlingit owners, who had a sizable seasonal fishing settlement of over one hundred residents at Sitkoh Creek (_Gaat Héeni_, or Sockeye Creek, a prime fishery). According to Price (1990:120), this conflict marked the first instance of U.S. military force employed against a Native group on behalf of a cannery. The _Alaskan_, a Sitka newspaper, reported on July 12, 1890, that Indians were preventing non-Natives from fishing in Sitkoh Bay, "claiming exclusive rights to its open and navigable waters." A week later, following the return of U.S. Marine Lt. Coontz, who was dispatched to adjudicate the situation, the _Alaskan_ (July 19, 1890) offered this synopsis:

> It appears that the present Native claimants of the exclusive right to fish in that bay are the descendants of the former villagers who had their permanent abode there while the present generation lives now across Chatham Straits in the Kootznahoo settlement.
>
> ... The Natives asked from every fisherman a royalty of 25 cents per day; which was not conceded. At last not being able to come to a mutual understanding in this imbroglio, the Lieut. proposed that the contesting Indians should proceed with him to Sitka in order to have the matter settled by the civil authorities. This proposition was readily accepted, and the Natives are now here awaiting the action of the civil government.

Lt. Coontz also recounted the incident in his autobiography, which provides additional details of the incident:

> When we reached our destination I found the white men in the upper part of the bay with their seines and everything ready to haul, and a band of one hundred and twenty-five Indians on a point of land where a little stream enters the bay. ... We saw that they were all armed with shotguns, rifles and other implements of war. I picked out the leader whom I found to be

Baptist Jim. . . . I demanded the surrender of the entire party at once. He demurred, but I told him that even if he did kill us, the federal government would sooner or later have its innings with them, and that if the Indians had real grievances, they could be adjusted by the governor [in Sitka]. . . .

. . . We chose about twenty of the leaders . . . and at midnight hove up anchor and started for Sitka, leaving the families behind to come on later as best they could. . . . Their troubles dragged for months, and the governmental investigation took so long that the poor Indians, who stayed with their friends at the Ranch in Sitka, gradually became discouraged and one by one went home.

As soon as the Indians surrendered I ordered the white men to start fishing, and I remember that on the first haul of the seine they took in more than a thousand salmon. (Coontz 1930:153–54)

Unable to forcibly resist or obtain legal recognition of their rights, the Deisheetaan risked losing their fishery altogether. In 1900, when a fish cannery was slated to be built at Sitkoh Bay below the Native village, the Deisheetaan owners contemplated further resistance, but chose to negotiate instead. According to Deisheetaan elder Mary Willis, an agreement was reached between the cannery operators and her uncles, the caretakers of the Sitkoh Creek: "They [the non-Native investors] asked them if they could put a cannery there. One of my uncles say 'No, they're going to take it [the territory] away from us!' The other uncles say 'We got lots of family. They always go to work to earn money . . . to Ketchikan . . . to Juneau, Petersburg. Over here, if they put the cannery here, the family gonna work here.' Then he okayed it, [the] other uncle. They put it there" (Thornton, Schroeder, and Bosworth 1990:43). Local employment was a quid pro quo for Deisheetaan acceptance of the cannery in their territory. Local employment would enable the Deisheetaan to maintain their seasonal productive and residential ties to Sitkoh Bay in the changing economy. Few groups were so fortunate; most found themselves going to canneries in alien territories for the summer fishing season.

In addition to an employment priority, the Sitkoh agreement also was said to have allowed for the Deisheetaan to retain ownership and control over their village and the bay. In fact, according to a recorded statement by Charlie Jim, Mary Willis's deceased brother, who assumed leadership over the territory after the death of Sitkoh Bay Chief (a nephew of Baptist Jim): "He [Sitkoh Bay Chief] also made clear that only the buildings would belong to the company, that the land would remain in the ownership of the [Deisheetaan] owners of the bay" (Alaska Consultants, Inc., 1976:27). In other words, the agreement was a lease arrangement rather than an outright sale or transfer of the territory. But in Sitkoh Bay, as elsewhere, such "leases" seem to have been made only out of expedience, to avoid initial confrontation, and "were abandoned as quickly as the cannery men could do so without endangering themselves" (Langdon 1989:317).

In many cases, Tlingit property rights were not recognized at all. The fate of another sockeye stream at Klag Bay on Chichagof Island is representative:

> About forty-four years ago, we put up a sign at the mouth of a sockeye stream at Klag Bay saying that the place belonged to us and the others should keep out. Some Government officials and men from the Dundas Bay cannery said we had no right to keep others out. So we had to take the sign down, although the place belonged to us from way back, and this was our one sockeye stream that gave us all the sockeyes we needed. (Goldschmidt and Haas 1998:62)

As the federal government assumed full control of the territory, federal agents consistently enforced the principles of common property over communal property with respect to fisheries.

As shown, however, Tlingits not only resisted this usurpation but continued to respect communal property rights among themselves. They also consistently pleaded their case to government officials (e.g., Moser 1899; U.S. Department of the Interior [1944]; Goldschmidt and Haas 1998). The following appeal, submitted on behalf of a Sitka group at the turn of the century was typical:

> We ask that Mr. Smith, the superintendent of the Baranof Packing Company, would be forbidden to take away our lagoons, bays and streams where we used to fish long before the arrival of white people. We wish that he would do the necessary fishing only with our consent. We demand that he stops throwing pieces of wood and tree trunks across the streams to prevent fish

from going there to spawn. His fishing methods in the last eight years have made such places as Redoubt Bay, Cross Sound, Hoonah, Whale Bay, Necker Bay, and Redfish Bay virtually empty. (In Kan 1985:135)

The Tlingits' concern was not only with property rights but also with the very survival of the fisheries, and by extension their own being. Moser (1899:43), who surveyed Alaska's salmon fisheries on behalf of the government in 1897, heard these concerns repeatedly and recognized the impending consequences if something was not done.

Whenever the "Albatross" anchored near any locality either permanently or temporarily inhabited by Natives, a delegation of the older men or chief came on board and requested an audience. The powwows which followed invariably took the form of relating the oppression of the white men. . . . These streams, under their own administration, for centuries have belonged to certain families or clans. . . . No Indians would fish in a stream not their own except by invitation, and they cannot understand how those of a higher civilization should be—as they regard it less honorable. . . . They claim the white man is crowding them from their houses, robbing them of their ancestral rights, taking away their fish by shiploads; that their streams must soon become exhausted; that the Indian will have no supply to maintain himself and family; and that starvation must follow. . . .

. . . My own sympathy is with the Indians and I would gladly recommend, if the way were clear, the establishment of ownership in streams; but it is impracticable, and I can only ask . . . whatever law is framed, that a liberal balance be thrown in his favor.

Tlingits and Haidas realized that the principle of common property was in the end not only unjust but unsustainable, leading ultimately to a tragedy of the commons (Hardin 1968). Non-Native resource managers, however, did not come to this realization until the 1960s. Ironically, as Langdon points out, the state of Alaska eventually adopted a limited-entry permit system, which constituted a "reinstitution of property rights to the salmon fisheries" (1989:328). But limited-entry imposed restrictions only on participation (a finite number of transferable, individual permits) and not on place (save for closures).[5] And this system has led to Native villagers' further alienation from fishing rights.

Under common property rule, Natives continued to assert their traditional rights, but, lacking economic alternatives, they had no choice but to participate in commercial fishing. As the Sitkoh Bay case shows, the primary goal was to maintain ties to traditional fishing grounds through the commercial fisheries. However, in most cases competition and the intensive and selective (with regard to salmon species) nature of the industry made this impossible over the long term. The traditional place-bound economy was replaced by a regional and global one characterized by the "flexible accumulation" (Harvey 1989) of salmon wherever they could be harvested most efficiently with commercial gear. The effect of this economic change was to further restructure Southeast Alaska Natives' productive relationships to places. In 1946, one Native fisherman with ties to Kegan Cove summed up the changes this way: "We never used to go anywhere else but fished only in this bay, but now I have to run all over with my gas boat to catch fish" (Goldschmidt and Haas 1998:84).

The contradictions between the traditional and modern economies created crosscutting tensions among Natives participating in the commercial fishery. Like trapping, commercial fishing increasingly became an individual or nuclear family enterprise rather than one carried on by the clan or house group. To succeed, commercial fishermen were constantly "prospecting" for fish in areas outside of their traditional territories. Nonlocals might be confronted by local Tlingits regarding their uninvited presence, creating tense situations. Mark Jacobs Sr., a Deisheetaan Tlingit from Angoon and Sitka, who was able to mitigate such a situation in Klawock through good humor, related the following account:

In 1918, I went fishing on a purse seine boat along with another fellow down to Klawock district, and when I entered the store I was talking with the storekeeper, and an old Indian asked me what I was. And I told him that I was Thlingit. And he asked me, "That is not the question I asked you. Do you belong to the Raven tribe or to the Eagle tribe?" And I told him that I did not know what he was talking about because I could not fly. That was my answer. And he laughed. And he says, "The people generally ask this question, and they don't insult each other when they ask it." So I told him, "I didn't come down here to insult anybody. I came down here to make a living." ["]Well,["] he says, ["]that is fine." And with that conversation he granted me the right to fish around Klawock district. (U.S. Department of the Interior [1944])

Another way to manage these contradictions intellectually was to distinguish between commercial fishing for market and fishing for one's own use (i.e., subsistence). In the context of the land claims investigation by Goldschmidt and Haas in 1946, statements such as "I have fished up Dolomi when purse seining *but never put up fish there for my own use*" (1998:174; emphasis added) implicitly conveyed that the individual was not asserting a claim to an area, though he used it for commercial purposes. Such a distinction maintained the concept of a home fishery, at which one partook directly of the fruits of production, rather than indirectly through the wage economy.[6]

The third wave of encroachers was that of settlers, including homesteaders, miners, fox farmers, and others seeking to capitalize on Alaska's land-based resources. Though their impacts were not as devastating in the short term as those of commercial fishing, in the long run they have proved most damaging to Tlingit place relations. The case of fox farms is illustrative and, like the commercial fishing situation, full of ironies. As with the fishing grounds, Natives' communal rights to hunting grounds were usurped on the basis of the common property principle, only to be leased to non-Native fox farmers, who then exercised territorial prerogatives to exclude Natives as trespassers. In many cases these farm sites were traditional settlements or hunting and gathering places. For example, Chilkat elder Mildred Sparks reported in 1946 that "Battery Point [near Haines] was formerly an important source of tideland foods, especially seaweed" but that "a fox farm at this place now . . . prevents its being used" (Goldschmidt and Haas 1998:34). Fox farmers and homesteaders not only ran Natives off but also tore down their cabins and smokehouses. When two Huna Tlingits living on Drake Island in Glacier Bay were run off their land and their houses destroyed, members of the T'akdeintaan clan protested, but the farmer "told the people the government had given him permission" (55). Similarly, in Kelp Bay, a Native camp on Crow Island was taken over by a fox farmer: "The Natives tried to tell the farmer to leave the place, but he told them that the island belonged to the government" (71). This pattern was repeated throughout Southeast Alaska by fox farmers, homesteaders, and miners (see Thornton 2004b), with the forces of the U.S. government aiding and abetting the process of usurpation of lands and the imposition of new property concepts.

The overall effect of such competition on production was one of inhibition and fragmentation. Time after time Tlingits were prevented from engaging in communal production activities on their traditional lands and waters. Their paths and projects were disrupted in space and time by encroaching competitors, changing property conceptions, and increasing regulation of the commons. Moreover, with the penetration of intensive, extractive industries, the resource base itself became increasingly unstable, even after corrective measures, such as limited entry, were implemented. Thus, even where they were allowed to continue to hunt and fish untrammeled, Tlingits often found a dwindling or undependable resource supply.

Given the centrality of salmon to Tlingit culture, changes in the salmon fisheries have been particularly disruptive. Today the state determines if, when, where, and how (e.g., gear type, proximity to stream, and targeted species) Alaskans fish, as well as how many fish they harvest. Assuming that one is eligible to participate in the commercial salmon fisheries, the fragmentation of these fisheries in time (openings as short as several hours), space (closed areas and other zoning), and participation (limited entry) precludes sustained productive interactions with place. Compare this to the traditional salmon harvest season, which involved two to six months of residence around spawning sites, or even to the pre-1960s commercial fishing era, which placed comparatively few restrictions on the paths and projects of fishermen and included seasonal employment and residence at canneries at least some of which—like Chatham in Sitkoh Bay—were located at or near traditional dwelling sites. The structure of the present commercial salmon fishing economy means that Tlingit fishermen spend many more hours in home ports than did their predecessors; consequently, their interactions with resources and productive sites tend to be shorter and often more intensive than in the past. Few can survive on fishing alone and must supplement their income with wage employment in other sectors of the economy. Such are the "changes in living," alluded to by Herman Kitka, that have taken place over the past century.

U.S. legal concepts with regard to property rights and inheritance also had a dramatic impact on traditional communal production and relationships to place. Property rights and inheritance under U.S. law stood in direct opposition to traditional Tlingit concepts. As de Laguna (Emmons 1991:287) points out,

> The teachings of the white missionaries and the imposition of our legal system caused the greatest confusion, often with bloodshed and misery, when the old matrilineal rules of succession and inheritance were shifting to our patrilineal inheritance with widow's rights to a share in her husband's property. These difficulties were particularly disruptive when clan or lineage heirlooms were involved. Thus sons took the clan or lineage property that their fathers had held in trust and sold it as if it were private property; widows hold on to their husband's regalia and were sometimes beaten by those who claimed it.

These conflicts also pervaded inheritance of productive lands. Instead of being transferred from mother (or mother's brother) to son, land and stewardship rights were transmitted from father to son, in effect transferring the property to another moiety and clan. This often exacerbated tensions between clans and weakened the foundational tenets of traditional Tlingit law. The federal Allotment Act, extended to Alaska in 1906, served to further undermine the Tlingit communal system of land and resource tenure by subdividing and individualizing title to land. Beyond this, clan territories were further undermined by the shift in sociopolitical organization away from the kin-based clans to territorially based k̲wáans, shaped by the Indian Reorganization Act and isomorphic with modern state-sanctioned villages (see Thornton 2002). In some cases communities moved to abandon clan territories altogether in favor of k̲wáan or village territories in which all members of the community were permitted to use an area in common without seeking any group's permission for access.

Changing property concepts also affected the social relations of production. Labor, traditionally recruited from the matrilineage, became much more of a nuclear family enterprise. Distribution also increasingly favored the nuclear family over the traditional clan or house group.

These changes in the relations of production tended to reinforce Euro-American concepts of property rights and inheritance.

To acknowledge the changes wrought by alien economic, social, and regulatory structures is not to suggest, however, that traditional structuring relationships toward places have been destroyed. On the contrary, traditional socioeconomic structures continue to play a strong role in Tlingit relations of production as well as in their political discourse about place and production. Although, under present subsistence law, harvesting privileges are accorded to residents of geographically localized communities that meet the criteria established by state law, regardless of ethnicity, moiety, clan, or house ties, and other principles of social organization continue to be emphasized by many Tlingits as important criteria for evaluating subsistence and territorial rights. Thus, at Sitkoh Bay (Thornton, Schroeder, and Bosworth 1990) Angoon elders were found to emphasize not only that the sockeye fishery was part of Angoon Ḵwáan but that it was Deisheetaan clan territory, and furthermore that only one "side" of that clan (i.e., a particular house group) had legitimate possessory rights to the bay.[7] Similarly, Sitka lineages with ties to the fishery continued to assert their claims.

Many Tlingits express dissatisfaction over the fact that their relatives, who meet Tlingit social criteria for subsistence use of an area, are denied access rights by the state simply because they reside outside of Angoon. The late Mark Jacobs Jr., a Daḵl'aweidí elder residing in Sitka but with ties to Angoon, put it this way: "My grandfather will not slap my hand if I reach into his bowl," implying that kinship ties are just as important as residence. Mr. Jacobs's metaphor reveals the durability not only of Native socioeconomic structures but of linguistic structures as well. Although the statement was made in English, the idiom of the (feast) bowl is clearly Tlingit. Just as people find meaning in two languages, so too do they reconcile participation in two economies: traditional subsistence and modern capitalism.

NEW TECHNOLOGY AND EFFECTS ON PATH AND PROJECT

As in the Industrial Revolution of the eighteenth century (see Polanyi 1944), the catastrophic dislocation experienced by Southeast Alaska

Natives in the late nineteenth and early twentieth centuries was partly attributable to vast improvements in the tools of production. New technologies generally allowed for increased access to hunting, fishing, and gathering sites as well as for increased efficiency of harvest, though the situation was by no means that simple. Some of the traditional technologies of the Tlingit, such as stream-mouth lattice traps and weirs, were outlawed in 1889 because they were too efficient when applied competitively and without escapement (a practice Natives had traditionally followed). Under a common property regime it looked as if such technologies might have to be abandoned in favor of less efficient means; yet this was not the case. Witness the disastrously efficient but unselective floating fish traps, introduced in 1907.

Langdon (1989) argues that the floating fish trap and gas-powered boat were the two technologies that most fundamentally altered traditional Tlingit relations of production. In the case of the gas-powered boats, the desire for young Tlingit men to strike out on their own in high-status jobs as independent fishing captains stimulated investment in motorized purse seine vessels. Though these boats constituted a considerable investment, cannery operators would finance the construction and purchase of the seiners on behalf of the fishermen; however, the debt incurred by the fishermen in effect indentured them to produce exclusively for the cannery. Some fishermen worked their whole lives without ever emerging from debt or gaining title to their boats. A major consequence of this dependence on the cannery, Langdon concludes, was withdrawal from the house group, although I would argue that this was not the most important outcome of this technology. In fact, in many cases the matrilineal labor structure of the house group was transferred to the seining crew, which in the early days typically required at least five or six men. Even today it is not uncommon to find maternal nephews crewing on their uncles' seine boats; in this regard purse seiners have been much more preservative of the house group than, say, trollers or other boat technologies.

Rather, the most important consequence of the gas-powered purse seine vessels was that they constrained fishermen to harvest more intensively and farther afield from their traditional production locales than ever before. In Southeast Alaska it was rarely possible to seine in one place all summer and make enough money to keep up with the debt; one had to move from place to place targeting the most abundant and lucrative (in terms of market price) stocks in order to compete in this capital-intensive and spatially flexible economy. As shown, many fishermen, because of their knowledge and traditional ties to these places and also because of the social tensions inherent in moving into other clan and ḵwáan territories, lamented the fact that they had to abandon their traditional fisheries and "go all over" to fish.

At the same time, the introduction of larger and faster boats did not always increase access. As one Taku Native noted, "I used to have a fish camp on Canyon Island and used it regularly until I got a larger boat with which I could not get up the river" (Goldschmidt and Haas 1998:42). Even where purse seiners could access traditional production sites, it meant exploiting them in a new way. And it was only after the adoption of larger gas-powered vessels that harvesters began to make a regular practice of sleeping on their boats rather than camping on land, which constituted yet another dislocation from traditional production locales and dwelling places.

The issues with commercial fish traps were more clear-cut: "Floating fish traps were capital-intensive gear; owned by the canneries, they could be operated by one man, who would live on the trap. . . . The fish trap put tremendous strains on the Tlingit and Haida fishermen who had committed themselves wholeheartedly to the purse seine vessel. The floating trap not only supplanted fishermen through its sheer efficiency in harvesting great quantities, but also drove those that remained in purse-seining to the edge of economic disaster through low prices for fish" (Langdon 1989:321). Fish traps also jeopardized subsistence harvests at terminal fisheries, as salmon bound for those locations were intercepted by the traps before they could enter the bays and streams. Weak returns to the streams precluded traditional levels of production, and many groups stopped traveling to their remote camps altogether because it was no longer deemed worthwhile (e.g., Goldschmidt and Haas 1998:71, 77, 80, 81, 84, 101). In a 1947 letter to the Commission of Indian Affairs an Angoon Tlingit committee summed up the situation this way: "Cannery fish traps have greatly interfered with all Native fishing in all areas claimed under our possessory rights" (154).

Southeast Alaska Natives protested vigorously against fish traps and took legal and extralegal measures to stop them. Acts of sabotage, such as the following, were widely reported: "About forty years ago [ca. 1906] while the chief of the clan who claimed Redfish Bay was still alive, a cannery put a fish trap there. The chief ordered the trap set out loose, and since that time there never has been a trap on Redfish Bay. The Natives responsible for destroying the trap were threatened with imprisonment, but nothing ever happened to them" (65). Despite such acts of resistance, the effort to curtail the use of traps was achieved only after statehood in 1949. By this time the damage done to fisheries and to the traditional social groups that used them was in many cases irreparable.

Changes in fishing production in many ways mirrored the transformation of place relations in commercial trapping. As Oberg (1973:60–61) points out, "With the introduction of firearms, steel traps and the great demand for fur, a new orientation was given to Tlingit production"; as the fur trade intensified, "fur bearing animals began to lessen in number with the consequence that the formerly undivided clan territories began to be cut up into small sections." Like the development of commercial fishing, this process severely weakened the house group as a productive unit controlling its own resource areas. Instead, the individual assumed more and more importance as a productive unit. In each case a change in property relationships led to changes in the relations of production, social and otherwise.

The adoption of modern technologies not only increased extraction of resources and the individualizing of production; it also had the effect of alienating people from the process of technological production. Guns and steel traps were bought in stores and manufactured elsewhere, while bows and arrows, spears, and deadfalls had been manufactured locally and hence were part of traditional productive relationships with place. Rendering technologies from the environment was a fundamental part of the traditional seasonal round. The introduction of new technologies altered this element of production permanently. Those craftsmen and craftswomen who continue to produce traditional technologies with local materials, such as spruce root baskets or Chilkat blankets from local mountain goat wool, cedar bark, and natural dyes, are highly respected for maintaining such knowledge, skills, and ties to the land.

As this discussion has demonstrated, production is a fundamental element of the experience of place. Over time Tlingit relationships to place have been altered by changes in the nature and level of production. But it is also important to recognize that the degree of change has varied considerably across communities and within communities to the level of the house group. Though a review of changes at the clan and house level is not possible here, production between communities can be compared. Variability in productive relations to traditional territories at the community level can be assessed in terms of three major factors: community integrity, environmental integrity, and subsistence production. Table 4.2 compares rural Southeast Alaska Native communities in terms of each of these factors.

Community integrity may be defined as the degree to which the traditional composition of community, including its population and social organization, has been maintained. Because consistent figures on clan and house-group composition within communities are not available, population composition figures (percent Native, column 4) are used as a proxy for assessing community integrity. It is assumed that these populations represent to a significant degree the traditional clan and house groups that occupied the village. While such an assumption cannot be made for urban communities, where substantial portions of the Native population are immigrants from the villages, rural villages generally have not had large influxes of Natives from nonlocal kin groups. Thus, any rural community that is more than 75 percent Native is considered to have a high degree of integrity.

Environmental integrity is more difficult to measure. A thorough analysis would evaluate all significant impacts to the physical environment of each ḵwáan, including natural and man-made changes. Obviously, those communities that have experienced less environmental degradation (such as Yakutat and Angoon) would be assumed to have higher production levels. I do not attempt such a complex assessment here. Rather, environmental integrity is evaluated here only on the basis of direct impacts on community location, undoubtedly a central dimension of the productive environment. Communities that have maintained

TABLE 4.2. Contemporary Subsistence Production and Native Community Integrity

Present Village	Historic Territory	Environment	Native Population*	Subsistence Production**		
Rural Native Community	Ḵwáan	Traditional (precontact) Settlement	Percent Native / percent Tlingit speakers*	Percent of Households Harvesting Subsistence Resources	Percent of Households Using Subsistence Resources	Per Capita Harvest (lbs)
Angoon	Xutsnoowú	Yes	82 (11)	99	100	242
Haines	Jilḵoot	Yes	18 (1)	82	92	104
Hoonah	Xunaa	Yes	67 (5)	95	100	388
Hydaburg	Kaigani	Yes	89 (<1)	91	100	337
Kake	Ḵéex'	Yes	73 (5)	91	97	159

Klawock	*Hinyaa*	Yes	54 (2)	97	100	223
Klukwan	*Jilkaat*	Yes	87 (8)	95	100	239
Metlakatla	Tsimshian	No	83 (<1)	77	100	71
Saxman	*Sanyaa*	No	77 (1)	83	97	89
Sitka	*Sheet'ka*	Yes	21 (3)	88	88	146
Wrangell	*Shtax'heen*	Yes	20 (1)	80	95	164
Yakutat	*Yakwdaat*	Yes	50 (5)	98	100	369

* Native population data are from the U.S. Census, 2000–2002. Percentage of Tlingit speakers among Native populations calculated from figures supplied by Sealaska Heritage Institute, August 2005.

** Subsistence production data are from the *Tongass Resource Use Cooperative Survey* (TRUCS 1988). Figures are for 1987.

themselves at or near traditional settlement sites are considered to have a high degree of environmental integrity, while those that have been moved in the past century are not.

Finally, production itself is evaluated in terms of 1987 "subsistence production" levels, measuring community harvest and consumptive use of the most common fish, wildlife, and plant resources in Southeast Alaska. Needless to say, these levels represent but a fraction of traditional production, in most cases less than 20 percent of precontact harvest levels.[8] Nevertheless, subsistence production remains a significant sector of the economy, and the vast majority of subsistence resources are gathered locally, that is, within traditional ƙwáan territories associated with each community. Therefore, subsistence production levels are a good way to compare present productive relations to place across communities. In the modern context, subsistence production in excess of one-half pound per day, or 182 pounds a year, per capita is considered a high level of production.

By these criteria, Angoon, Hoonah, Hydaburg, Klawock, Klukwan, and Yakutat continue to have the most productive subsistence relations with their traditional environment. These communities also all have a high degree of environmental integrity and a high or moderate level of community integrity.[9] Another interesting pattern also emerges: those communities with a low degree of environmental integrity, Metlakatla and Saxman, correspondingly have the lowest levels of subsistence production (though each has a special set of circumstances: Metlakatla is a reservation with its own commercial fish traps—thus fewer households participate in harvests, but 100 percent use wild foods—and Saxman is a village within the larger city of Ketchikan). Those communities with high levels of subsistence production are also typically the most zealous in protecting their resource sites and their traditional subsistence patterns.

Though there is no time-allocation study comparable to Oberg's for contemporary subsistence communities, it is clear that substantially less time is allocated to these activities than in 1931 or before. The reduction of time commitments is a result of the consolidation of residence, increased regulation, increased efficiency in production, and a general lessening of dependence on subsistence foods, among other factors. This is not to say that every family's production level has dropped, but rather that most typically spend less time engaged in the process of harvesting and processing country foods. This, in turn, has typically led to an overall reduction in the duration of engagements with the places of production.

CONTEMPORARY SUBSISTENCE, RESISTANCE, AND THE ECOLOGICAL INDIAN

The struggles of Tlingit clans, house groups, and tribes to maintain their traditional productive ties to place are struggles not only of collectives but of extraordinary individuals as well. Herman Kitka (b. 1914) is one such individual. Through modern and traditional means of property law and resource stewardship, he has steadfastly maintained his family's land base and subsistence camp at Deep Bay. Recently, Mr. Kitka succeeded in gaining a 160-acre allotment, after nearly a century and three generations of jumping bureaucratic hurdles laid down by various federal agencies charged with administering and conveying these lands through the allotment program.

Although he became a very successful commercial fisherman and general contractor, Mr. Kitka continued to take care of Deep Bay, conserving and even enhancing its subsistence values. As shown, one way he did this was through indigenous aquaculture. More than a half century ago, using traditional ichthyological knowledge, Herman Kitka and his father Frank transplanted fall dog salmon from Excursion Inlet to Deep Bay in order to lengthen the subsistence-fishing season beyond the close of commercial fishing. Within several years a successful run of these late salmon was established, and the Kitkas and other families were able to fish for subsistence well into October, whereas previously the salmon runs were exhausted as early as August. Like the Deisheetaan in Sitkoh Bay, the Kitkas were motivated by a strong desire to continue their subsistence ties to sacred lands in the face of alienating changes wrought by the new industrial economy. In the Kitkas' case, participation in an ever-lengthening commercial fishing season had increasingly curtailed their opportunities to subsist at Deep Bay during the traditional peak runs. By transplanting the run of fall dog salmon, they revitalized this opportunity by creating a late fishery at Deep Bay that subsistence users could rely on after the commercial fishing season closed.

In addition, Herman Kitka has taken care to protect Deep Bay from ecological damage. One example of this was in the early 1990s when the U.S. Forest Service proposed to clear-cut tens of millions of board feet of timber in Deep Bay as part of its Ushk Bay timber sale. One alternative even included a road running right by Mr. Kitka's smokehouse. In July 1993 a public hearing was held in Sitka to take testimony on the proposed action and its potential impacts on subsistence. The event was extraordinary in that many people, Native and non-Native alike, came to testify not only about potential negative impacts of the timber sale but also about Herman Kitka's profound ties to Deep Bay and how they would be jeopardized by this action. It was moving to see how this recognition of the integrity of Herman Kitka's relationship with Deep Bay transcended cultural boundaries. Characteristically, when Herman rose to speak, he modestly chose not to emphasize his own family ties to Deep Bay but rather to stress the potential environmental destruction that would occur if the sale went forward and how this would hurt all users of the bay, including commercial, recreational, and subsistence groups. His assessment was based on a Native science, including his own systematic observations of the Deep Bay watershed over eight decades and traditional ecological knowledge that had been passed down from his father and grandfathers. This is part of what he said:

Deep Bay is a . . . very unique river; it's very sensitive to temperature. The river itself is not snow-fed, so if the Forest Service do some logging action in that area, I'm afraid if they warm up the streams, it will finish the run that's in there. To the commercial fisherman, it produces a lot of pink salmon. This last opening, three boats from Puget Sound got 8,000 humpies apiece in that area. This is the thing commercial fishermen going to lose. The river produces a lot of cohos. The stream is full of cohos in the fall and the culprit to the death of all salmon in streams is temperature. Some algae grows in the stream [if it's too warm], and the stream turns brown and everything that's in that stream—eggs, salmon, everything—dies. They float out without even spawning. . . . To log . . . [the bark] would destroy the King crab and the Dungeness that sportsmen and subsistence users come to Deep Bay to fish in the fall. When I'm there, they ask permission; even though I don't own the water, they come to my cabin and ask me if they could fish that King crab off the flats. I tell them, "Go ahead, I don't own it." These are the things I want to protect. I know the bark from the trees will destroy like it done in Poison Cove. . . . So I oppose any activity in Deep Bay. And this I'm going to stand firm on it, even if I have to go take action against the Forest Service on that activity they're planning there. I prefer that the Forest Service leave Deep Bay alone because the river is too sensitive. (Thornton 2000:84)

Fortunately, this story has a happy ending. The timber sale was put on hold and Deep Bay was not clear-cut logged or crosscut by roads. It remains a productive cultural and biological habitat because of conservation efforts spearheaded by a Tlingit leader committed to his ancestors' land.

At the same time, recent events at Deep Bay serve as a cautionary tale that highlights the limitations of present law to protect relationships between traditional Tlingit social groups and their sacred landscapes. As well, it underscores the need for contemporary Tlingit leaders like Mr. Kitka, who know and use the land and resources, to continue their struggles to "take care of the land" in the face of incursions, so as not to "diminish its generosity" (Soboleff 1992). This is what it means to be an ecological Indian in the postcolonial age.

The image of the ecological Indian has been under attack of late, however. Some critics (e.g., Krech 1999) have sought to explode the image as a distortion, if not complete mischaracterization, of Indian environmental relations, highlighting evidence of profligacy and resource depletion in the historical and archeological record to make their case. Unfortunately, much of this literature suffers from selective historicizing, weak theorizing, and unrealistic expectations. A recent study of Tlingit bird-egg harvesting in Glacier Bay (Hunn et al. 2003) rebuts the critique of the ecological Indian, in part based on strong data showing a wide range of Tlingit resource practices to be conservation oriented. But successful conservation depends on a range of variables beyond ideology, such as whether or not the resource in question is *depletable* and under the group's *effective control* (see also Berkes 1999:110; Smith and Wishnie 2000). As the record clearly shows, salmon were both depletable—aboriginal peoples of the Northwest Coast had weir and trap technologies to exploit salmon for some four thousand years—and under Native effective control, until that control was wrested from them by non-Native private and state interests in the name of common property, with disastrous results. In Deep Bay, where Tlingit territorial control over the river and knowledge of its salmon stocks were maintained comparatively well through cultural and practical means, deliberate conservation techniques developed to insure adequate fish stocks and productive habitat. Herman Kitka and his father employed such techniques in their successive roles as *héen s'áati* (stream master or river keeper), taking care of Deep Bay. Unfortunately, in recent years not all streams in Tlingit country have had such stern river keepers. Resource managers would do well to keep the Tlingit model of "taking care" of places in mind in developing future watershed conservation regimes.

CONCLUSION: THE CONSUBSTANTIAL ACT OF PRODUCTION

This chapter has stressed the importance of production in Tlingit senses of place. As a fundamental element of experience, production—the paths and projects pursued in nourishing and sustaining human life—is central to the process of perceiving and conceptualizing the landscape. Subsistence production especially (as opposed to commercial production for markets) was celebrated as communion with place, consummated in particular locales, seasons, and social milieus. The connections between production, identity, and being were everywhere reinforced. Far from being drudgery, traditional Tlingit production was conceived as having a sacramental quality in that projects were performed in a recurring sacred context, on the same lands and along the same paths as those of one's ancestors, whose spirits still dwell there. At the same time, detailed knowledge of the history and ecology of specific environments facilitated subsistence production and engendered feelings of comfort and topophilia. To a very large degree these interactive contexts, as much as some innate "power" of place, are what made such locales "sacred" sites—fundamental components of identity and being worthy of protection, stewardship, and honor. This fact, unfortunately, has seldom been recognized in the conventional defining of sacred sites or in their "preservation," the latter commonly being achieved by outlawing harvesting activities on sacred sites (cf. Stoffle and Evans 1990; Kelley and Francis 1994; Gulliford 2000).

Tlingit relationships with place have been altered by changes in the demographic, social, and technological relations of production. Competition for resources, dispossession of lands, regulatory encroachments, and other impacts have made resource harvesting activities more fragmented and fleeting. Though subsistence production is still a vital component of the annual cycle, levels of production and especially time allocations toward productive activities have dropped. Changes in the technological and social relations of production have similarly had the effect of disembedding people from traditional places of production. A contemporary assessment of production shows that communities with a high degree of environmental, community, and linguistic integrity generally have the highest levels of production and, correspondingly, a strong sense of place.

This integrity resonates especially in individuals, like Fred Friday and Herman Kitka, who maintain productive ties to their traditional lands and attend to their conservation ecology. Through productive engagement, valuable aspects of culture, language, and environment are conserved, and understanding of *ecological* linguistics is enhanced, as the mapping and exegesis of the Aak'wtaatseen Salmon Boy story in the last chapter revealed. Without the synesthetic, experiential understanding of the land that comes through living on it, stories and TEK tend to become disembedded from place and one's understanding of the ecological wisdom they contain is diminished. Robert Bringhurst (2002:21) makes this point forcefully in an essay on ecological linguistics:

Oral culture means much more and less than simply talking. Rekindling oral culture means rejoining the community of speaking beings—sandhill cranes, whitebark pines, coyotes, wood frogs, bees and thunder [and, one might add, salmon].

Oral culture also means much more than telling stories. It means learning how to hear them, how to nourish them, and how to let them live. It means learning to let stories swim down into yourself, grow large in there and rise back up again. It does not—repeat, does not—mean memorizing the lines so you can act the script you've written or recite the book you've read . . .

If you embody an oral culture, you are a working part of a place, a part of the soil in which stories live their lives.

Herman Kitka, who remains very much "a working part of a place," makes the same point in his own way: "If I ever lost sight of how to put up our customary cultural food, I don't think the stories they told me at those camps would ever stay alive. Because when I testify for our people on subsistence it all comes back to that—what our old people used to tell us" (Thornton 2000:85).

5 RITUAL AS EMPLACEMENT

The Potlatch / *Ku.éex'*

Tleil dagák' ahawateeni yík [Don't leave insulted like those little sockeyes].
—Ritual oratory of Sitka Tlingits (HERMAN KITKA SR.)

On ritual occasions such as the memorial potlatch, or *ku.éex'*, Sitka
Tlingits sometimes distinguish themselves as magnanimous, emplaced
hosts by regaling guests with this aphorism: *Tleil dagák' ahawateeni
yík*, or "Don't leave insulted like those little sockeyes." It is a humble
way of saying to guests from the opposite moiety, "I hope I have not
offended you," or "I hope I have treated you with respect so that you
will return." In effect, "It means they [the hosts] want them [the guests]
back at the next gathering," according to Herman Kitka. But without
some knowledge of Sheet'ka Ḵwáan as a place, the aphorism's meaning is hardly transparent. This is because it is rooted in an ecological
fact unique to Sitka: the presence and disappearance of a species of small
sockeye salmon known as *dagák'*.

These little sockeye, which Tlingits differentiate from regular sockeye
(*gaat*) with a separate lexeme (unlike Western science, which lumps them
under one species), are found only in Sitka territory, presently just in
Necker Bay, known as *Dagák' Ḡeeyí* (Little Sockeye Bay) in Tlingit. In
the past, the little sockeye attempted to populate several other streams
in the area, including ones in Silver Bay (Green Lake), Shamrock Bay,
and Suloia Bay; however, their presence in these streams was disrupted
by humans. In the case of the creek at Green Lake, known as *Dagák'
Ahawateeni Héen* (Little Sockeyes Left the Creek), local Tlingits failed
to provide escapement for the run of sockeye, instead blocking the whole
creek with their weir. As a result, the sockeye became insulted and left,
never to return to that stream. According to Herman Kitka, "Those lit-

tle sockeye get offended if you don't leave them a hole in your [fish] weir; they won't come back if it [the stream] is all blocked off." Thus, this unique bit of traditional ecological knowledge and wisdom becomes immortalized in a place-name, embodied in ritual oratory as a metaphor of social relations, and encoded as a moral-ecological principle regarding escapement and conservation of salmon in a particular fishery. In its ecological context, it speaks volumes about the particular character of Sitka Tlingit country; in its ceremonial use it speaks volumes about the character of the Tlingit hosts. They have learned an important moral and ecological lesson through the fate of the little sockeye, just as they did through the fate of the salmon boy, and seek to apply it in the realm of social relations.

RITUAL AS AN EMPLACEMENT SUPERSTRUCTURE

Ritual is perhaps the ultimate human emplacement structure. More than any other human institution, ritual reflects and shapes the order of things. In ritual the cognitive, social, and material elements of human existence are combined and fused in powerful, participatory, and symbolic means. The ordinary existential constraints of time and space and corporeal existence are superseded, transcended, and reordered—literally re-placed—to mark and achieve important transformations in society and nature. As Roy Rappaport (1999:164) states, "There is in ritual not only a representation of creation, but a re-creation of the primordial order, the primordial union of form and substance which forever comes apart as the usages of life depart from the order that should be." In the primordial order of ritual, people are brought together in a communal place, often an ancestral landscape or place, where *communitas* prevails (Turner 1969), and, ideally, guests—human and other—never leave insulted like those little sockeye.

The memorial potlatch, which traditionally marked the (approximately one-year) anniversary of the death of a prominent individual (an *aanyádi*, or aristocrat) and the distribution of the deceased's *at.óow* to successors, was and remains the most important public venue for configuring *shagóon* (see Kan 1989). Here, the immortality and primacy of the social structure are celebrated and substantiated through the

FIG. 5.1. A rock in the river. Ties to sacred sites are celebrated in Tlingit art as *at.óow* (owned things). This Chilkat blanket (known as *Yaaw Teiyí Naaxein,* or Herring Rock Robe), woven from mountain goat wool and cedar bark and worn by the late Sitka Kiks.ádi leader Al Perkins, features Herring Rock *(Yaaw Teiyí),* the site where Kiks.ádi ancestors learned to harvest herring roe and where a woman was turned into an owl for selfishly harvesting too much. The carved wooden hat represents a frog, the main crest of Kiks.adi, at Indian River *(Kasdahéen,* Man's Stream), for it was the frog people who led the Kiks.adi to settle by the Indian River in Sitka. Donning this regalia and displaying it as *at.óow* in ritual integrates personhood into place and place into personhood in a way that Tlingits still celebrate. Photo by T. Thornton

liturgical ordering of time and space wherein matrilineal ancestors' spirits (and landscapes) are invoked and made present and their material and symbolic possessions (*at.óow*) transferred to, literally re-placed upon, new ranks of living matrikin. Here, too, notions about the ideal Tlingit person as a thoroughly emplaced, knowledgeable, heavy, *at.óow*-laden, pure, and rocklike "high-class" person are celebrated, reconfirmed, and naturalized as part of the ethnogeographic order (see fig. 5.1). Finally, here, too, subsistence foods are linked eternally and consubstantially with ancestral spirits, social identity, and sacred lands to forge a profound sense of participants' place and being in the world. In short, memorial potlatches create a setting, that is, a place or a superstructure, for all of the cultural structures that have been examined—social organization and property (*at.óow*), cognition and language (ritual oratory and iconography), and economic production (subsistence foods and gifts)—to interact in a powerful nexus of maintenance and exchange, gathering and redistribution, and conservation and succession. The potlatch constitutes not only a "total social phenomenon" (Mauss 1967; Kan 1989) but also a cosmic one, a phenomenon wherein the *Logos*, defined by Rappaport (1999:218–19) as the "all encompassing rational order uniting nature, society, individual humans and divinity into a 'great cosmos' . . . which is eternal, true, moral, and in some sense harmonious," is consummated and given blessing (*laxeitl*) and strength (*latseen*).

This chapter examines more closely the three emplacement structures in action within the *ḵu.éex'*, or potlatch ritual.

SOCIAL STRUCTURE IN RITUAL

Social structure defines and places ritual participants according to their nested layers of identity (nation, moiety, ḵwáan, clan, house, and person) and collective *shagóon*. Moieties form the reciprocal exchange partners in ritual. In the memorial potlatch, the host clan (or clans), bolstered by moiety affiliates, honors and regales guests, and guest clans respond as the opposite side, the "outer shell" (*ax daakanóox'u*) or "container" (*daakeidí*), to validate, substantiate, and make whole the host's prerogatives, *at.óow*, and *shagóon*. In the funerary services held a year or more prior to the memorial party, the opposites "handled the deceased's polluted outside [body], allowing the mourners to concentrate on his pure inside, i.e., those aspects of his total social person that were immortal and derived from his matrilineal group's *shagóon*" (Kan 1989:52–53). The opposites also comforted the deceased's kin with gifts and speeches of condolence, bolstered by their own *shagóon* and *at.óow*, elements of which are offered as support to those in grief. This condolence oratory remains a powerful feature of the memorial potlatch.

Though today many rituals are staged in larger venues, the ritual space of the memorial ḵu.éex' was traditionally the clan house (or *hít*), itself a manifestation of the social body and its *shagóon*. The homology between the social body and the clan house, including links between the eight major joints in the house frame and the eight major long, jointed bones of the body, has been remarked on by Kan (1989:51). Along with its "bones" the house also contains major *at.óow*, including crest objects, which become the face and expressive force of the social group in ritual. In this embodied ritual landscape, each moiety, clan, house group, and ranked member has a place, reflecting both the symmetry of the opposing host-guest moieties and the asymmetry of social rank.

In this way the ritual space aligns and sanctifies the social structure as an emplacing force. The Logos of s*hagóon* as community, heritage, and destiny is made tangible by the presencing of ancestral spirits and sacred landscapes through *at.óow*. In the most poignant moments of ritual, the ancestors and the land may present themselves as one, as in the following lines from a L'uknaẖ.ádi mourning song, composed by Dry Bay Chief George for a memorial potlatch (de Laguna 1972, 3:1164): "When I look out at the mountains of my grandfather's land, I imagine that my grandfathers are still alive," meaning "he sees a big rock standing up, just like a man walking, just as though his grandfathers had all come alive and were walking across from the other side of the bay." In combination with the embodying architecture of the clan house, the homology between land, ancestors, and the living social body framed in oratory, song, and other *at.óow* serve as a powerful vehicle for emplacing social group members, as well as for bolstering them in times of stress, thus insuring their continued well-being in the world. Indeed Tlingit phenomenology and eschatology contrast the relative immortality of ancestors as rock with the fragile mortality of human life as leaf: "Raven tried to make them [humans] out of a rock and a leaf at the same time, but the rock was slow while the leaf was very quick. Therefore human beings came from the leaf. . . . That is why there is death in the world. . . . Years ago people used to say when they were getting old, 'We are unfortunate in not having been made from a rock. Being made from a leaf, we must die'" (Swanton 1909:81; see also Kan 1989:57–58). Of course, the organic and perennial qualities of the leaf also imply renewal and reincarnation, another goal of the memorial potlatch.

The late Lukaax̱.ádi leader Austin Hammond, *Daanaawáak̲*, once defined *haa* (our) *shagóon* as "what we are now, what we have been since the beginning, and everything that our children must become" (Kawaky 1981). Ritual consummates this being and becoming by enacting and affirming what Tlingit social groups have been since the beginning, who they are now, and what their descendants must become. This is why the names and property of the deceased are brought forth and passed on in the eternal, timeless frame of the memorial potlatch. The ritual forges *shagóon* through *at.óow* as an inalienable and indissoluble component of identity through naming. Significantly, the most literal gloss of *shagóon* is "head bridge," most likely an anatomical reference to the atlas bone that connects the head to the spine and body.[1] The link between the common use of the term to refer to heritage and destiny, on the one hand, and the more literal anatomical reference, on the other, resides in the metaphoric connections between the individual and the larger social body and physical landscape. These connections and symmetries are made explicit and substantial through the process of ritual.

But so, too, are the asymmetries made clear. Drawing on Bourdieu's (1977) theory of practice, Kan (1989:290) emphasizes that those aristocratic matrikin who were the custodians and controllers of their matrilineal relatives' *at.óow* and *shagóon* strategically used the hallowed structure of ritual to legitimize their dominant role in society: "Because they controlled much of *shagóon*, the *aanyátx'i* [children of the land] appeared to be the ancestors' mouthpieces. . . . Thus, their coercion of their lower-ranking matrikin was exercised not through brute force but mainly through "symbolic violence," i.e., oratory and other forms of ritual/symbolic action. . . . The hierarchical nature of this society was linked to and reinforced by the formalized language and ritual, so prominent in Tlingit life." By couching strategic political acts in the culturally reified and empathetic formats of ritual language and action, such as oratory, song, dance, cooperative feasts, and gift giving, members of the dominant strata could not only demonstrate their status and influence but also raise and expand it in Big Man–like fashion (see also Boelscher 1989).

Yet, as Kan and others (see de Laguna 1972, 2:606-51; Dauenhauer and Dauenhauer 1990) demonstrate, this framework of interpreting the potlatch as primarily about politics and rivalry is too limited. Kan (1989:272) suggests that "it would be a mistake . . . to see the potlatch rhetoric of love and respect for the dead and the living participants as only a mask hiding the brute facts of power, inequality, and competition." Indeed the ritual format can just as easily be seen as an institutional check on the worst forms of domination and self-aggrandizement, and other sociopolitical and even emotional excesses. Olson (1956:686) emphasized that in ceremonies, as elsewhere, "character [*shagóon*] was channeled to harmonize with the most important social group, the clan, and for most individuals the participation which they experienced was rewarding and satisfying." In sum, the potlatch and other ceremonies offered ample room for individuals to realize the Logos of social character and *shagóon* for collective and personal ends and also to extend and shape it in new and positive ways that were consonant with clan and individual interests and often transcended them.

One powerful means of extending and reconfiguring the social order was by using the transcendent capacity of ritual to create what I term "linking landscapes" to overcome social group distance, physically, emotionally, and spiritually. A linking landscape is a terrain of the imagination, based on a geographic landscape, that is designed to bring people together. In making ancestral spirits and landscapes present in ritual space, ritual participants within this extraordinary setting could link with one another in *communitas*, as a unified whole. Often this was consummated by invoking historical sites of cohabitation as linking landscapes for clans now separated, and then celebrating their unity in those places. Thus phrases like *Ch'a Tleix' Kax̱'nuwḵweidí* (We who are still one People of Grouse Fort), *Ch'a Tleix' Xakwnukeidí* (We who are still one People of *Xakwnoowú*), or *Ch'a Tleix' Shangukeidí* (We who are still one People of *Shank'w*) served to re-emplace matrikin now separated in time and space in the original, ancestral dwelling places they shared, so as to foster feelings of continued solidarity and harmonious dwelling.

The best of Tlingit oratory and ritual action is filled with linking land-scapes brought forth to promote solidarity, sharing, remembering, com-passion, peace, healing, and other social, political, intellectual, material, and emotional ends. The form and character of condolence speeches have been explored in some depth by Dauenhauer (1975), Dauenhauer and Dauenhauer (1990), and Kan (1983, 1989), so here I emphasize only the role of place in this genre. Specifically, I examine the rhetorical construction of a speech for the removal of grief, which was given by T'akdeintaan clan mother (*Naa Tláa*) Jessie Dalton and has been carefully translated and annotated by the Dauenhauers (1990:243–57, 385–97).

Jessie Dalton's oration was delivered at an October 1968 memorial party for Jim Marks, a member of the Chookaneidí clan of the Eagle moiety and a child of the Lukaax.ádi clan of the Raven moiety, who died in October 1967. Mrs. Dalton was chosen to make the central speech in the "removal of grief" portion of the ceremony in part because of her social position as an elder and clan mother (head of the T'akdein-taan women, collectively known as the *K̲'eik̲'w Shaa*, or "Seagull [Kit-tiwake] Ladies") with ties to both hosts and guests, but also because of her outstanding individual character as a compassionate person and skilled orator. As the Dauenhauers (1990:81) explain:

> An orator such as Jessie Dalton is selected to speak because of his or her sensitivity, and the orator is compared in Tlingit to someone who brings a very long pole into a house. In handling words, as in handling a pole, a speaker must be careful not to strike or hit anyone's face, or to break anything by accident. Referring to oratory during an interview, her own words were, "It is difficult to speak to someone who is respected. It is very difficult." Deliv-ered carelessly, words can be dangerous and detrimental. But when deliv-ered carefully, oratory can be a soothing medicine, a healing power and balm to one who is in pain. It can give spiritual strength. In Tlingit one says, *k̲aa toowú kei altseench*, "people gain spiritual strength from it," or *toowú lat-seen k̲aa jeex̲ atee*, "it gives strength to the spirit." The effect of words in a good speech is described as *yándei kdusyaa yáx̲ yatee du yoo x̲'atángi*, "his words were like cloth being gently spread out on a flat service."

FIG. 5.2. *K̲'eik̲'w X'óow* (Black-Legged Kittiwake Blanket) refers to a sacred geographic site of the T'ak̲deintaan clan known as *G̲aanax̲áa* and is the central *at.óow* and key feature in the linking landscape employed by Jessie Dalton in her speech for the removal of grief at a 1968 memorial potlatch. Photo by R. Dauenhauer

Alternatively, a well-delivered oration may also be seen as a "supportive wedge" or bridge linking two things—the past and the future (*shagóon*), the living and the dead, the grievers and the consolers, the hosts and the guests, and so on. In this respect, Tlingits often characterize successful oratory as "imitating their ancestors," as a realization of their *shagóon*.

Jessie Dalton's speech builds on *at.óow* worn by her clansmen, some of which have been referenced by earlier speakers. A button blanket, *K̲'eik̲'w X'óow* (Black-Legged Kittiwake Blanket; see fig. 5.2), commemorating an ancestral T'ak̲deintaan settlement located by a prominent rock outcropping and kittiwake rookery named *G̲aanax̲áa* on the outer coast of Glacier Bay National Park, becomes the central encapsulating image in the linking landscape that she lays out to clothe her hosts and aid in the removal of their grief.[2] After invoking the central and supporting *at.óow* and the ancestral spirits they represent, Jessie

Ritual as Emplacement 181

Dalton transports her listeners to the landscape at _Gaanaxáa_ for the purpose of healing:

K̲'eik̲'w X'óow
Yes . . .
A person who is feeling like you
Would be brought by canoe,
yes,
to your father's point,
Gaanaxáa.
That is when
the name would be called out, it is said,
of the person who is feeling grief.
Yes.
    (In Dauenhauer and Dauenhauer 1990:245–47)

She completes the setting with references to other _at.óow_, which are similarly tied to T'ak̲deintaan land and _shagóon_ and also "show their faces" at _Gaanaxáa_, before she consummates the image of the healing landscape by recalling the consoling acts of her ancestors, the kittiwakes— referenced here as "your father's sisters"—to embrace the hosts of the opposite moiety (whose grateful responses are included in the excerpt)— at this sacred site.

These terns [kittiwakes]
Your father's sisters would fly out over the person
who is feeling grief.
    (Willie Marks) _Áawé._
Then
they would let down fall
like snow
over the person who is feeling grief.
    (George Dalton) _Your brother' children are listening to you._
    (Harry Marvin) _Thank you._
That's when their down
isn't felt.
That's when

I feel it's as if your fathers' sisters are flying
back to their nests
with your grief.
    (Harry Marvin) *Thank you indeed.*
(250–51)

Thus, in the climax of Jessie Dalton's oratorical-linking landscape for the removal of grief, the sacred _k̲'eik̲'w_ literally cushion and absorb her host relatives' sadness and tears with their downy feathers and carry away their grief back to their nests at _G̲aanax̲áa._ She follows this with an extensive genealogical catalog of the bereaved hosts, whom she identifies, like the kittiwakes, by name and appropriate kin term, before ending with a reference to another *at.óow* representing a mountain pass (_G̲éelak'w_) near _G̲aanax̲áa_ from which the ancestors also "reveal their faces." In completing the genealogical catalog of relatives, as with the inventory of *at.óow* and sacred geography, Jessie Dalton effectively transcends or bridges the divisions of social groups just as she transcends the divisions of time, space, and body in transporting her audience to the spiritual landscape of her ancestors at _G̲aanax̲áa._ At the same time she reinforces the homologous linkages between the sociological landscape of those present at the memorial and the spiritual, temporal, and geographical healing landscape that she has fashioned through her skillful oratory and mediation of *at.óow.* _G̲aanax̲áa_ and other linking landscapes, then, serve as chronotopic touchstones of communal significance, endurance, and strength on the land.

The powerful embracing and emplacing effect of Jessie Dalton's oratory in combination with her invocation and mediation of *at.óow* and ancestral landscapes is nicely summed up by the Dauenhauers (1990:96):

> All of these at.óow capsulize the history of the T'ak̲deintaan people and others in the community to whom they are related. They anchor the people in place (Gaanax̲áa, G̲éelákw, Mt. Fairweather), recall physical and spiritual events that happened on the land (the Tern [Kittiwake] Blanket, the Mt. People's Dog Hat, etc.), and remember the ancestors to whom things happened and to whom the at.óow belonged. By focusing on an at.óow while addressing the people present, the speaker metaphorically conveys her listeners to the place the at.óow represents and gathers them among the ancestors and spir-

its who are there. The community is thus made complete: its members are together. Jessie Dalton does this when she focuses on the G̲aanax̲áa Blanket, which she turns to first. Through this blanket, physically present in the room, she will eventually bring all of the living people present, as well as the spirits of the human departed, and various other disembodied spirit powers, to the rookery at G̲aanax̲áa. This at.óow (The blanket and the design on it) becomes the place to which the speaker gathers people, both physically and spiritually. In all of this, we are reminded of the serious word play in English: the connection of the words "heal," "whole," and "holy," and of the words "re-member" and "remember."

Beyond the skillful mediation of word, image, and place, the beauty of this kind of oratory is that it both requires and engenders individual and social character as *shagóon*. One learns what it means to be human, to be Tlingit, to be T'ak̲deintaan, as well as to be grief stricken, to possess *at.óow*, and to be possessed by *shagóon*. With hardly a reference to "I," one also learns what it means to be Jessie Dalton, a clan mother and orator with particular relationships and responsibilities, who must rise to the occasion and weave a healing, linking landscape into being with her own traditional knowledge and the materials (words, people, *at.óow*, *shagóon*, etc.) at hand. Furthermore, one sees that she must commence the speech from her own location—her own place in Tlingit geography and social structure—but also transcend those structures in meaningful ways through words and images that inspire and move the assembly to new horizons of insight and terrains of being. For *k̲u.éex'* participants, such oratory can truly be a blessing, for *toowú latseen k̲aa jeex̲ atee*, "it gives strength to the spirit."

FOODWAYS AS A FORCE IN RITUAL EMPLACEMENT

The unique Logos and locus of ritual is further consummated by the communal harvest, preparation, and consumption of foods from ancestral lands. Herman Kitka observes,

Everything stems back, all of our religion stems to the use of the cultural foods. No memorial party is ever given without each clan bringing all their

Native dishes together. You see, the Eagle clan [moiety] is a large group, different clans, different houses, they have different names. But they all live under one, the Eagle clan. So when the Eagle clan [or] any member is giving a party, the whole works come and join. The Ravens did the same thing. It's a community affair. And they make sure everything is the cultural food prepared the old way at this memorial party.

In the memorial potlatch, both the living and the deceased are treated to subsistence foods—*their* foods of place and being. And the links between sustenance, spirit, and place are alluded to, if not made explicit, in the context of the ritual.

This was brought home to me in the mid-1990s, when I attended a ceremonial gathering in Hoonah to which Glacier Bay National Park personnel and a few "higher-ups" from the National Park Service in Washington, D.C. (including the assistant secretary of Interior for Fish, Wildlife and Parks), were invited and cultural foods, including harbor seal meat, were served. A rumor began to circulate that this seal was "especially good" and "must have come from Glacier Bay." When it reached the Park Service table, I remember one of the higher-ups momentarily blanching aghast upon learning this news, before recomposing himself and resuming his repast in assiduous avoidance of the seal meat. Then I noticed how many other Tlingits, having heard the same rumor, also were looking curiously at the same Park Service official. I never could verify whether the rumor was true, but that did not detract from its value as a statement about who the Huna Tlingit are and how they see and value Glacier Bay, where harbor seal thrive and have been hunted by Natives for centuries. Park Service personnel, however, were shocked and embarrassed to learn that they might be consuming the meat of an animal they are charged with protecting. Only a year or so before this, park rangers had cited a Tlingit hunter for killing a seal within the park in violation of federal regulations. This act evoked a strong negative response from the Tlingit community, especially because the seal, which was confiscated, had been designated for a memorial potlatch in honor of a descendant of Glacier Bay. The hosts had to apologize for its absence and felt bad that this important consubstantial link with their homeland had been taken away.

Why did it have to be a Glacier Bay harbor seal and not one from elsewhere in the clan and or ḵwáan territory? Perhaps it did not have to be, as accommodations are often made in ritual as in other spheres of life. But when the Logos of ritual is understood as all encompassing and emplacing order, one can see why it would have been ideal for the Glacier Bay descendant to be honored in his memorial with a Glacier Bay seal, especially one from his old hunting territory. When I asked Huna Kaagwaantaan elder Frank White why it is important to have food from Glacier Bay at a memorial for a Glacier Bay descendant, he gave this response: "It's hard to explain, but Glacier Bay foods are . . . special. At a party [potlatch] we like to serve [gull] eggs, salmon, seal, and berries from there not just 'cause they taste the best, but 'cause they're part of who we are. It makes us feel good. . . . Even the deceased is fed this food to make him feel good and guide him on his journey. . . . The spirits of our ancestors are in Glacier Bay. And when we're there subsisting, we feel them." In this context one can see how subsistence becomes a sacred act of emplacement not just in the consumption and distribution phases of the ritual but also in the production phase, in the act of harvesting itself.

As Frank White makes clear, when subsisting on your own land, you can "feel" the ancestors. This is one reason why the spirits of the ancestors, as elements of the landscape, are given offerings by relatives seeking to hunt, fish, or gather on ancestral lands, and why their blessings, like the blessings of other nonhuman persons on the land (e.g., bears, mountains, glaciers), are sought. Such connections can be especially powerful when one is visiting the hunting territory of a recently deceased clan member, as was true in the case of Greg Brown, the Hoonah seal hunter who was prosecuted by the Park Service. He was hunting on Chookaneidí ancestral lands and at a particular hunting site used for generations by Huna seal hunters, including his uncle, who had successfully instructed his nephew on the significance of the site and on how to use the site to hunt seal accurately and effectively (i.e., without striking and losing them), just prior to the run-in with park officials. If Greg Brown's seal had made it to the potlatch it would have been recognized as a Glacier Bay seal, a gift from Chookaneidí traditional cultural property, land that still provides sustenance, where the memories and spirits of ancestors still dwell and where younger hunters like Greg Brown follow in their elders' footsteps. In short, it would have been recognized as a beautiful act, pregnant with symbolic as well as material significance, exquisite in its balance and symmetry.

In the context of the potlatch the seal also would have given special comfort to the deceased. For the ancestors can feel the nourishment and comfort of foods (and other gifts, such as blankets) bestowed upon them (and other guests) as part of the ritual. Such gifts from the homeland help to guide and sustain the deceased on their arduous journey to the land of the dead (*daganḵú*, "inland from water to shore," or *s'igeeḵáawu aaní*, "land of the deceased"; see Kan 1989:115), where they will continue to dwell and be sustained by future offerings of living matrikin. This is a matter of reciprocity and respect toward the ancestors and their eternal presence on the land, which continues to nourish and sustain the people. In this context, it is sometimes said of both human and nonhuman inhabitants of the cosmos, *At yaa aya goonei* (Whatever it may be as a whole, it also has a face, and thus a spirit). Thus, the deceased and sentient features of the ancestral landscapes were themselves respected and vital participants in the memorial potlatch rather than mere impersonal forces of emplacement. Together with the human hosts and guests, they formed a covenant. Accordingly, if the covenant were violated they would feel disrespected and might disrupt the proceedings, withdraw their support, or depart the venue insulted and never to return, like those little sockeye at *Dagák' Ahawateeni Héen*.

CONCLUSION

Highlighting the all-important memorial potlatch, or *ḵu.éex'*, this chapter has demonstrated how the three fundamental structures of emplacement—social organization, language and symbol, and subsistence production of food—dynamically combine in ritual to integrate person and place in profound social, cognitive, and material ways. Building on Mauss, one might describe the potlatch not only as a "total social phenomenon" but as a *total emplacement phenomenon*. With these emplacement structures potently aligned in the potlatch, ritual participants could not help but feel the powerful embrace of their social networks, their ancestry, and their land. The *longue durée* of Tlingit webs of existence in places became in ritual a controlling force that could be gathered to transcend the limits of everyday life and link people in powerful new ways.

Unfortunately, as with social structure, language, and economic production, there have been substantial changes in the Tlingit potlatch in the postcontact era, particularly in the past one hundred years. As Tlingit social structure has become overlayered, weakened, and stretched; Tlingit language, ritual oratory, and metaphysics undermined, diluted, and threatened; and Tlingit food production increasingly attenuated, regulated, and alienated from traditional places and social milieus, the ability of these structural forces to magnificently fuse in ritual likewise has been diminished. And yet they do continue to potently combine in ritual. For, just as Howard Morphy (1995:204) points out for the Yolngu, "in reality places are continually being formed into sets," and "the presentation in ceremonies of these new orders of relationship between ancestral past and social group is public confirmation of their existence."

The memorial potlatch remains the central ceremonial setting for the emplacement of twenty-first-century Tlingits. What is more, the number of ku.éex' scheduled each year is increasing, as are the number of attendees. Each fall and winter dozens of memorials are staged involving thousands of Tlingit and non-Tlingit participants and hundreds of thousands of dollars' worth of food and other gifts. In addition, movements in recent decades to revitalize language and culture, to protect subsistence foodways, and to repatriate (with the aid of NAGPRA, the Native American Graves Protection and Repatriation Act of 1990) sacred at.óow have placed renewed emphasis on making use of these vehicles of cultural expression and Logos in the context of ritual. Accordingly, as Tlingit senses of place are continually being reconfigured in new constellations of relationships, Tlingit ritual continues to answer, forcefully, questions of how Tlingits belong to places and how ancestral places continue to define their identity, community, and cosmos.

6 CONCLUSION

Toward an Anthropology of Place

Our history and our personal connections to the land are out there waiting for each of us. —ALBERT (SONNY) MCHALSIE

This study began with Gabriel George's statement that "these lands are vital not only to our subsistence, but also to our sense of being as Tlingit people." Accepting this autoethnographic thesis, this project has been an attempt to examine what cultural institutions most profoundly shape Tlingit senses of being and place. Defining place as a combination of three crucial elements—time, space, and experience—four major structuring institutions were identified as being especially influential and revelatory in forging Tlingit senses of place: social organization, language and cognition, material production, and ritual. In each case, I have analyzed how these evolving structures and elements of place intersect at the level of individuals and social groups to create distinctively Tlingit senses of being in place.

If one accepts that places mark the intersection and fusing of space, time, and experience, one can appreciate, with Aristotle, their ontological and epistemological authority. It is, indeed, impossible to talk of space without envisioning a concrete place as a point of departure. Each person conceptualizes places in unique ways according to his or her knowledge and experience. Part of that knowledge and experience is shared, but one's individual sum total is unique. How memory, experience, and one's sense of being become inextricably linked to places depends on a person's particular time-space biography and the cultural structures that configure that biography in relation to places real and imagined, earthly and cosmic.

In his marvelous study *Wisdom Sits in Places: Language and Land-*

scape among the Western Apache, Keith Basso (1996:148) observes that the exploration of cultural senses of place should begin not

> solely for the purpose of enlarging our knowledge of particular social groups. For as surely as place is an elemental existential fact, sense of place is a universal genre of experience, and therefore, as more and more work gets done, it may be found to exhibit transcultural qualities. . . . Ubiquitously accepted as natural, normal, and unexceptional, sense of place is variously trained, variably intense, and having grown to mature proportions, stoutly resistant to change. Its complex affinities are more an expression of community involvement than they are of pure geography, and its social and moral force may reach sacramental proportions, especially when fused with prominent elements of personal and ethnic identity.

I have argued that Tlingit geography and senses of place, particularly knowledge and experience of named places and the stories behind them, form an important basis for the development and interpretation of Tlingit individual and social character and identity. Like Aristotle and the Apache, Tlingits recognize the primacy and revelatory logic of places and their vessel-like qualities as containers of wealth and wisdom. Thus, geographic knowledge and experience go hand in hand with Tlingit social (*at.óow, shagóon, shuká*), linguistic (place-names, stories), ecological (TEK, subsistence), and ritual (protocol, oratory, dance) knowledge and experience to support Tlingit being in the world. Moreover, although the place-making dynamics of Tlingit social organization, linguistics, production, and ritual are unique, the structures themselves are transcultural and seem central to forging place connections of "sacramental proportions" between personal, social, and ethnic identity across cultures.

Indeed, comparative evidence suggests that social, linguistic, economic, and ritual structures are vitally important vehicles for place making among indigenous peoples from the Americas to Eurasia to Africa to Oceania, and even for immigrant and diasporic peoples no longer tied to their original lands, who must continue to make individual and communal sense or their place(s) in this world. Everywhere, these structures make some places, some pasts, some beings, and some products more salient, more memorable, more integral, and more organic to one's

heritage and destiny than others. And yet they all respond to a fundamental human need to have meaningful places in this world.

What happens when these cultural structures of place making
become altered, break down, or lose their original ties to geographic
places? Clearly, vital senses of place begin to be lost. As seen in the Salmon
Boy story, when indigenous place-names and other "ecological linguistics" become decoupled from the story, when the story becomes
increasingly detached from the subsistence and experience of dwelling
in place, critical aspects of its meaning may become obscured, generalized, or abstracted. Perhaps only the basic plot, or the moral of the
story, remains. The problem is particularly acute among people who
have been dispossessed of their land, as James Weiner (2001:243) emphasizes in the Australian indigene context: "Anthropologists who have
worked in Australia will attest that what is lost in the first instance as
a result of dispossession is knowledge of places. What is apparently
retained for a much longer period is knowledge of the songs and the
stories associated with these places. What people lose is the relationship between the stories and the particular portion of the ground."
Alternatively, if a story can be unpacked—as was done with the Deikeenaak'w's Salmon Boy story in Sitka—with culture bearers who know
the names, geography, history, language, and lessons of place, then the
story resonates much deeper and in many more ways. It remains "alive
in the eddy" rather than atrophying into a "moldy end," out of place.
Ultimately, a healthy sense of place requires participatory engagement in
the plots, characters, and settings that comprise ancestral landscapes
as cultural-ecological systems. Tlingit place intelligence cannot be reduced
to a set of facts because it is a complex, relational way of knowing.

Skillful ritual experts like Jessie Dalton intuitively know how to sense
Tlingit places and apply place intelligence in creative and transforma-
tive ways. They can channel and amplify the power and resonance of
place through oratory, image, song, food, and other modes of expressive culture to create linking landscapes—places of *communitas*—that
are both conservative and generative of *shagóon*, of heritage and destiny, of being in the world. Rituals can also be employed to heal human
relations with places. Austin Hammond carried out such a ritual at
Chilkoot Lake in the early 1980s (Kawaky 1981). Concerned by non-
Native destruction of local ancestral landmarks, graves, and fish habi-

tats, he conceived of a unique peace ceremony that would repair the place damage at Chilkoot; revitalize Tlingit language, kinship, and subsistence values as means of attending to places; and emplace all local residents—Native and non-Native—as *aanyatx'i saaní*, or children of the land. Significantly, however, the ceremony required a response and reparations on the part of the state in order to be completed. To this day it remains uncompleted because of the state's failure to remove a restrictive fish weir, which Tlingits believe interferes with salmon reproduction and subsistence fishing.

Recognizing the power of place in human life leads to an important corollary and subtheme of this study: the health of places and the health of people are integrally related. This connection would seem to be so obvious and commonsensical that it could hardly be ignored. And yet fragmented, bureaucratized public policy organs consistently have failed to grasp it, especially as it concerns indigenous people. States might recognize physically "toxic" landscapes like Love Canal through their departments of environmental monitoring and protection, or socially "dysfunctional" neighborhoods through their police and social services divisions, but seldom do these bureaucratic units go beyond the limited statistics they gather to assess the small but tangible reality defined for them by the state. Seldom, if ever, do they combine to explore the cultural structures that dynamically shape lived experiences and senses of place among individuals and social groups. Such an approach means going beyond conventional environmental protection, normative social indicators, and standard approaches to space and to health. As a recent book title suggests, it requires *putting health into place* (Kearns and Gesler 1998) and, I would add, *putting place into health*. In all, it requires an anthropological and ethnographic approach.

Indigenous peoples whose dwelling connections to ancestral lands have been diminished or lost, and whose cultural structures of emplacement have been weakened, often suffer health crises, even if they enjoy a comparable or even higher level of material security—food, shelter, and income—than in the past. This is especially true of those groups that have been *forcibly* removed from their land and forbidden to speak their languages, structure their social life, harvest their foods, and practice their rituals. The tragic story of gas sniffing and suicidal Canadian

Innu youth in the Labrador community of Davis Inlet is an extreme example, one that has drawn international media attention (e.g., *New York Times Magazine*, March 12, 2001). Unfortunately, in highlighting the tragic details of dysfunction in this indigenous community, much of the coverage lost sight of the defining moment for the group's health: a government-initiated relocation, consolidation, and sedentarization of the Innu community into a shantytown at Davis Inlet in 1967, and the consequent alienation from their traditional dwelling places, paths, and projects. All of this was done in the name of progress, of course, and development and civilization. And yet, following displacement came mostly dependency, despondency, and despair. One Innu leader summed up the problem in ultimate terms of displacement: "We are a lost people," he said. Another relocation, to Natuashish, has not solved the problem, and one woman involved in healing the community opined, "You always go back to the land to find peace and serenity. . . . I love everything about the land; it represents us, the Innu people, and our culture, and it's where we came from and it's where we'll go back. You're dignified in the country, you're important in the country, because you need that to survive as Innu" (CBC Archives 2004). There is in this tragedy recognition of the importance of a strong sense of place to human health and community.

The situation among the Tlingit is not so dire, although processes of displacement, in the name of progress and development, proceed apace in Alaska, too. Fortunately, the Tlingit have not been forcibly relocated and to a large degree remain on their land base, controlling significant portions of it through corporate ownership of lands gained through the Alaska Native Claims Settlement Act of 1971 (ANCSA) and various cooperative land management agreements. Critics of ANCSA corporations argue that these institutions have undermined Tlingit senses of place and, in their own quest for profit and development, have begun to replace Tlingit communal values with corporate values, which commodify the land and its resources for profit maximization at the expense of sustainable and healthy relationships fostered by more subsistence-oriented economies (cf. Thornton 2007). It is true that ANCSA corporations have generated conflict and new hierarchies and modes of exploitation (cf. Dombrowski 2001, 2002), but, significantly, those conflicts have been most spirited among corporations that have either controlled lands out-

FIG. 6.1. Herman Kitka Sr. drying salmon at his smokehouse in Deep Bay, 1994. Photo by T. Thornton

side of their traditional territories (i.e., "in another ḵwáan's backyard') or been controlled by nonlocal segments of the population (i.e., "in my ḵwáan's backyard that I no longer dwell in"). As unseemly as these conflicts are, at base they are indicative of the strong, stoutly resistant senses of place that still exist among Tlingit tribes and clans, especially those that still dwell in their traditional homelands. At the same time ANCSA corporations are doing much to engender new Tlingit senses of place through their own investments, employment, heritage programs, architecture, symbols, and other activities. The role of place in aboriginal autonomy and development is a key issue in contemporary studies of northern indigenous peoples (cf. Scott 2001).

I once asked Herman Kitka (fig. 6.1)—a man still healthy in his ninety-third year, who has served as vice president of his ANCSA corporation, Shee Atika, Inc. (from the aboriginal name for Sitka), and been a successful commercial fisherman, boatbuilder, logger, general contractor, and Christian (first Russian Orthodox and, after marriage, Presbyterian)—how he managed to hold on to his subsistence camp in Deep Bay, whereas nearly every other remote camp in the region had been destroyed or appropriated (largely by the federal government), or otherwise abandoned. His answer, parts of which I have cited already, was a poignant one and worth considering in full:

The reason my smokehouse is still there is because when Forest Service said we were trespassing, I was the only one who testified. I told them if they touched and burned my place, I'm going to take the federal government to court because my family was there even before United States came into existence. My dad couldn't swallow it when the latecomers tried to claim the early settlers' land. [He told them,] "Which grandfather gave you that place that you can claim it?" After the Forest Service started burning the old cabins and smokehouses, I got a BIA [Bureau of Indian Affairs] lawyer and applied for the land [through the allotment process]. So they left it alone.

And the others, they didn't say nothing. It wasn't just because of the policy [that people stopped going to their fish camps]; it had to do with the federal government and Christianity being opposed to all Tlingit ways of living. Even when I was going to school, if I spoke Tlingit, you know the teacher plastered my mouth and made me stand in front of the class with the plaster over my mouth. They were that strict. They wanted all the Tlingit culture wiped out. What they kept saying was that they didn't want the Indian pagan worship existing. But we never worshipped any idols. The Tlingit, they prayed to the Holy Spirit only—just one. Western man came among us, the missionaries told us there was three that you pray to. My grandfather, when we caught fish in Deep Bay, stood on the sandbar and prayed to the Holy Spirit, thanking the Holy Spirit for allowing us to get our food easily. And he'd hold his hands up this way [outstretched toward the sky]. And he prayed in Tlingit out loud. But at the same time he was an elder in the [Russian] Orthodox Church. He prayed the Orthodox way. But when he gets fish he prays to the Holy Spirit, thanking the Holy Spirit.

The families didn't like to have their children suffering like that; everybody was aware of what they were doing to the children in school. So when the Alaska Native Brotherhood endorsed that we move forward only, to lift our morals and . . . standards up with the cultivated races of the world, most families just dropped the old ways. They started buying food from the stores instead of putting it up. . . . My family never quit because they always claimed that without the foods we'd never have any culture among our people.

Everything stems back, all of our religion stems to the use of the cultural foods. No memorial party is ever given without each clan bringing all their Native dishes together. You see, the Eagle clan is a large group, different clans, different houses, they have different names. But they all live under one, the Eagle clan. So when the Eagle clan [or] any member is giving a party, the whole works come and join. The Ravens did the same thing. It's a community affair. And they make sure everything is the cultural food prepared the old way at this memorial party. If I ever lost sight of how to put up our customary cultural food, I don't think the stories they told me at those camps would ever stay alive. Because when I testify for our people on subsistence it all comes back to that—what our old people used to tell us. (Thornton 2000:84–85)

Mr. Kitka suggests that "progress" is not a zero-sum game. Natives do not have to give up their language, their social structure, their foodways, or their religious rituals even as they adopt new ways to join "the cultivated races of the world." To do so, in fact, risks decline rather than progress, dysfunction rather than accommodation, becoming a "lost people" rather than an emplaced people. Indeed, without a strong sense of place and integrative intellectual, social, and material structures to maintain it, personal health and communal well-being are at stake. Fortunately, for Tlingits these emplacement structures, like Tlingit places themselves, remain vital, though to varying degrees all have been altered and compromised, if not undermined and threatened, over the past two centuries. And yet they persist and adapt, and even revitalize, as axes of identity, community, and place building; as cultural frames for navigating heritage and destiny and the terrains of relations that constitute *shagóon*; and as sources not merely of social capital (Putnam 2000) but of real organic bonds—in short, as wellsprings of being.

The key to future success lies in cross-cultural recognition of biological and cultural health as two sides of the same entity: place. Environmental health and communal health were never separate in Tlingit place consciousness. "Taking care" of places and communities meant never going "against nature" (*ligaas'*, the Tlingit word for "taboo") and cultivating places through respectful engagement with their constituent beings as a means of promoting *biocultural health*. Transgressions, as in Aak'wtaatseen's insulting the salmon, brought serious negative consequences, sometimes even cosmic repercussions. These events, too, became embedded in the landscape through commemorative geographic names, narratives, and other genres of place, thus serving to enlarge place intelligence and refine techniques of engagement. Social structure, language, subsistence production, and ritual remain the critical tools in this ongoing process of sensing and tending to places and of nurturing place intelligence, just as they are critical components in efforts to promote cultural survival and revitalization.

We should all be so aware of *being in place* and of *place in our being* as *aanyatx'u saaní*, children of the land.

APPENDIX

Tlingit Resources with Seasonality

Tlingit Resources with Seasonality (X = primary harvest periods, x = secondary harvest)

Resource	Tlingit Name	Scientific Name	Spring	Summer	Fall	Winter
FISH						
Cod, black	Ishkeen	Anoplopoma fimbria	x	X	x	X
Cod, ling	X'áax'w	Ophiodum elongatus		X	x	
Cod, Pacific	S'áax'	Gadus macrocephalus	x	X	x	X
Flounder	Dzánti	Plattichthys stellatus	x	X	X	X
Halibut	Cháatl	Hippoglossus stenolepsis	X	X	x	X
Herring	Yaaw	Culpea harengus pallasi	x	X	x	X
Herring eggs	Gáax'w	Valenciennes	X			
Eulachon	Saak	Thaleichthys pacificus	X			
Red snapper	Léik'w	Sebastes ruberrimus	X	X	x	X
Salmon eggs	Kabáakw	All salmon species		X	x	
Salmon, chum	Téel'	Oncorhynchus keta		X	x	
Salmon, coho	L'ook	Oncorhynchus kisutch		X	x	

Resource	Tlingit Name	Scientific Name	Spring	Summer	Fall	Winter
Salmon, king	T'á	Oncorhynchus tshawytscha	x	X	x	x
Salmon, pink	Cháas'	Oncorhynchus gorbushka		X		
Salmon, red	Gaat	Oncorhynchus nerka	x	X	x	x
Smelt	Shách'	Osmeridae	X			
Steelhead	Aashát	Salmo gairdnerii	X			x
Trout, cutthroat	X'éitaa	Oncorhynchus clarki	X	X	x	X
Trout, Dolly Varden	X'wáat'	Salvelinus malma	X	X	x	
LAND MAMMALS						
Beaver	S'igeidí	Castor canadensis	X		X	x
Black bear	S'eek	Ursus americanus	X	X	X	x
Brown bear	Xóots	Ursus arctos	x	X	X	x
Caribou	Watsíx	Rangifer tarandus		X	X	X
Deer	Guwakaan	Odocoileus hemionus sitkensis		X	X	X
Fox	Naagas'éi	Vulpes vulpes	x		x	X

Resource	Tlingit Name	Scientific Name	Spring	Summer	Fall	Winter
Land otter	Kóoshdaa	*Lutra canadensis*	x		X	x
Lynx	<u>G</u>aa<u>k</u>	*Lynx canadensis*	x		X	x
Marmot	S'aa<u>x</u>	*Marmota caligata*	x		X	X
Marten	K'óox	*Martes americana*	x		X	X
Mink	Nukshiyáan	*Mustela vision*	x		X	X
Moose	Dzísk'w	*Alces alces*	x		X	X
Mountain goat	Jánwu	*Oreamnos americanus*	X		x	X
Mountain sheep	Wanadóo	*Ovis dalli dalli*	X		x	X
Musk ox	Xaas	*Ovibos moschatus*			X	X
Muskrat	Tsín	*Ondatra zibethica*	X		x	X
Porcupine	<u>X</u>ala<u>k</u>'ách'	*Erethizon dorsatum*			X	X
Rabbit	<u>G</u>áa<u>x</u>	*Lepus americanus*	x		X	X
Squirrel, ground	Kanals'áak	*Spermophilus parryii*	x		X	X
Squirrel, red	Tsálk	*Tamiasciurius hudsonicus*	x		X	X

Resource	Tlingit Name	Scientific Name	Spring	Summer	Fall	Winter
Weasel	Dáa	Mustela spp.	x			X
Wolf	Gooch	Canis lupus	x			X
Wolverine	Núskw	Gulo gulo	x			X
MARINE MAMMALS						
Seal, fur	X'óon	Callorhinus ursinus	x			X
Seal, harbor (hair)	Tsaa	Phoca vitulina	X		X	x
Sea lion	Taan	Eumetopias jubata	X		X	X
Sea otter	Yáxwch'	Enhydra lutris	x	X	X	X
BIRDS						
Bird eggs	K'wát'	[Mostly] Larus spp.	x			
Canada goose	T'aawák	Branta candensis	x		X	
Duck	Gáaxw	Various	x		X	
Grouse, spruce	Káax' (f.), Núkt (m.)	Canachites Canadensis	x		X	X
Ptarmigan, willow	X'eis'awáa	Lagopus lagopus	x		X	X

Resource	Tlingit Name	Scientific Name	Spring	Summer	Fall	Winter
INTERTIDAL						
Abalone	Gúnxaa	Haliotis kamtschatkana	x	x		
Clam, butter	Gáal'	Saxidomus giganteus	X	x	X	X
Clam, horse	Yeis	Tresus capax	X	x	X	X
Clam, littleneck	Tl'ildaaskeit	Protobaca staminea	X	x	X	X
Clams, razor	Ḵalkátsk	Siliqua	X		X	X
Cockle	Yalooleit	Clinocardium nuttali	X	x	X	X
Crab, Dungeness	S'áaw	Cancer magister	X	x	X	X
Crab, king	X'eix	Parlithodes camtschatica	X	x	X	X
Gumboot (chiton)	Shaaw	Katherina tunicata	X	x	X	X
Mussel, California	Yées'	Mytilus californianus	X	x	X	X
Mussel, Pacific	Yaak	Mytilus trossulus	X	x	X	X
Octopus	Náakw	Octupus dofleini (liederma)	x	x	X	
Sea cucumber	Yéin	Parastichopus spp.	x	x	X	

Resource	Tlingit Name	Scientific Name	Spring	Summer	Fall	Winter
Sea ribbon	K̲'aach'	Rhodymenia pacmata (Palmeria palmate)	x			X
Sea urchin	Nées'	Strongylocentrotus sp.	x	x		X
Seaweed, black	Laak̲'ásk	Porphyra spp.	x			
Seaweed, hair	Né	Obelia	x			
Seaweed, yellow	Tayeidí	Fucus gardneri	x			
Shrimp	S'éex'át	Pandalus spp.	x	x	x	
Squid	Dak̲saa	Cephalopoda	x	x	x	x
PLANTS *(not including berries)*						
Alder, beach or Sitka	Keishísh	Alnus sinuate				
Alder, red	Shéix'w	Alnus rubra				
Birch	At Daayí	Betula papyrifera				
Carrot, Indian	S'ín	Canioselinum pacificum	x			
Cedar, yellow (bark)	X̲áay (Teey)	Chamaecyparis nootkatensis				
Cottonwood	Dúk̲	Populus balsamifera				

Resource	Tlingit Name	Scientific Name	Spring	Summer	Fall	Winter
Crabapple	X'ús (Kaxwats' [Oberg 1973])	Malus fusca				X
Devils club	S'áxt'	Oplopanax horridus	x	x	x	X
Fern, (root/fiddlehead)	K'wálx	Polypodiaceae (family)	x			
Fireweed	Lóol	Epilobium angustifolium	X		X	X
Firewood	Gán	Various	X	X	X	X
Goosetongue	Suktéitl'	Plantago maritime	X			
Hemlock (sap)	Yán (Sáx')	Tsuga heterophylla	X			
Hudson's Bay tea	S'ikshaldéen	Ledum palustre	X	X	x	X
Maple	X'aalx'éi	Acer glabrum spp.				
Mountain ash	Kalchaneit	Sorbus spp.				
Rice, Indian	Kóox	Fritillaria camschatcensis	X			
Saxifrage (heart-leaved)	Katkashaaya Náakw	Saxifraga nelsoniana (s. punctata?)	X	X		

Resource	Tlingit Name	Scientific Name	Spring	Summer	Fall	Winter
Skunk cabbage	X̱'áal'	Lysichiton americanum	X	X	x	
Spruce	Shéiyi	Picea sitchensis	X	X		
Wild (Indian) celery (cow parsnip)	Yaana.eit	Heracleum lanatum	X	X		
Wild rhubarb	Tl'aak'wách'	Polygonum alaskanum	X	X		
Wild sweet potato (sweet-vetch)	Tséit	Hedysarum alpinum	X	X		
Willow	Ch'áal' (xi'sis, in Oberg 1973)	Salix myrtillifolia	X	X		
BERRIES						
Bearberry (aka Stoneberry or Kinnikinnick)	Tínx	Arctostaphylos uva-ursi		X	x	
Blueberry (generic and oval-leaved)	Kanat'á	Vaccinium ovalifolium		X		
Blueberry, Alaskan (ripens later)	Naanyaa Kanat'áayí	Vaccinium alakaense		X	x	

Resource	Tlingit Name	Scientific Name	Spring	Summer	Fall	Winter
Blueberry, bog	Tsʼeekáx̱kʼw or Láx̱ʼloouní	Vaccinium uliginosum		X	x	
Blueberry, dwarf	Kakatlaax̱	Vaccinium caespitosum		X		
Cloudberry, yellow	Néx̱ʼw or Tá Kaháakw (salmon eggs)	Rubus chamaemorus		X		
Cranberry, bog	K̲ʼeishkaháagu	Oxycoccus microcarpus		X	x	
Cranberry, high-bush	Kaxwéix̱	Vibrium edule		X	x	
Cranberry, low-bush (Duckberry? [Oberg 1973])	Dáx̱w	Vaccinium vitis		X	x	
Currant, gray	Shaax̱	Ribes bracteosum		X	x	
Currant, swamp	Kaneiltsákw	Ribes lacustre		X	x	
Elderberry	Yéilʼ	Sambucus racemosa		X		
Huckleberry	Tleikatánk	Vaccinium parvifolium		X		
Jacobberry, bunchberry	K̲ʼeikax̱etlʼk	Cornus canadensis		X		

Resource	Tlingit Name	Scientific Name	Spring	Summer	Fall	Winter
Mossberry	XitliwAs'i (McClellan 1975:201)	Empetrum nigrum L.		X		
Nagoonberry	Neigóon	Rubus arcticus		X		
Nettleberry	Xaxiyuleko? (Oberg 1973)	Urtica dioica		X		
Pigeonberry	Xel taktsasi? (Oberg 1973)	Rivina humilis		X		
Raspberry	Tlekw Yádi	Rubus idaeus (pedatus)		X		
Redberry	Slaki? bayo-lelho? (Oberg 1973)	Cornus canadensis?		X		
Rose hip	K'inchéiyi/ Kanyeilw.aas'i (McClellan 1975:201)	Rosa species	X			
Salmonberry	Was'x'aan tléigu	Rubus spectabilis	shoots	X		

Resource	Tlingit Name	Scientific Name	Spring	Summer	Fall	Winter
Saskatoon berry	Gáaxw Wakx̱' (McClellan 1975:201)	Amelanchier alnifolia				
Serviceberry	Gaawák	Amelanchier Medik				
Soapberry	Xákwl'i	Shepardia Canadensis		X		
Strawberry	Sháku	Fragaria chiloensis		X		
Swampberry	Nux̱? (Oberg 1973)	Oxycoccus spp?		X		
Thimbleberry	Ch'eex'	Rubus parviflorus		X		

SOURCES: Oberg (1973), McClellan (1975, 1981), Newton and Moss (2005, 1983), Cruikshank (1990b, 1991), Thornton (2004b).

NOTES

1 INTRODUCTION

1. In other cases places have even come to stand for ethnographic ideas themselves: for example, India = hierarchy (Appadurai 1988), or the Pacific Northwest Coast = potlatch.

2. It follows then that, as the composition and structure of society change, so do conceptions of place. This is one reason why, as Tlingit groups have evolved and relocated, so have their myths been re-localized. For example, the Tlingit story known as "The Woman Who Married the Bear" is localized in at least five different places (see Thornton 1992).

3. In strict terms, it is possible that human variables such as overharvest or other ecological disturbances could affect the environment, especially in the short term.

4. Of course, every experience of the physical world is at some level mediated by culture. Even when one directly confronts a landscape, one always experiences it *as something*, that something being largely defined by culture. Nevertheless, the distinction is useful here in demonstrating the extent to which cultural values and perceptions of place are constructed and reproduced through means other than physical encounters.

5. For reviews of anthropological and linguistic studies of Native American place-names, see Afable and Beeler (1996), Thornton (1997b), and Jett (2001).

2 KNOW YOUR PLACE

1. Dauenhauer and Dauenhauer (1990:19) define *shuká* as "'ahead' or 'before' . . . those born ahead of us who are now behind us, as well as those unborn who wait ahead of us." Thus, the term is temporally ambiguous and "faces two directions," referring both to the past—that which came before— and to the future—that which lies ahead.

2. Transfer of land was permitted under certain circumstances, however (see, e.g., Garfield 1947).

3. In addition to these fundamental units other important dimensions of Tlingit social structure during the pre- and early contact period included slavery, shamanism, gender, and confederations (de Laguna 1983; Thornton 2002). Shamans were especially important in shaping senses of place because of their acute perception of the cosmos and abilities to mediate between the human and spirit worlds to achieve important ends such as protecting and healing people and places, locating precious resources, controlling weather, battling enemies, and the like. Even in death shamans remained powerful: they were not cremated like ordinary Tlingits, but instead were placed on remote islands, caves, or bluffs, which themselves became potent shamanic landscapes that were respected, if not taboo, among the living. Shamanism declined in the postcontact era, as it proved less effective in maintaining human-place relations in the face of non-Native incursions and the introduction of new technologies, medicines, and religion.

4. With one anomalous exception, the Neix̱.ádi (probably of southern origin; see Olson 1967), who called themselves Eagles and intermarried with both Raven and Wolf.

5. The content and use of metaphor and other tropes in Tlingit oratory have been carefully analyzed by Dauenhauer (1975) and Dauenhauer and Dauenhauer (1987, 1990).

6. In addition to *at.óow* names, original pet names were also given, often by the father's side of the family; generally these names were inspired by unique characteristics of the child.

7. For a comparative perspective on "the embrace of names," see Richard Nelson's (1994) article, with that title, on Inupiaq and Athabascan place-names and Howard Morphy's work (e.g., 1995) on Yolngu personal naming in relation to place.

8. In certain ways, these leaders resembled the so-called Big Men of Oceanic societies (Johnson and Earle 1987). In return for some measure of economic control, Tlingit elites provided their clan members with security, prestige, social networks, and valuable nonlocal goods. If they failed in these duties, or otherwise shamed their clan, status could also be taken away.

9. See Thornton (2004a) for an extended discussion of Tlingit character. Hillman's emphasis on the individuality of character offers an important corrective to the more totalizing national character studies that tended to portray character as a reflection of dominant personality traits, which, in turn, were molded in cookie-cutter-like fashion by certain cultural institutions or enculturation practices. A good example of this in the Tlingit literature is Ronald Olson's (1956) study on how Tlingit character is "channeled." Alternatively, Hillman (1999:197) argues, "Unlike 'personality,' character is impersonal. Rocks, paintings, houses,

even kinds of bacteria and logical propositions demonstrate character. The discourse of personality is human psychology; of character, imaginative description." To the extent that his conceptualization of character extends beyond persons to aspects of the natural and built environment, it is well suited to the study of indigenous peoples, for whom character is typically viewed not merely as a manifestation of humanity but also as a force of nature.

10. In addition there is a Chookaneidí version of the story. See Willie Marks's story in Dauenhauer and Dauenhauer (1987:152–65). Interestingly, his story begins at _Gathéeni_ (Sockeye Creek), a stream at Cape Spencer, rather than at Dundas Bay.

11. Archeological investigations have shown Ground Hog Bay, the location of the Grouse Fort remains, to be one of the earliest Native settlements in Southeast Alaska, dating to 9,000–10,000 BP (Ackerman 1968; Ackerman, Hamilton, and Stuckenrath 1979).

12. Wayne Howell, personal communication, Gustavus, Alaska, 1996.

3 WHAT'S IN A NAME?

1. The place-name data come from a gazetteer I compiled of more than three thousand place-names in Tlingit territory from primary and secondary sources. A small percentage of these names are not Tlingit, especially at the northern and southern extremes, where Chugash, Eyak, Haida, or Tsimshian intersect. My interest in Tlingit place-names began with research on Sitkoh Bay in 1989 (Thornton, Schroeder, and Bosworth 1990), where I first learned that Tlingit elders had extensive undocumented toponymic knowledge. This was followed by further ethnogeographic work with elders from Angoon, Hoonah, Kake, Sitka, and Yakutat in the course of mapping projects and other research between 1990 and 1994, which yielded approximately 650 additional place-names in Northern Tlingit country. Between 1995 and 2001 I coordinated a comprehensive survey of indigenous place-names for the Southeast Native Subsistence Commission (SENSC) in collaboration with tribal governments in the region (Thornton 1999c). This project yielded hundreds of new names and clarified locations, pronunciations, and meanings of over a thousand toponyms in the existing literature, including several rich sources of ethnogeographic information, especially Thomas Waterman's (n.d.; 1922) work documenting over 860 place-names in the southern Tlingit country and Frederica de Laguna's ethnographic studies of Angoon (1960) in central Southeast Alaska and Yakutat (1972) in the north. A number of linguists (e.g., Leer [1985]; Naish and Story [1960s]), explorers (e.g., Glave 1890), teachers (e.g., Campen n.d.), mis-

sionaries and government officials (e.g., Brady n.d.), and Tlingit scholars (e.g., Shotridge n.d.; Joseph n.d.) also recorded place-names in these and other communities, as did the ethnographers George Emmons ([1916–45]), John Swanton (1908, 1909), Ronald Olson (1967), Walter Goldschmidt and Theodore Haas (1998), and others besides de Laguna. In some cases these names were unmapped and recorded in idiosyncratic, sometimes fragmentary, script. Consequently, their proper spellings, meanings, and locations had to be deciphered (or not) from contextual clues, or re-elicited from knowledgeable elders. Fortunately, through the SENSC research and other projects, the majority of these names have been re-elicited and verified. Emmons ([1916–45]) and Olson (1967; n.d.) each recorded hundreds of names, though neither is completely reliable for providing accurate locations, transcriptions, or translations. Olson was best as a source for the communities in which he conducted fieldwork: Klawock and Klukwan. Linguists Jeff Leer and Nora Dauenhauer, active in recording Tlingit texts for many years, have maintained place-name files, which they also shared with me. Both also contributed their talents in helping me make sense of unusual orthographies and arcane place-names, especially those that the richly ethnogeographic witness statements contained in the Goldschmidt and Haas 1946 manuscript (published in 1998).

2. This map is now housed at the Bancroft Library at the University of California, Berkeley (see Hope and Thornton 2001 for a reproduction and discussion).

3. For a full-length study of "maps of experience" in a colonial and post-colonial context among the Secwepemc of Alkali Lake, British Columbia, see the recent book of Andie Diane Palmer (2005).

4. If conjugations and other forms are considered, this represents but a fraction of the total. Compare Gary Witherspoon's (1977:21) calculation that there are some 356,200 distinct conjugations of the Navajo verb "to go."

5. Yet, it is not clear that a cross-cultural pattern has been identified, for in Sahaptin one finds that the aorta of rivers, the Columbia, is one of the few tagged with a generic (cf. Hunn 1990).

6. Though perhaps more or less prominently employed. A related issue that is important to consider is whether certain constructions are opaque in the sense that they contain semantic references that are not necessarily evoked when the name is spoken. For example, few people think of "pacificity" or "peaceful" when they hear the name "Pacific Ocean."

7. Emmons [1916–45]; J. Marks, personal communication, 2000.

8. Measuring toponymic density in Tlingit country is complicated by the fact that there have been exhaustive inventories conducted of some areas and little or no toponymic surveys in others. Similarly, research has been conducted

in various postcontact stages of non-Native intrusion with informants having suffered varying degrees of toponymic loss as a result of language and lifestyle shifts. Recovering significant numbers of indigenous names in these areas today is not possible. In addition, ḵwáan boundaries, while generally encompassing lands and waters used by clans residing in a particular winter village, may not include all lands used and often include significant acreage that was used little or not all (e.g., mountain ranges and ice fields). Despite these limitations, ḵwáans are the most logical existing area units for calculating toponymic density.

9. Thus far, I have encountered only a few toponyms that refer to internal bodily features; of these, the majority refer to the heart or the stomach.

10. Clarence Jackson, personal communication, 1997.

11. Lilly White, personal communication, Hoonah Alaska, 1993.

12. Glacier Bay itself, as Scidmore observed, was a merciful exception to the littering of biographical names on the landscape: "By his own personal insistence and a determined stand made at the Coast Survey office, Captain Beardslee had his very apt name of Glacier bay retained on official charts instead of giving it the name of some inconsequent and now forgotten statesman whom it seemed officially desirable to flatter at the time. All Alaska tourists owe it to Captain Beardslee that this reserve of such unparalleled scenic grandeur is not vulgarized by some great misnomer" (1896:143).

13. For an extended discussion of European imperialistic patterns of naming and otherwise appropriating and domesticating indigenous landscapes in Australia, see Carter (1987).

14. "Hoonah" is the modern spelling of the original Tlingit town name. The spelling "Huna" also is used to refer to the Tlingit inhabitants of this settlement.

4 PRODUCTION AND PLACE

1. This speech has been reproduced in several publications (Kitka 1999, 2000). This version is based on my original transcription of a taped interview with Herman Kitka in 1995.

2. Indeed, the names of the months of the year were often expressions of activities and vary by community (cf. Emmons 1991).

3. For an excellent discussion on the agency of glaciers, see Julie Cruikshank's (2005) recent study.

4. Swanton (1911:172); J. Marks, personal communication, 2000.

5. For other ethnographic case studies concerning common property resources, see McCay and Acheson (1987), Ostrom (1990), Agrawal and Gibson (1999), and Acheson (2003).

6. This is not to say, however, that Tlingits did not retain commercial fish for their own use; on the contrary, they did and still do to a great degree. Rather, it was a distinction between primary and secondary purposes of specific fishing activities.

7. Some groups in Sitka contested this, however.

8. If one accepts Ivan Petroff's inflated figures for traditional production levels, present harvest levels represent an even smaller percentage. Leaving other resources aside, in 1880 he ventured that "each individual man, woman, or child consumes the equivalent of between 3,000 and 4,000 fish" a year (1884:70). This estimate is likely ten to thirty times too high. Still, there has been a significant decline in subsistence food production over the past century by any measure.

9. Unfortunately, in those communities with a proportionately low Native population (Haines, Sitka, and Wrangell), there are no comparative figures to determine whether Native households are producing at a higher per capita level than the non-Native ones (although in Sitka, for example, this seems to be the case).

5 RITUAL AS EMPLACEMENT

1. Jeff Leer, personal communication, 1999.

2. See Thornton (2004a:384) for a discussion of my translation of $\underline{K}$'eik'w X'óow as "Black-Legged Kittiwake Robe" rather than as the Dauenhauers' "Tern Robe."

BIBLIOGRAPHY

Abram, David. 1996. *The Spell of the Sensuous*. New York: Vintage Books.

Acheson, James M. 2003. *Capturing the Commons: Devising Institutions to Manage the Maine Lobster Industry*. Lebanon, NH: University Press of New England.

Ackerman, Robert E. 1968. *The Archeology of the Glacier Bay Region, Southeastern Alaska*. Washington State University, Laboratory of Anthropology, Report of Investigations no. 44. Pullman: Washington State University.

Ackerman, Robert E., Thomas D. Hamilton, and Robert Stuckenrath. 1979. "Early Cultural Complexes of the Northern Northwest Coast." *Canadian Journal of Archaeology* 3:195–209.

Afable, Patricia O., and Madison S. Beeler. 1996. "Place-Names." In *Handbook of North American Indians*, vol. 17, *Languages*, ed. Ives Goddard, 185–99. Washington, DC: Smithsonian Institution.

Agnew, John A., and James S. Duncan. 1989. *The Power of Place: Bringing Together Geographical and Sociological Imaginations*. Boston: Unwin Hyman.

Agrawal, Arun, and Clark Gibson. 1999. "Enchantment and Disenchantment: The Role of Community in Natural Resource Conservation." *World Development* 27 (4): 629–49.

Alaska Consultants, Inc. 1976. *City of Angoon, Comprehensive Development Plan*. Report on file with Angoon Community Association, Angoon, AK.

Alaska Fisheries Board and Alaska Department of Fisheries. 1949. 1949 Annual Report, no. 1. Juneau, AK.

Allaire, Louis. 1984. "A Native Mental Map of Coast Tsimshian Villages." In *The Tsimshian: Images of the Past, Views for the Present*, ed. Margaret Seguin, 82–98. Vancouver: University of British Columbia Press.

Altman, Irwin, and Setha M. Low. 1992. *Place Attachment*. New York: Plenum Press.

Ames, Kenneth M. 1994. "The Northwest Coast: Complex Hunter-Gatherers, Ecology, and Social Evolution." *Annual Review of Anthropology* 23:209–29.

Ames, Kenneth M., and Herbert D. G. Maschner. 1999. *Peoples of the Northwest Coast: Their Archaeology and Prehistory*. London: Thames and Hudson.

Appadurai, Arjun. 1988. "Putting Hierarchy in Its Place." *Cultural Anthropology* 3 (1): 36–49.

———. 1996. *Modernity at Large: Cultural Dimensions of Globalization*. Minneapolis: University of Minnesota Press.

Appleton, Jay. 1975. *The Experience of Landscape*. London: John Wiley and Sons.

Atkins, John R. 1973. "On the Fundamental Consanguineal Numbers and Their Structural Basis." *American Ethnologist* 1:1–31.

Auge, Marc. 1995. *Non-Places: Introduction to an Anthropology of Supermodernity*. New York: Verso.

Bakhtin, Mikhail. 1981. *The Dialogic Imagination: Four Essays by M. M. Bakhtin*. Ed. M. Holmquist. Austin: University of Texas Press.

Basso, Keith. 1984a. "Stalking with Stories: Names, Places, and Moral Narratives among the Western Apache." In *Text, Play, and Story: The Construction and Reconstruction of Self and Society*, ed. Stuart Plattner, 19–53. Washington, DC: American Ethnological Society.

———. 1984b. "Western Apache Place-Name Hierarchies." In *Naming Systems*, 1980 Proceedings of the American Ethnological Society, ed. Elisabeth Tooker, 78–94. Washington, DC: American Ethnological Society.

———. 1988. "'Speaking with Names': Language and Landscape among the Western Apache." *Cultural Anthropology* 3 (2): 99–130.

———. 1996. *Wisdom Sits in Places: Language and Landscape among the Western Apache*. Albuquerque: University of New Mexico Press.

Bateson, Gregory. 1979. *Mind and Nature: A Necessary Unity*. New York: Dutton.

Beardslee, L. A. 1882. *Reports of . . . relative to affairs in Alaska, and the operations of the U.S.S. Jamestown under his command, while in the waters of the Territory, 1882*. Forwarded by William H. Hunt, Secretary of the Navy. Senate Executive Document no. 71, in vol. 4, 47th Cong., 1st sess.

Bender, Barbara, and Margot Winer, eds. 2001. *Contested Landscapes: Movement, Exile and Place*. Oxford: Berg.

Berkes, Fikret. 1999. *Sacred Ecology: Traditional Ecological Knowledge and Resource Management*. Philadelphia: Taylor and Francis.

Berlin, Brett. 1992. *Ethnobiological Classification: Principles of Categorization*. Princeton, NJ: Princeton University Press.

Berlin, Brett, and Paul Kay. 1969. *Basic Color Terms: Their Universality and Evolution*. Berkeley: University of California Press.

Berry, Wendell. 1977. *The Unsettling of America*. New York: Avon.

Betts, Martha, Matthew Kookesh, Robert F. Schroeder, Thomas F. Thornton, and Anne-Marie Victor. 1992. *Subsistence Resource Use Patterns in South-*

east Alaska: Summaries of 30 Communities. Technical Paper no. 216. Juneau: Alaska Department of Fish and Game, Division of Subsistence.

Bicker, Alan, Paul Sillitoe, and Johan Pottier. 2004. *Development and Local Knowledge: New Approaches to Issues in Natural Resources Management, Conservation, and Agriculture*. New York: Routledge.

Bierwert, Crisca. 1999. *Brushed by Cedar, Living by the River: Coast Salish Figures of Power*. Tucson: University of Arizona Press.

Bird-David, Nurit. 1992. "Beyond 'the Hunting and Gathering Mode of Subsistence': Culture-Sensitive Observation on the Nayaka and Other Modern Hunter-Gatherers." *Man*, n.s., 27:583–603.

———. 1999. "'Animism' Revisited: Personhood, Environment, and Relational Epistemology." *Current Anthropology* 40:S67–S91.

Birdsell, Joseph B. 1953. "Some Environmental and Cultural Factors Influencing the Structuring of Australian Aboriginal Populations." *American Naturalist* 87:171–207.

Black, Mary B. 1977. "Ojibwa Taxonomy and Percept Ambiguity." *Ethos* 5 (1): 90–118.

Boas, Franz. 1917. "Grammatical Notes on the Language of the Tlingit Indians." *University of Pennsylvania Museum, Anthropology Papers* 7 (1): 1–179.

———. 1934. *Geographical Names of the Kwakiutl Indians*. Columbia University Contributions to Anthropology, no. 20. New York: Columbia University Press.

Boelscher, Marianne. 1989. *The Curtain Within: Haida Social and Mythical Discourse*. Vancouver: University of British Columbia Press.

Bourdieu, Pierre. 1973. "The Berber House of the World Reversed." In *Rules and Meaning*, ed. Mary Douglas. Harmondsworth, UK: Penguin.

———. 1977. *Outline of a Theory of Practice*. Cambridge: Cambridge University Press.

Brady, John G. n.d. "Place Names in the Vicinity of Sitka." Manuscript, John G. Brady Papers (WA MSS-1206), Beinecke Rare Book and Manuscript Library, Yale University. Microfilm on file at the Alaska State Historical Library, Juneau.

Braudel, Fernand. 1972. *The Mediterranean and the Mediterranean World in the Age of Philip II*. New York: Harper and Row.

Bringhurst, Robert. 2002. "The Tree of Meaning and the Work of Ecological Linguistics." *Canadian Journal of Environmental Education* 7 (2): 9–22.

Brody, Hugh. 1981. *Maps and Dreams*. Toronto: Douglas and McIntyre.

Brown, Cecil H. 1985. "Mode of Subsistence and Folk Biological Taxonomy." *Current Anthropology* 26 (1): 43–62.

Brown, Steve. 2000. "Comments on the Northern Style, Northwest Coast Art."
In Fair and Worl, *Celebration 2000*, 107–12.

Buttimer, Anne, and David Seamon, eds. 1980. *The Human Experience of Space
and Place*. London: St. Martin's Press.

Caldwell, William E. 1998. "'Reasonable Opportunity' versus 'Customary and
Traditional' in Lime Village." *Cultural Survival Quarterly* 22 (3): 63–65.

Campen, Brenda. n.d. "Tlingit Place Names in the Angoon Area, Sitka, Alaska."
Manuscript in author's possession.

Carpenter, Edmund. 1977. "Some Notes on the Separate Realities of Eskimo
and Indian Art." In *The Far North: 2000 Years of American, Eskimo and
Indian Art*, ed. Henry B. Collins, Frederica de Laguna, Edmund Carpenter,
and Peter Stone, 281–89. Bloomington: Indiana University Press.

Carrier, James A. 1987. "Marine Tenure and Conservation in Papua New Guinea:
Problems of Interpretation." In *The Question of the Commons: The Cul-
ture and Ecology of Communal Resources*, ed. Bonnie J. McCay and James
M. Acheson, 142–67. Tucson: University of Arizona Press.

Carter, Paul. 1987. *The Road to Botany Bay*. London: Faber.

Casey, Edward S. 1993. *Getting Back into Place: Toward a Renewed Understanding of the Place-World*. Bloomington: Indiana University Press.

———. 1997. *The Fate of Place: A Philosophical History*. Berkeley: University
of California Press.

CBC (Canadian Broadcasting Corporation) Archives. 2004. *A Glimmer of Hope*.
Broadcast October 25, 2004. http://archives.cbc.ca/IDC-1-70-1671-11525/
disasters_tragedies/davis_inlet/clip8 (accessed July 15, 2005).

Coontz, Robert. 1930. *From the Mississippi to the Sea*. Philadelphia: Dorrance
and Company.

Cruikshank, Julie. 1981. "Legend and Landscape: Convergence of Oral and Scientific Traditions in the Yukon Territory." *Arctic Anthropology* 18 (2): 67–93.

———. 1990a. "Getting the Words Right: Perspectives on Naming and Places
in Athapaskan Oral History." *Arctic Anthropology* 27 (1): 52–65.

———. 1990b. *Life Lived like a Story: Life Stories of Three Yukon Native Elders*.
In collaboration with Angela Sidney, Kitty Smith, and Annie Ned. Lincoln:
University of Nebraska Press.

———. 1991. *Dän Dhá Ts'edenintth'é: Reading Voices; Oral and Written Inter-
pretations of Yukon's Past*. Vancouver, BC: Douglas and McIntyre.

———. 1998. *The Social Life of Stories: Narrative and Knowledge in Yukon
Territory*. Lincoln: University of Nebraska Press.

———. 2005. *Do Glaciers Listen? Local Knowledge, Colonial Encounters, and
Social Imagination*. Vancouver: University of British Columbia Press.

Culp, Wanda, Richard Sheakley, Wilbur James, Kenneth Grant, Mary Rudolph, and Amy Marvin. 1995. "Presentation of the Huna Tlingits." In *Proceedings of the Third Glacier Bay Science Symposium, 1993*, ed. Daniel Engstrom, 302–8. Anchorage, AK: National Park Service.

Curry, James E., and I. S. Weissbrodt. n.d. Curry-Weissbrodt Papers of the Tlingit and Haida Indian Tribes of Alaska. Manuscript on file at Sealaska Heritage Institute, Juneau, AK.

Dauenhauer, Nora Marks, and Richard Dauenhauer. 1981. *"Because We Cherish You . . .": Sealaska Elders Speak to the Future.* Juneau, AK: Sealaska Heritage Foundation.

———, eds. 1987. *Haa Shuká, Our Ancestors: Tlingit Oral Narratives.* Seattle: University of Washington Press; Juneau, AK: Sealaska Heritage Foundation.

———, eds. 1990. *Haa Tuwunáagu Yis, for Healing Our Spirit: Tlingit Oratory.* Seattle: University of Washington Press; Juneau, AK: Sealaska Heritage Foundation.

———, eds. 1994. *Haa Ḵusteeyí, Our Culture: Tlingit Life Stories.* Seattle: University of Washington Press; Juneau, AK: Sealaska Heritage Foundation.

———. 1998. "Technical, Emotional, and Ideological Issues in Reversing Language Shift: Examples from Southeast Alaska." In *Endangered Languages: Language Loss and Community Response*, ed. Lenore A. Grenoble and Lindsay J. Whaley, 57–98. Cambridge: Cambridge University Press.

Dauenhauer, Richard. 1975. "Text and Context of Tlingit Oral Tradition." PhD diss., University of Wisconsin, Madison.

Davidson, George. 1901. "Explanation of an Indian Map . . . from the Chilkaht to the Yukon Drawn by the Chilkaht Chief, Kohklux, in 1869." *Mazama* 2 (2): 75–82.

Davis, Robert H. 1989. "Saginaw Bay: I Keep Going Back." In *Ḵeex̱' Ḵwaan: In Our Own Words: Interviews with Kake Elders*, 57–60. Kake, AK: Organized Village of Kake.

De Laguna, Frederica. 1954. "Tlingit Ideas about the Individual." *Southwestern Journal of Anthropology* 10 (2): 172–91.

———. 1960. *The Story of a Tlingit Community: A Problem in the Relationship between Archeological, Ethnological, and Historical Methods.* Bureau of American Ethnology, Bulletin 172. Washington, DC: Government Printing Office.

———. 1972. *Under Mount Saint Elias: The History and Culture of the Yakutat Tlingit.* 3 vols. Washington, DC: Smithsonian Institution Press.

———. 1983. "Aboriginal Tlingit Sociopolitical Organization." In *The Development of Political Organization in Native North America*, 1979 Proceedings of the American Ethnological Society, ed. Elisabeth Tooker, 71–85. Washington, DC: American Ethnological Society.

———. 1990. "Tlingit." In *Handbook of North American Indians*, vol. 7, *Northwest Coast*, ed. Wayne Suttles, 203–28. Washington, DC: Smithsonian Institution Press.

Descola, Philippe, and Gísli Pálsson. 1996. *Nature and Society: Anthropological Perspectives*. London and New York: Routledge.

Dombrowski, Kurt. 2001. *Against Culture: Development, Politics, and Religion in Indian Alaska*. Lincoln: University of Nebraska Press.

———. 2002. "The Praxis of Indigenism." *American Anthropologist* 104 (4): 1062–73.

Donald, Leland. 1997. *Aboriginal Slavery on the Northwest Coast of North America*. Berkeley: University of California Press.

Drucker, Phillip. 1951. *The Northern and Central Nootkan Tribes*. Bureau of American Ethnology, Bulletin 144. Washington, DC: Government Printing Office.

———. 1958. *The Native Brotherhood: Modern Intertribal Organization on the Northwest Coast*. Bureau of American Ethnology, Bulletin 168. Washington, DC: Government Printing Office.

———. 1983. "Ecology and Political Organization on the Northwest Coast of America." In *The Development of Political Organization in Native North America*, 1979 Proceedings of the American Ethnological Society, ed. Elisabeth Tooker. Washington, DC: American Ethnological Society.

Durkheim, Émile. [1915] 1965. *The Elementary Forms of Religious Life*. Trans. Joseph Ward Swain. New York: Free Press.

Dyson-Hudson, Rada, and Eric A. Smith. 1978. "Human Territoriality: An Ecological Reassessment." *American Anthropologist* 80:21–41.

Eliade, Mircea. 1959. *The Sacred and the Profane*. New York: Harper.

Ellana, Linda, and George Sherrod. 1986. *Timber Management and Fish and Wildlife Utilization in Selected Southeast Alaska Communities: Klawock, Prince of Wales Island, Alaska*. Technical Paper no. 126. Juneau: Alaska Department of Fish and Game, Division of Subsistence.

Ellen, Roy, Peter Parkes, and Alan Bicker, eds. 2000. *Indigenous Environmental Knowledge and Its Transformations: Critical Anthropological Perspectives*. Amsterdam: Harwood.

Emmons, George T. 1911. "Native Account of the Meeting between La Perouse and the Tlingit." *American Anthropologist* 13:294–98.

———. 1916. *The Whale House of the Chilkat*. American Museum of Natural History, Anthropological Papers, vol. 19, pt. 1, 1–33. New York: American Museum of Natural History.

———. [1916–45]. "The History of Tlingit Tribes and Clans." Manuscript on file at American Museum of Natural History archives, New York.

———. 1991. *The Tlingit Indians*. Edited with additions by Frederica de Laguna. American Museum of Natural History Anthropological Papers, vol. 70. Seattle: University of Washington Press and the American Museum of Natural History.

Entrikin, J. Nicholas. 1991. *The Betweenness of Place: Toward a Geography of Modernity*. Baltimore: Johns Hopkins University Press.

Escobar, Arturo. 2001. "Culture Sits in Places: Reflections on Globalism and Subaltern Strategies of Localization." *Political Geography* 20:139–74.

Evans-Pritchard, E. E. 1940. *The Nuer*. Oxford: Oxford University Press.

Fabian, Johannes. 1983. *Time and the Other: How Anthropology Makes Its Object*. New York: Columbia University Press.

Fair, Susan, and Rosita Worl, eds. 2000. *Celebration 2000: Restoring Balance through Culture*. Juneau, AK: Sealaska Heritage Foundation.

Feld, Steven, and Keith H. Basso, eds. 1996. *Senses of Place*. Santa Fe, NM: School of American Research Press.

Firman, Anne S. 1986. *Harvest and Use of Fish and Wildlife Resources by Residents of Kake, Alaska*. Technical Paper no. 145. Juneau: Alaska Department of Fish and Game, Division of Subsistence.

Fladmark, Knut R. 1975. *A Paleoecological Model for Northwest Coast Prehistory*. National Museum of Man, Mercury Series. Archaeological Survey of Canada, Paper no. 43. Ottawa: National Museum of Man.

Foucault, Michel. 1980. *Power and Knowledge*. Brighton, UK: Harvester Press.

———. 1984. *The Foucault Reader*. Ed. Paul Rabinow. New York: Pantheon.

Garfield, Viola E. [1945]. "Fieldnotes from Kake, Alaska." Manuscript on file at University of Washington Archives, Seattle.

———. 1947. "Historical Aspects of Tlingit Clans in Angoon, Alaska." *American Anthropologist* 9 (3): 438–542.

———. n.d. "Ownership of Food Producing Areas." Manuscript on file at University of Washington Archives, Seattle.

Geertz, Clifford. 1973. *The Interpretation of Cultures: Selected Essays by Clifford Geertz*. New York: Basic Books.

———. 1996. Afterword. In *Senses of Place*, ed. Steven Feld and Keith H. Basso, 259–62. Santa Fe, NM: School of American Research Press.

George, Gabriel D., and Robert G. Bosworth. 1988. *Use of Fish and Wildlife by Residents of Angoon, Admiralty Island, Alaska*. Technical Paper no. 159. Juneau: Alaska Department of Fish and Game, Division of Subsistence.

Gibson, James J. 1979. *The Ecological Approach to Visual Perception*. Boston: Houghton Mifflin.

Gibson, James R. 1992. *Otter Skins, Boston Ships, and China Goods: The Maritime Fur Trade of the Northwest Coast, 1785–1841*. Seattle: University of Washington Press.

Giddens, Anthony. 1984. *The Constitution of Society: Outline of a Theory of Structuration*. Cambridge, UK: Polity Press.

———. 1985. "Time, Space, and Regionalization." In *Social Relations and Spatial Structures*, ed. Derek Gregory and John Urry, 265–95. New York: Palgrave Macmillan.

Glave, Edward J. 1890. "Our Alaska Expedition." *Frank Leslie's Illustrated Newspaper*, July–September.

Gmelch, George, Sharon Bohn Gmelch, and Richard Nelson. 1984. *Sitka: Resource Use in a Small Alaskan City*. Technical Paper no. 90. Juneau: Alaska Department of Fish and Game, Division of Subsistence.

Goffman, Erving. 1974. *Frame Analysis: An Essay on the Organization of Experience*. Cambridge, MA: Harvard University Press.

Goldschmidt, Walter R., and Theodore R. Haas. 1998. *Haa Aaní, Our Land: Tlingit and Haida Land Rights and Use*. Edited with an introduction by Thomas F. Thornton. Seattle: University of Washington Press; Juneau, AK: Sealaska Heritage Foundation. Original report titled "Possessory Rights of the Natives of Southeastern Alaska: A Report to the Commissioner of Indian Affairs," 1946.

Goulet, Jean-Guy. 1998. *Ways of Knowing: Experience, Knowledge, and Power among the Dene Tha*. Lincoln: University of Nebraska Press.

Greer, Sheila. 1995. *Skookum Stories on the Chilkoot/Dyea Trail*. Carcross, YT: Carcross-Tagish First Nation.

Gregory, Derek. 1994. *Geographic Imaginations*. Cambridge, MA: Blackwell.

Gulliford, Andrew. 2000. *Sacred Objects and Sacred Places: Preserving Tribal Traditions*. Boulder: University Press of Colorado.

Gupta, Akhil, and James Ferguson, eds. 1997. *Anthropological Locations: Boundaries and Grounds of a Field Science*. Berkeley: University of California Press.

Hägerstrand, Torsten. 1975. "Space, Time, and Human Conditions." In *Dynamic Allocation of Urban Space*, ed. A. Karlqvist, L. Lundqvist, and F. Snickars. Farnborough, UK: Saxon House; Lexington, MA: Lexington Books.

———. 1982. "Diorama, Path and Project." *Tijdschrift voor Economische en Sociale Geografie* 73:323–39.

Hall, George. 1962. "Report of a Visit to Hoonah, Alaska, July 1960." Manuscript on file at Sitka National Historical Park, Sitka, AK.

Hallowell, A. Irving. 1967. *Culture and Experience*. New York: Schocken Books.

Hardin, Garrett. 1968. "The Tragedy of the Commons." *Science* 162:1243–48.

Harrington, John. n.d. Unpublished notes and vocabulary from George Johnson, Jack Ellis, and others, 1939–40. Copy of manuscript on file at Alaska Native Language Center, University of Alaska, Fairbanks.

Harvey, David. 1989. *The Condition of Postmodernity: An Enquiry into the Origins of Culture Change*. London: Basil Blackwell.

Heidegger, Martin. 1962. *Being and Time*. New York: Harper and Row.

———. 1971. "Building Dwelling Thinking." In *Basic Writings*. London: Routledge.

———. 1977. *"The Question Concerning Technology" and Other Essays*. Trans. William Lovitt. New York: Harper Colophon Books.

HIA (Hoonah Indian Association). 1994. "ANILCA Glacier Bay National Park '2nd Ice Age' Continues: A Plan to Thaw the '2nd Ice Age.'" Hoonah, Alaska. Manuscript in author's possession.

———. 2006. *Tlingit Place Names of the Huna Káawu*. Map. Hoonah, AK: Hoonah Indian Association.

Hillman, James. 1999. *The Force of Character, and the Lasting Life*: New York: Ballantine.

Hinckley, Ted C. 1970. "The Canoe Rocks———We Do Not Know What Will Become of Us. . . ." *Western Historical Quarterly* 1 (July): 265–90.

———. 1996. The *Canoe Rocks: Alaska's Tlingit and the Euroamerican Frontier, 1800–1912*. Lanham, MD: University Press of America.

Hirsch, Eric, and Michael O'Hanlon. 1995. *The Anthropology of Landscape: Perspectives on Space and Place*. Oxford: Oxford University Press.

Hope, Andrew, III, and Thomas F. Thornton, eds. 2000. *Will the Time Ever Come? A Tlingit Source Book*. Fairbanks: University of Alaska, Alaska Native Knowledge Network.

Hufford, Mary. 1986. *One Space, Many Places: Folklife and Land Use in New Jersey's Pinelands National Reserve*. Washington, DC: American Folklife Center, Library of Congress.

———. 1987. "Telling the Landscape: Folklife Expressions and Sense of Place." In *Pinelands Folklife*, ed. Rita Zorn Moonsammy, David Steven Cohen, and Lorraine Williams, 13–42. New Brunswick, NJ: Rutgers University Press.

———. 1990. "'One Reason God Made Trees': The Form and Ecology of the Barnegat Bay Sneakbox." In *Sense of Place: American Regional Cultures*, ed. Barbara Allen and Thomas J. Schlereth, 40–57. Lexington: University of Kentucky Press.

———. 1992. "Thresholds to an Alternate Realm: Mapping the Chaseworld in New Jersey's Pine Barrens." In *Place Attachment*, ed. Irwin Altman and Setha M. Low, 231–52. New York: Plenum Press.

Hunn, Eugene S. 1982. "The Utilitarian Factor in Folk Biological Classification." *American Anthropologist* 84 (4): 830–47.

———. 1990. *Nch'i-Wána, "The Big River": Mid-Columbia Indians and Their Land.* Seattle: University of Washington Press.

———. 1993. "What Is Traditional Ecological Knowledge?" In *Traditional Ecological Knowledge: Wisdom for Sustainable Development,* ed. Nancy Williams and Graham Baines, 13–15. Canberra: Centre for Resource and Environmental Studies, Australian National University.

———. 1994. "Place Names, Population Density, and the Magic Number 500." *Current Anthropology* 35 (1): 81–85.

———. 1996. "Columbia Plateau Indian Place Names: What Can They Teach Us?" *Journal of Linguistic Anthropology* 6 (1): 3–26.

Hunn, Eugene S., and David H. French. 1984. "Alternatives to Taxonomic Hierarchy: The Sahaptin Case." *Journal of Ethnobiology* 4:73–92.

Hunn, Eugene S., Darryll R. Johnson, Priscilla N. Russell, and Thomas F. Thornton. 2003. "Huna Tlingit Environmental Knowledge, Conservation, and the Management of a 'Wilderness' Park." *Current Anthropology* 44 (December): S79–S103.

Ingold, Tim. 2000. *The Perception of the Environment: Essays in Livelihood, Dwelling, and Skill.* London: Routledge.

Jett, Stephen. 2001. *Navajo Placenames and Trails of the Canyon de Chelly System, Arizona.* New York: Peter Lang.

Johnson, Allen W., and Timothy Earle. 1987. *The Evolution of Human Societies: From Foraging Group to Agrarian State.* Stanford, CA: Stanford University Press.

Johnson, Leslie Main. 2000. "'A Place That's Good': Gitksan Landscape Perception and Ethnoecology." *Journal of Human Ecology* 28 (2): 301–25.

Johnson, Mark. 1987. *The Body in the Mind: The Bodily Basis of Reason and Imagination.* Chicago: University of Chicago Press.

Jonaitis, Aldona. 1981. "Tlingit Halibut Hooks: An Analysis of Visual Symbols of a Rite of Passage." American Museum of Natural History, Anthropological Papers, vol. 57, pt. 1. New York: American Museum of Natural History.

Jordan, Peter. 2003. *Material Culture and Sacred Landscape: The Anthropology of the Siberian Khanty.* Walnut Creek, CA: AltaMira Press.

Joseph, Charlie. n.d. Map and audiotape recordings of Tlingit place-names around Sitka. Map, tapes, and transcriptions on file at Sitka Native Education Program and Sitka Tribe of Alaska.

Kahn, Miriam. 1990. "Stone-Faced Ancestors: The Spatial Anchoring of Myth in Wamira, Papua New Guinea." *Ethnology* 29:51–66.

Kan, Sergei. 1983. *Words That Heal the Soul: Analysis of the Tlingit Potlatch Oratory. Arctic Anthropology* 20 (2): 47–59.

———. 1985. *Tlingit Indians of Alaska by Anatolii Kemenskii.* Translated with an introduction and supplementary material by Sergei Kan. Fairbanks: University of Alaska Press.

———. 1989. *Symbolic Immortality: The Tlingit Potlatch of the Nineteenth Century.* Washington, DC: Smithsonian Institution Press.

Kant, Immanuel. 1956. *The Critique of Pure Reason.* Translated with an introduction by Lewis White Beck. Indianapolis: Bobbs-Merrill.

Kari, James. 1987. "Some Principles of Alaska Athabaskan Toponymic Knowledge." In *General and Amerindian Ethnolinguistics: In Remembrance of Stanley Newman,* ed. Mary R. Key and Henry Koenigswald, 129–49. Berlin: Mouton de Gruyter.

Kawaky, Joseph, producer. 1981. *Haa Shagóon.* Film presented by Chilkoot Indian Association. Juneau, AK: Sealaska Heritage Foundation.

Kay, Paul, and C. K. McDaniel. 1978. "The Linguistic Significance of the Meanings of Basic Color Terms." *Language* 54:610–46.

Kearns, Robin A., and Wilbert M. Gesler. 1998. *Putting Health into Place: Landscape, Identity, and Well-Being.* Syracuse, NY: Syracuse University Press.

Kelly, Klara Bonsack, and Harris Francis. 1994. *Navajo Sacred Places.* Bloomington: Indiana University Press.

Kitka, Herman, Sr. 1999. "Deep Ties to Deep Bay: A Tlingit Elder's Training." *Cultural Survival Quarterly* 22 (3): 47–48.

———. 2000. "A Tlingit Elder's Training." In Fair and Worl, *Celebration 2000,* 77–78.

Krause, Aurel. 1956. *The Tlingit Indian.* Trans. Erna Gunther. Seattle: University of Washington Press.

Krause, Aurel, and Arthur Krause. 1981. *Journey to the Tlingits by Aurel and Arthur Krause, 1881/1882.* Trans. Margot Krause McCaffrey. Haines, AK: Centennial Commission.

Krech, Shepard. 1999. *The Ecological Indian: Myth and History.* New York: W. W. Norton.

Kroeber, Alfred. 1916. "California Place Names of Indian Origin." *University of California Publications in American Archeology and Ethnology* 12:31–69.

———. 1939. "Cultural and Natural Areas of North America." *University of California, Publications in American Archeology and Ethnology* 38.

Kruger, Linda Everett. 1996. "Understanding Place as a Cultural System: Implications of Theory and Method." PhD diss., University of Washington, Seattle.

Lakoff, George. 1987. *Women, Fire, and Dangerous Things: What Categories Reveal about the Mind.* Chicago: University of Chicago Press.

Lakoff, George, and Mark Johnson. 1980. *Metaphors We Live By*. Chicago: University of Chicago Press.

———. 1999. *Philosophy in the Flesh: The Embodied Mind and Its Challenge to Western Thought*. New York: Basic Books.

Langdon, Stephen J. 1977. *Technology, Ecology, and Economy: Fishing Systems in Southeast Alaska*. PhD diss., Stanford University. Ann Arbor, MI: UMI Dissertation Services.

———. 1989. "From Communal Property to Common Property to Limited Entry: Historical Ironies in the Management of Southeast Alaska Salmon." In *A Sea of Small Boats*, ed. John Cordell, 304–32. Cambridge, MA: Cultural Survival.

———. 2000. "Then, Now, and Always: Names among Tlingit and Haida People." In Fair and Worl, *Celebration 2000*, 149–54.

———. 2002. "Construing 'Conservation': An Examination of Conceptual Construction and Application to Yup'ik Cultural Practice." Paper presented to the Ninth International Conference on Hunting and Gathering Societies, Edinburgh. Manuscript in author's possession.

Leer, Jeff. [1985]. "Tlingit Tribes and Clans." Manuscript, Alaska Native Language Center, University of Alaska, Fairbanks.

———. 1991. *The Schetic Categories of the Tlingit Verb*. PhD diss., University of Chicago. Ann Arbor, MI: UMI Dissertation Services.

Lefebvre, Henri. 1991. *The Production of Space*. Trans. Donald Nicholson-Smith. Malden, MA: Blackwell.

Lèvi-Strauss, Claude. 1966. *The Savage Mind*. Chicago: University of Chicago Press.

Littlefield, Roby, Ethel Makinen, Lydia George, Nora Marks Dauenhauer, and Richard Dauenhauer, eds. 2003. "Aak'wtaatseen, 'Shanyaak'utlaax' told by Deikeenáak'w, Sitka, 1904. Transcribed by John R. Swanton, 1904. Published in Swanton, *Tlingit Myths and Texts* (1909), as Story #99, 'Moldy End,' pp. 301–310." Working draft. Transliterated into modern orthography by Roby Littlefield and Ethel Makinen. http://www.ankn.uaf.edu/curriculum/Tlingit/Salmon/graphics/swanton.pdf.

Lopez, Barry. 1986. *Arctic Dreams: Imagination and Desire in a Northern Landscape*. New York: Bantam.

Low, Setha M. 2000. *On the Plaza: The Politics of Public Space and Culture*. Austin: University of Texas Press.

———. 2003. "Anthropological Theories of Body, Space, and Culture." *Space and Culture* 6 (1): 9–18.

Low, Setha M., and Denise Lawrence-Zúñiga, eds. 2003. *The Anthropology of Space and Place: Locating Culture*. Malden, MA: Blackwell.

Maffi, Louisa, ed. 2001. *On Biocultural Diversity: Linking Language, Knowledge, and the Environment.* Washington, DC: Smithsonian Institution Press.

Malinowski, Bronislaw. 1922. *Argonauts of the Western Pacific.* London: Routledge and Kegan Paul.

Matson, R. G., and Gary Coupland. 1995. *The Prehistory of the Northwest Coast.* San Diego, CA: Academic Press.

Mauss, Marcel. 1967. *The Gift.* Trans. Ian Cunnison. New York: W. W. Norton.

———. 1979. "The Notion of Body Techniques." In *Sociology and Psychology: Essays.* London: Routledge and Kegan Paul.

McCay, Bonnie J., and James M. Acheson, eds. 1987. *The Question of the Commons: The Culture and Ecology of Communal Resources.* Tucson: University of Arizona Press.

McClellan, Catherine. 1970. *The Girl Who Married the Bear.* National Museum of Man, Publications in Ethnology, no. 2. Ottawa: National Museums of Canada.

———. 1975. *My Old People Say: An Ethnographic Survey of Southern Yukon Territory.* 2 vols. National Museum of Man, Publications in Ethnology, no. 6. Ottawa: National Museums of Canada.

McHalsie, Albert (Sonny). 2001. "Halq'eméylem Place Names in Stó:l_ Territory." In *A Stó:l_ Coast Salish Historical Atlas,* ed. Keith Thor Carlson et al., 134–35. Vancouver, BC: Douglas and McIntyre; Seattle: University of Washington Press; Chilliwack, BC: Stó:l_ Heritage Trust.

Meining, D. W., ed. 1979. *The Interpretation of Ordinary Landscapes.* Oxford: Oxford University Press.

Merleau-Ponty, Maurice. 1962. *The Phenomenology of Perception.* London: Routledge and Kegan Paul.

Mills, David, and Anne S. Firman. 1986. *Fish and Wildlife Use in Yakutat, Alaska.* Technical Paper no. 131. Juneau, AK: Department of Fish and Game, Division of Subsistence.

Milton, Kay. 2002. *Loving Nature: Towards an Ecology of Emotion.* London and New York: Routledge.

Momaday, Scott. 1974. "Native American Attitudes to the Environment." In *Seeing with a Native Eye: Essays on Native American Religion,* ed. Walter Capps, 79–85. New York: Harper and Row.

Monmonier, Mark. 1991. *How to Lie with Maps.* Chicago: University of Chicago Press.

Morphy, Howard. 1995. "Landscape and the Reproduction of the Ancestral Past." In *The Anthropology of Landscape: Perspectives on Space and Place,* ed. Eric Hirsch and Michael O'Hanlon, 184–209. Oxford: Oxford University Press.

Moser, Jefferson F. 1899. *The Salmon and Salmon Fisheries of Alaska*. Washington, DC: Government Printing Office.

Moss, Madonna L. 1993. "Shellfish, Gender, and Status on the Northwest Coast: Reconciling Archeological, Ethnographic, and Ethnohistorical Records of the Tlingit." *American Anthropologist* 95 (3): 631–52.

———. 1998. "Northern Northwest Coast Overview." *Arctic Anthropology* 35 (1): 88–111.

Moss, Madonna, and Jon M. Erlandson. 1992. "Forts, Refuge Rocks, and Defensive Sites: The Antiquity of Warfare along the North Pacific Coast of North America." *Arctic Anthropology* 29 (2): 73–90.

Muir, John. 1895. "The Discovery of Glacier Bay, Alaska." *National Geographic*, April.

Munn, Nancy. [1973] 1986. *Walbiri Iconography*. Chicago: University of Chicago Press.

———. 1996. "Excluded Spaces: The Figure in the Australian Aboriginal Landscape." *Critical Inquiry* 22 (3): 446–65.

Myers, Fred. 1982. "Always Ask: Resource Use and Land Ownership among Pintupi Aborigines of the Australian Western Dessert." In Williams and Hunn, *Resource Managers*.

———. 1986. *Pintupi Country, Pintupi Self: Sentiment, Place, and Politics among Western Desert Aborigines*. Washington, DC: Smithsonian Institution Press.

———. 1989. "Burning the Turck and Holding the Country: Pintupi Forms of Property and Identity." In *We Are Here: Politics of Aboriginal Land Tenure*, ed. Edwin M. Wilmsen, 15–42. Berkeley: University of California Press.

Naish, Constance M., and Gillian L. Story. [1960s]. Excerpts from notebooks based on fieldwork in Angoon. Manuscript on file at the Alaska Native Language Center, University of Alaska, Fairbanks.

———. 1973. *Tlingit Verb Dictionary*. Fairbanks: Alaska Native Language Center, University of Alaska.

———. 1976. *Tlingit Noun Dictionary*. 2nd ed. Revised and expanded by Henry Davis. Sitka, AK: Sheldon Jackson College.

Nelson, Richard. 1994. "The Embrace of Names." In *Northern Lights: A Selection of New Writing from the American West*, ed. Deborah Clow and Donald Snow, 14–21. New York: Vintage Books.

Newton, Richard G., and Madonna L. Moss. 1983. *The Subsistence Lifeway of the Tlingit People*. Juneau, AK: U.S. Department of Agriculture, Forest Service.

———. 2005. *Haa Atxaayí Haa Kusteeyíx Sitee, Our Food Is Our Tlingit Way of Life*. Juneau, AK: U.S. Department of Agriculture, Forest Service.

Niblack, Albert P. [1890] 1970. *The Coast Indians of Southern Alaska and Northern British Columbia*. U.S. National Museum Annual Report, 1888, 225–386. Reprint, New York: Johnson Reprint Corporation.

Nyman, Elizabeth, and Jeff Leer. 1993. *Gágiwdul.àt: Brought Forth to Reconfirm; The Legacy of a Taku River Tlingit Clan*. Whitehorse: Yukon Native Language Centre, Yukon College; Fairbanks: Alaska Native Language Center, University of Alaska.

Oberg, Kalervo. 1973. *The Social Economy of the Tlingit Indians*. Seattle: University of Washington Press.

Olson, Ronald L. 1956. "Channeling of Character in Tlingit Society." In *Personal Character and Cultural Milieu*, ed. D. G. Haring, 675–87. 3rd rev. ed. Syracuse, NY: Syracuse University Press.

———. 1967. *The Social Structure and Social Life of the Tlingit in Alaska*. University of California, Anthropological Records 26. Berkeley: University of California Press.

———. n.d. Unpublished field notes on the Tlingit of Southeastern Alaska. Bancroft Library Archives, University of California, Berkeley.

Orth, Donald J. 1971. *Dictionary of Alaska Place Names*. Geological Survey Professional Paper 567. Washington, DC: Government Printing Office.

Ostrom, Elinor. 1990. *Governing the Commons: The Evolution of Institutions for Collective Action*. New York: Cambridge University Press.

Palmer, Andie Diane. 2005. *Maps of Experience: The Anchoring of Land to Story in Secwepemc Discourse*. Toronto: University of Toronto Press.

Paul, William. n.d. *The Alaska Tlingit: Where Did They Come From?* National Anthropological Archives, MS 7077. Washington, DC: Smithsonian Institution Press.

Peirce, Charles S. 1960. *Collected Papers of Charles Sanders Peirce*. Vols. 1–8. Ed. C. Hartshorne and P. Weiss. Cambridge, MA: Harvard University Press.

Petroff, Ivan. 1884. *Report on Population, Industries and Resources of Alaska*. U.S. Census Office, 10th Census, 1880. Washington, DC: Government Printing Office.

Pickles, John. 1985. *Phenomenology, Science, and Geography: Spatiality and the Human Sciences*. Cambridge: Cambridge University Press.

Pinker, Steven. 1999. *How the Mind Works*. New York: W. W. Norton.

Polanyi, Karl. 1944. *The Great Transformation*. New York: Farrar and Rinehart.

Pred, Allan. 1986. "Place, Practice and Structure: Social and Spatial Transformation in Southern Sweden, 1750–1850." Cambridge, UK: Polity Press.

———. 1990. *Making Histories and Constructing Human Geographies: The Local Transformation of Practice, Power Relations, and Consciousness*. Boulder, CO: Westview Press.

Price, Robert. 1990. *The Great Father in Alaska: The Case of the Tlingit and Haida Salmon Fishery*. Juneau, AK: First Street Press.

Putnam, Robert. 2000. *Bowling Alone: The Collapse and Revival of American Community*. New York: Touchstone.

Rappaport, Roy A. 1999. *Ritual and Religion in the Making of Humanity*. Cambridge: Cambridge University Press.

Relph, Edward. 1976. *Place and Placelessness*. London: Pion.

———. 1987. *The Modern Urban Landscape*. London: Croom Helm.

Richardson, Allan S. 1982. "The Control of Productive Resources on the Northwest Coast of North America." In Williams and Hunn, *Resource Managers*.

Ridington, Robin. 1990. *Little Bit Know Something: Stories in a Language of Anthropology*. Iowa City: University of Iowa Press.

Rodman, Margaret C. 1992. "Empowering Place: Multilocality and Multivocality." *American Anthropologist* 94:640–56.

Rosaldo, Renato. 1980. *Ilongot Headhunting, 1883–1974: A Study in Society and History*. Stanford, CA: Stanford University Press.

Ryden, Kent C. 1993. *Mapping the Invisible Landscape: Folklore, Writing, and the Sense of Place*. Iowa City: University of Iowa Press.

Sack, Robert D. 1997. *Homo Geographicus: A Framework for Action, Awareness, and Moral Concern*. Baltimore: Johns Hopkins University Press.

Sackett, Russell. 1979. *The Chilkat Tlingit: A General Overview*. Fairbanks: Anthropology and Historic Preservation, Cooperative Park Studies Unit, University of Alaska.

Sapir, Edward. 1912. "Language and Environment." *American Anthropologist* 14:226–42.

———. 1915. "The Na-Dene Languages: A Preliminary Report." *American Anthropologist* 17 (3): 534–58.

Sauer, Carl O. 1927. "Recent Developments in Cultural Geography." In *Recent Developments in the Social Sciences*, ed. E. C. Hayes, 154–212. New York: Lippincott.

Schalk, Randall. 1977. "The Structure of an Anadromous Fish Resource." In *For Theory Building in Archeology*, ed. Lewis R. Binford, 207–49. New York: Academic Press.

Schama, Simon. 1995. *Landscape and Memory*. London: Harper Collins.

Schroeder, Robert F., and Matthew Kookesh. 1988. *Subsistence Harvest and Use of Fish and Wildlife Resources by Residents of Hoonah, Alaska*. Technical Paper no. 142. Juneau: Alaska Department of Fish and Game, Division of Subsistence.

Scidmore, Eliza R. 1896. "The Discovery of Glacier Bay, Alaska." *National Geographic* 7 (April).

Scott, Colin, ed. 2001. "Aboriginal Autonomy and Development in Northern Quebec and Labrador." Vancouver: University of British Columbia Press.

Seamon, David. 1980. "Body-Subject, Time-Space Routines, and Place-Ballets." In *The Human Experience of Space and Place*, ed. Anne Buttimer and David Seamon. London: St. Martin's Press.

SENSC (Southeast Native Subsistence Commission). 1995–2002. *Native Place Names Project: Final Reports*. Maps and data on file at Central Council of Tlingit and Haida Tribes of Alaska, Juneau.

Service, Elman R. 1962. *Primitive Social Organization: An Evolutionary Perspective*. New York: Random House.

Sharp, Henry S. 2001. *Loon: Memory, Meaning and Reality in a Northern Dene Community*. Lincoln: University of Nebraska Press.

Shotridge, Louis. 1920. "Ghost of Courageous Adventurer." *Museum Journal* 11 (1): 11–26.

———. n.d. "Tlingit Geographical Names." Manuscript, Alaska State Historical Library, Juneau.

Silko, Leslie Marmon. 1990. "Landscape, History, and the Pueblo Imagination." In *The Norton Book of Nature Writing*, ed. Robert Finch and John Elder, 882–94. New York: W. W. Norton.

Smith, Eric Alden, and Mark Wishnie. 2000. "Conservation and Subsistence in Small-Scale Societies." *Annual Reviews in Anthropology* 29:493–524.

Soboleff, Walter A. 1992. "Tlingit Values." Manuscript, Sealaska Heritage Foundation, Juneau, AK.

Stedman, Richard C. 2002. "Toward a Social Psychology of Place: Predicting Behavior from Place-Based Cognitions, Attitude, and Identity." *Environment and Behavior* 34 (5): 561–81.

Stern, Pamela R. 1999. "Learning to Be Smart: An Exploration of the Culture of Intelligence in a Canadian Inuit Community." *American Anthropologist* 101 (3): 502–14.

Steward, Julian. 1955. *Theory of Culture Change: The Methodology of Multilinear Evolution*. Urbana: University of Illinois Press.

Stoffle, Richard W., and Michael J. Evans. 1990. "Holistic Conservation and Cultural Triage: American Indian Perspectives on Cultural Resources." *Human Organization* 49 (2): 91–99.

Strehlow, T. G. H. 1947. *Aranda Traditions*. Melbourne: Melbourne University Press.

Suttles, Wayne. 1968. "Coping with Abundance: Subsistence on the Northwest Coast." In *Man the Hunter*, ed. Richard B. Lee and Irven De Vore, 56–68. Chicago: Aldine Press.

———. 1974. "Variation in Habitat and Culture on the Northwest Coast." In

Man in Adaptation: The Cultural Present, ed. Yehudi Cohen, 93–106. Chicago: Aldine Press.

Swanton, John R. 1908. *Social Condition, Beliefs and Linguistic Relationships of Tlingit Indians*. Twenty-sixth Annual Report, Bureau of American Ethnology, 391–485. Washington, DC: Government Printing Office.

———. 1909. *Tlingit Myths and Texts*. Bureau of American Ethnology, Bulletin 39. Washington, DC: Government Printing Office.

———. 1911. "Tlingit." In *Handbook of American Indian Languages*. Pt. 1. Bureau of American Ethnology, Bulletin 10. Washington, DC: Government Printing Office.

Thornton, Thomas F. 1992. *Subsistence Use of Brown Bear in Southeast Alaska*. Technical Paper no. 214. Juneau: Alaska Department of Fish and Game, Division of Subsistence.

———. 1995. "Tlingit and Euro-American Toponymies in Glacier Bay." In *Proceedings of the Third Glacier Bay Science Symposium, 1993*, ed. Daniel Engstrom, 294–301. Anchorage, AK: National Park Service.

———. 1997a. "Anthropological Studies of North American Indian Place Naming." *American Indian Quarterly* 21 (2): 209–28.

———. 1997b. "Know Your Place: The Organization of Tlingit Geographic Knowledge." *Ethnology* 36 (4): 295–307.

———, ed. 1998. "Crisis in the Last Frontier: The Alaskan Subsistence Debate." *Cultural Survival Quarterly* 22 (3).

———. 1999a. "Subsistence: The Politics of a Cultural Dilemma." In *Public Policy Issues in Alaska: Background and Perspectives*, ed. Clive S. Thomas. Juneau, AK: Denali Press.

———. 1999b. "*Tleik̲w Aaní*, The 'Berried' Landscape: The Structure of Tlingit Edible Fruit Resources at Glacier Bay, Alaska." *Journal of Ethnobiology* 19 (1): 27–48.

———. 1999c. "What's in a Name? Indigenous Place Names in Southeast Alaska." With Harold P. Martin. *Arctic Research of the United States* 13 (Spring/Summer): 40–48.

———. 2000. "Person and Place: Lessons from Tlingit Teachers." In Fair and Worl, *Celebration 2000*, 79–86.

———. 2001. "Subsistence in Northern Communities: Lessons from Alaska." *Northern Review* 23 (Summer): 82–102.

———. 2002. "From Clan to K̲wáan to Corporation: The Continuing Complex Evolution of Tlingit Political Organization." *Wicazo Sa Review* 17 (2): 167–94.

———. 2004a. "The Geography of Tlingit Character." In *Coming to Shore: Northwest Coast Ethnology, Traditions, and Visions*, ed. Marie Mauzé,

Michael Harkin, and Sergei Kan, 363–84. Lincoln: University of Nebraska Press.

———. 2004b. *Klondike Gold Rush National Park: Ethnographic Overview and Assessment*. Anchorage, AK: National Park Service, Department of the Interior.

———. 2007. "Alaska Native Corporations and Subsistence: Paradoxical Forces in the Making of Sustainable Communities." In *Sustainability and Communities of Place*, ed. Carl Maida, 41–62. Oxford and New York: Berghahn Books.

———. n.d. "Animals in Their Place: The Localization of Traditional Ethological Knowledge." Paper presented at the Shelby Cullom Davis Center for Historical Studies Seminar, "Animals and Human Society," Princeton University, January 10, 1997.

Thornton, Thomas F., Robert F. Schroeder, and Robert G. Bosworth. 1990. *Use of Sockeye Salmon at Sitkoh Bay, Alaska*. Technical Report no. 174. Juneau: Alaska Department of Fish and Game, Division of Subsistence.

Tilley, Christopher. 1994. *A Phenomenology of Landscape: Places, Paths and Monuments*. Oxford: Berg.

A Time of Gathering: Tlingit Berry Picking in Glacier Bay National Park. 1999. Video. Thomas F. Thornton, executive producer. Juneau: University of Alaska, Southeast Library and Media Services. Distributed by Hoonah Indian Association, Hoonah, AK.

TRUCS. 1988. *1988 Tongass Resource Use Cooperative Survey*. Juneau: Alaska Department of Fish and Game, Division of Subsistence; U.S. Department of Agriculture, Forest Service; Anchorage: Institute of Social and Economic Research, University of Alaska.

Tuan, Yi-Fu. 1974. *Topophilia: A Study of Environmental Perception, Attitudes, and Values*. Englewood Cliffs, NJ: Prentice-Hall.

———. 1975. "Place: An Experiential Perspective." *Geographic Review* 65:151–65.

———. 1977. *Space and Place: The Perspective of Experience*. Minneapolis: University of Minnesota Press.

Turner, Victor. 1969. *The Ritual Process: Structure and Anti-Structure*. Chicago: Aldine Press.

U.S. Department of the Interior. [1944]. Hearings upon claims of natives of Alaska pursuant to the provisions of section 201.21b of the regulations for protection of the commercial fisheries of Alaska 1944: petition of Indians of Hydaburg, Alaska; petition of Indians of Klawock, Alaska; and petition of Indians of Kake, Alaska. Transcripts of hearings under Judge Hanna on file at the Alaska State Historical Library, Juneau.

Varela, Francisco J., Evan Thompson, and Eleanor Rosch. 1991. *The Embodied Mind: Cognitive Science and Human Experience*. Cambridge, MA: MIT Press.

Walens, Stanley. 1981. *Feasting with Cannibals: An Essay on Kwakiutl Cosmology*. Princeton, NJ: Princeton University Press.

Wallace, Anthony F. C. 2003. *Revitalizations and Mazeways: Essays on Culture Change*. Vol. 1., ed. Robert S. Grumet. Lincoln: University of Nebraska Press.

Walter, E. V. 1988. *Placeways: A Theory of the Human Environment*. Chapel Hill: University of North Carolina Press.

Waterman, Thomas T. 1920. "Yurok Geography." *University of California, Publications in American Archaeology and Ethnology* 16:177–314.

———. 1922. "The Geographic Names Used by the Indians of the Pacific Coast." *Geographical Review* 12 (2): 175–94.

———. n.d. "Tlingit Geographic Names for Extreme Southeast Alaska, with Historical and Other Notes." Bureau of American Ethnology. Manuscript on file at the National Anthropology Archives, Smithsonian Institution, Washington, DC.

Weiner, James F. 2001. Afterword. In *Emplaced Myth: Space, Narrative, and Knowledge in Aboriginal Australia and Papua New Guinea*, ed. Alan Rumsey and James Weiner. Honolulu: University of Hawai'i Press.

Williams, Nancy M., and Eugene S. Hunn. 1982. *Resource Managers: North American and Australian Hunter-Gatherers*. American Association for the Advancement of Science, Selected Symposium 67. Boulder, CO: Westview Press.

Witherspoon, Gary. 1977. *Language and Art in the Navajo Universe*. Ann Arbor: University of Michigan Press.

Wolf, Eric. 1982. *Europe and the People without History*. Berkeley: University of California Press.

INDEX

Lightning Source UK Ltd.
Milton Keynes UK
UKHW011948010322
399399UK00002B/64